NAVIGATING
ENGLISH
GRAMMAR

T0373202

ANNE LOBECK and KRISTIN DENHAM

NAVIGATING ENGLISH GRAMMAR

A Guide to Analyzing Real Language

Second Edition

WILEY Blackwell

This edition first published 2025
© 2025 Anne Lobeck and Kristin Denham

Edition History
[Anne Lobeck and Kristin Denham, 1e, 2014]

All rights reserved. No part of this publication may be reproduced, stored in a retrieval system, or transmitted, in any form or by any means, electronic, mechanical, photocopying, recording or otherwise, except as permitted by law. Advice on how to obtain permission to reuse material from this title is available at http://www.wiley.com/go/permissions.

The right of Anne Lobeck and Kristin Denham to be identified as the authors of this work has been asserted in accordance with law.

Registered Offices
John Wiley & Sons, Inc., 111 River Street, Hoboken, NJ 07030, USA
John Wiley & Sons Ltd, The Atrium, Southern Gate, Chichester, West Sussex, PO19 8SQ, UK

For details of our global editorial offices, customer services, and more information about Wiley products visit us at www.wiley.com.

Wiley also publishes its books in a variety of electronic formats and by print-on-demand. Some content that appears in standard print versions of this book may not be available in other formats.

Trademarks: Wiley and the Wiley logo are trademarks or registered trademarks of John Wiley & Sons, Inc. and/or its affiliates in the United States and other countries and may not be used without written permission. All other trademarks are the property of their respective owners. John Wiley & Sons, Inc. is not associated with any product or vendor mentioned in this book.

Limit of Liability/Disclaimer of Warranty
While the publisher and authors have used their best efforts in preparing this work, they make no representations or warranties with respect to the accuracy or completeness of the contents of this work and specifically disclaim all warranties, including without limitation any implied warranties of merchantability or fitness for a particular purpose. No warranty may be created or extended by sales representatives, written sales materials or promotional statements for this work. This work is sold with the understanding that the publisher is not engaged in rendering professional services. The advice and strategies contained herein may not be suitable for your situation. You should consult with a specialist where appropriate. The fact that an organization, website, or product is referred to in this work as a citation and/or potential source of further information does not mean that the publisher and authors endorse the information or services the organization, website, or product may provide or recommendations it may make. Further, readers should be aware that websites listed in this work may have changed or disappeared between when this work was written and when it is read. Neither the publisher nor authors shall be liable for any loss of profit or any other commercial damages, including but not limited to special, incidental, consequential, or other damages.

Library of Congress Cataloging-in-Publication Data
Names: Lobeck, Anne C., author. | Denham, Kristin E., 1967– author.
Title: Navigating English grammar : a guide to analyzing real language /
    Anne Lobeck and Kristin Denham.
Description: Second edition. | Hoboken, NJ : Wiley Blackwell, 2025. |
    Includes index.
Identifiers: LCCN 2024013948 (print) | LCCN 2024013949 (ebook) | ISBN
    9781119944430 (paperback) | ISBN 9781119944447 (adobe pdf) | ISBN
    9781119944454 (epub)
Subjects: LCSH: English language–Grammar. | English
    language–Grammar–Problems, exercises, etc. | English
    language–Grammar–Study and teaching. | English language–Variation. |
    English language–Social aspects.
Classification: LCC PE1112 .L587 2025 (print) | LCC PE1112 (ebook) | DDC
    425–dc23/eng/20240415
LC record available at https://lccn.loc.gov/2024013948
LC ebook record available at https://lccn.loc.gov/2024013949

Cover Design: Wiley
Cover Image: © seksan Mongkhonkhamsao/Getty Images

Set in 9.5/12pt Palatino LT Std by Straive, Pondicherry, India
Printed and bound by CPI Group (UK) Ltd, Croydon, CR0 4YY

C9781119944430_061024

To our moms, Isabelle Lobeck and Rachel Denham

Contents

Preface

Goals of the Book

When you think of studying English grammar, what comes to your mind? *Mad Libs*? Learning parts of speech and punctuation? Diagramming sentences? Does the study of grammar interest you, or do you find it tedious and boring? Why do you study grammar? Because you have to? Because you want to?

There are as many different reasons to study grammar as there are ways to study it. We know, for example, that we need to study the grammar of another language in order to learn to speak or sign it. But what about the grammar of a language you already speak? Is there any reason to study that? You're probably familiar with the idea that we study English grammar to learn how to speak and write it "correctly." But can we learn anything else from studying the grammar of a language? In fact, the study of this dynamic system can be quite revealing and useful and provides insights into how language, your own and others', whether spoken or signed, actually works.

As you progress through this book, you will discover the grammatical rules of English that users already know, though they may not be aware of them. We approach the study of language and grammar through inquiry; you will discover, by analyzing your own and others' linguistic systems, the grammatical categories and principles of language. You will also find that the idea that some version of grammar is more "correct" than another has no basis in linguistic fact and that all language varieties are equally valid grammatical systems worthy of study. The approach we take here therefore encourages you to challenge and question social perceptions of language (as "good" or "bad," "lazy" or "sloppy"), perceptions that are often based on stereotypes about speakers, rather than on any deficiency in the language they use.

This book is not designed to teach you how to become a better writer, nor is it designed to teach you how to speak English "correctly." The goal of this book is to provide you with tools to analyze the language you use every day, in a variety of registers, genres, and styles, discovering the categories and concepts that underlie users' unconscious knowledge of language. With an understanding of how language actually works, and a concise vocabulary to talk about it, you will be equipped to make more informed decisions and choices about grammar and usage and to tease out linguistic fact from linguistic fiction. You will be able to navigate the study of grammar in all its diverse incarnations.

Changes and Revisions to the Second Edition

In this second edition, we have made significant changes to the way in which we approach language "data," the language examples used to illustrate grammatical terms and concepts. Rather than marginalizing variation in English to boxed sections in the text, we integrate examples of this variation throughout and show how this variation informs the description of English as an ever-changing linguistic system. We label the varieties of English we draw from (and acknowledge that there are many others not represented here) in an effort to recognize the communities who use them and to decenter the so-called "mainstream" varieties of English that are typically taken as the norm in discussions of grammatical structure. For this same reason, we focus on spoken rather than written English. That said, we acknowledge that we are two senior, white, tenured university professors, writing a college textbook in an edited written English that reproduces many of the norms we strive to decenter. We realize our approach here is only a first step in making the study of English, and the way we write and teach about it, more inclusive.

Other changes to the second edition include a **References** section at the end of the book (rather than citing references chapter by chapter). Almost all the **exercises** at the end of each chapter are revised, and each chapter includes new and updated **text excerpts** by a diverse set of authors in each practice section. We have also significantly revised the **boxed material** in each chapter to address related topics of interest. Boxes no longer focus exclusively on language variation and change, as examples of both make up the examples discussed throughout the text. As in the first edition, each chapter includes a **summary** with important terms in bold. Throughout, we introduce **basic phrase structure rules** and **tree diagrams** to provide accessible graphic representations of language structure.

Chapter Organization and Other Changes

Grammatical categories and concepts cannot be taught in isolation – nouns without adjectives or verbs without clauses – and each chapter (despite their simple titles) introduces concepts that we build on in subsequent chapters. We therefore recommend that chapters be studied in order. We provide chapter overviews below, where we also highlight changes and revisions in this second edition.

Note: We approach the grammar of English descriptively here, with an eye toward not just description but explanation. We therefore strike a balance between **basic syntactic structure** and **syntactic theory**, introducing the reader not just to the structure of English but also to *why* English has the structure it does. Some of the theoretical concepts we introduce (in accessible and useful ways) include movement, ellipsis, proform substitution, and null (unpronounced) heads and phrases, among others. We believe this is one of the strengths of this book, as it underscores the approach to grammatical analysis through inquiry rather than memorization, and it provides accessible insights into the study of language beyond basic sentence analysis. Readers are then prepared to pursue further study of grammar more deeply if they wish to.

Chapter 1: This chapter provides an overview of the primarily descriptive approach to grammar we take in this book, using tools of scientific inquiry to learn about how language works. We also discuss prescriptivism (rules of grammar prescribed by language authorities) and Standard Language Ideology in some depth, including the origins of these perspectives on language and their relevance to the study of grammar today. Rather than taking a binary approach to description versus prescription, we show that we learn from both, about grammatical structure, language change and variation, and the origins of the language attitudes that still shape how we judge and value language(s) and users of those languages today.

Chapters 2–5: These chapters investigate the basic semantics, morphology, and syntax of English noun phrases and verb phrases and include discussion of examples from a range of varieties of English to illustrate grammatical concepts, including (but not limited to) variation in inflectional morphology. Both Chapters 4 and 5 on verbs and verb phrases, respectively, are substantially revised to highlight variation in English verb morphology and in the tense and aspect system, including verb strings with null auxiliaries, and variation in subject–verb agreement.

Chapter 6: This chapter is significantly revised and streamlined to focus more on the structure of the independent clause rather than on theoretical aspects of the English verb string (as in the first edition). We focus on grammatical functions of subjects, complements (in this chapter, direct objects), and predicates and on basic evidence for the Tense position (subject–auxiliary inversion, tag question formation and negation). The chapter provides students with the tools to diagram independent clauses, including those with the complex verb strings discussed in Chapter 5, and prepares students to move on to complementation, subordination, and coordination in subsequent chapters.

Chapters 7–9: These chapters are each updated with new examples and exercises and introduce students to the basic semantics, morphology, and syntax of adjective phrases, adverb phrases, and prepositional phrases (and particles) and how these phrases function as modifiers and complements. These chapters introduce a range of different complements, including subjective complements, objects of prepositions, and indirect objects. We also show how the theoretical concept of syntactic movement (Passive, Indirect Object Movement, Particle Shift) can be used as a tool to distinguish among different complements.

Chapter 10: This chapter is significantly revised to focus first on coordination and then on subordination, acquainting students with the structure of more complex clauses. The section on different types of subordinate clause complements, complementizers, and PRO subjects of infinitival clauses is revised to be more accessible.

Chapter 11: This chapter is the most significantly revised of all the chapters in the book, and it now connects more seamlessly with Chapter 10. From the discussion of subordinate clause complements in Chapter 10, we move on in this chapter to explore subordinate clause modifiers, namely restrictive and nonrestrictive relative clauses. From there, we investigate a range of other nonrestrictive modifiers, what we call "movable modifiers."

Chapter 12: This completely new chapter provides an overview of the book, pulling together concepts, terms, and tools introduced in earlier chapters. We briefly review syntactic categories and phrases, the functions of those phrases as complements and modifiers, and subordination and coordination. The chapter is designed as a capstone, revisiting familiar concepts but concluding with a set of challenging exercises that encourage students to apply the tools they have learned to explore and analyze language.

Acknowledgments

This book grew out of our longtime experience teaching *The Structure of English*, a course on English descriptive grammar, but it is also influenced by other courses we teach: on language change and the history of English, linguistics in education, and generative syntactic theory. Our students in these classes have made an enormous contribution to this book, and it is shaped by their insights (sometimes about our oversights), comments, and feedback, and we are deeply indebted, first and foremost, to them.

We also thank each other. Two heads are definitely better than one, especially when those two heads collaborate as compatibly and productively as our two heads do.

Anne Lobeck and Kristin Denham
December 2023

What is Grammar and How Do We Study It?

Introduction

Humans have always been fascinated by language, and the study of language has always been a fundamental part of intellectual inquiry. In fact, the study of language forms the core of the social and behavioral sciences as

Navigating English Grammar: A Guide to Analyzing Real Language, Second Edition.
Anne Lobeck and Kristin Denham.
© 2025 Anne Lobeck and Kristin Denham. Published 2025 by John Wiley & Sons Ltd.

well as the humanities and is unique in crossing such interdisciplinary boundaries; we can study the psychology of language, how children acquire language, and how speakers and signers process it and understand it; we can study the biology and neurology of language, and what it tells us about the organization of the brain; we can study language as a social tool, how we use it to express our identities as members of different social groups; and we can study the language of literature and artistic expression.

We can also study the internal structure, or *grammar*, of language, which is what we focus on in this book. Our goal is to help you discover some of the organizing principles of grammar by studying how English works. This book is neither a "how-to" book on "good English" nor is it a comprehensive or precise description of English grammar. In fact, we use the term "English" broadly here; what we call a single language is more accurately described as a (vast) collection of different varieties spoken by both native and non-native speakers around the globe. We will provide you with some tools to help you explore the structure of whatever variety of English you speak; you will become familiar with syntactic categories (parts of speech), heads and phrases, subordination, coordination, modification, and complementation. Our approach to grammatical structure is descriptive; we will explore and describe language data, data that helps reveal some of our intuitive knowledge of grammar. That said, because "English" is a dynamic, changing system, we cannot attempt to provide any kind of comprehensive set of rules or principles that define it (nor could we, even if we wanted to!). This scientific approach to the study of grammar will be different from the more familiar "school" approach, in which you learn grammar and usage rules with the goal of learning to speak and write "correctly." Rather, we hope that what you learn here will provide you with important tools of critical analysis to make your own informed decisions about grammar and usage.

Along with our study of the structure of English, we explore how language changes over time and varies from community to community. We'll show that although social value may be attached to one way of using language over another, the scientific study of language reveals that all language varieties are equally expressive, and all are rule-governed systems. Our focus here is on oral language, though what we say here about grammar, as a linguistic system, applies to any language, signed or oral. All language users have intuitive knowledge of language, and all languages can be studied scientifically in the way we discuss here. This book will therefore not only introduce you to the structure of English but will also provide you with an important context for the study of grammar, its influence on other areas of modern thought, and the study of language more generally. In the course of navigating English grammar, we also think that you will find that the study of language is fascinating and often really fun.

2

What is English? Language Change and Variation

Before we tackle what we mean by *grammar* in more detail, we need to explore what we mean by *English*. It's actually quite difficult to explain what English is once you think about it; English (like other languages) is a continuum of (many) different language varieties or dialects. According to *Ethnologue*, as of 2023, English has more speakers than any other language in the world, when factoring in not only native speakers but also those who speak English in addition to other languages.

With nearly 1.5 billion speakers of English around the world (about 15% of the world's population), it's no surprise that there may be varieties of English that sound familiar to you, and others that you have never encountered before. Here are a few examples of sentences from varieties of English from both inside and outside the United States.

What is Grammar and How Do We Study It?

That's me away. (Scots English)
That house looks a nice one. (varieties of British English)
I asked him where does he work. (Indian English)
She'll be right. (Australian English)
He be working. (African American English)
We might should do that. (varieties of Southern US English)
They went a-fishin' yesterday. (Appalachian English)

Complicating the notion of what we think of as "English" is that languages change, sometimes quite dramatically, over time. Any of you who have studied Old English (spoken around 445–1000 CE), for example, know that Old English looks very little like modern, or Present Day English. Yet, we still call Old English "English." Consider these lines from the Old English poem *Beowulf*, written in about 700.

Hwæt! We Gardena in geardagum,
Listen! We of the Spear-Danes in days of yore,

Þeodcyninga, Þrym gefrunon,
Of those folk-kings, the glory have heard,

hu ða æÞelingas ellen fremedon.
How those noblemen brave-things did.

Middle English (spoken around 1100–1400) looks more like Present Day English but is still clearly not what we would consider contemporary. Here is an excerpt from Geoffrey Chaucer's *The Wife of Bath's Tale*, from his famous *Canterbury Tales* written at the end of the fourteenth century.

> Experience, though noon auctoritee
> *Experience, though no authority*
>
> Were in this world, is right ynogh for me
> *Were in this world, were good enough for me*
>
> To speke of wo that is in mariage;
> *To speak of woe that is in marriage;*

And Early Modern English (1500–1700), though much more familiar, is still a little different. Here is an excerpt from Shakespeare's *Hamlet*. We may not need a translation anymore, but this 400-year-old version of English is still quite different from English spoken today.

> To be, or not to be: that is the question:
> Whether 'tis nobler in the mind to suffer
> The slings and arrows of outrageous fortune,
> Or to take arms against a sea of troubles,
> And by opposing end them?

We learn from studying language change and variation that not all of us speak the same variety or dialect of English, and whatever variety we do speak continues to change. As we will see as we progress through this book, all varieties, or dialects of English are worthy of investigation and can be explored using the tools of analysis we will introduce to you here. This is something of a departure from what you may have learned, namely, that studying English grammar means learning a single set of rules in order to avoid errors. An approach to English as a set of rules to memorize doesn't tell you very much about how English actually works, nor do such rules accurately describe the grammar of the language.

Throughout the exploration of the grammar of English in this book, we will draw examples (or "data") from a range of varieties of American English to illustrate grammatical features and concepts. Our goal is two-fold: one is to highlight the diverse ways in which English speakers use language, and another is to highlight the principles that are common to all varieties. This approach to the study of language in turn sheds light on how (all) languages work.

What is Grammar?

When you hear the word *grammar*, what comes to mind? Over the years, we have asked countless students this question, and most agree that in school, the study of grammar seems to be connected to the study of writing. "Grammar" covers a broad range of rules, including punctuation rules (where to put commas and apostrophes, for example), vocabulary rules (use *active* verbs rather than *be* verbs; avoid "slang;" use "academic" vocabulary), spelling rules (don't mix up *they're, their,* and *there* or *you're* and *your*), as well as other injunctions such as "Never start a sentence with *because;*" "Never end a sentence with a preposition;" "Don't use first person;" "Don't use passive voice;" "Avoid fragments;" "Use *I* instead of *me* and *whom* instead of *who;*" and so on. You have also probably heard certain words or phrases labeled as "correct" or "incorrect" grammar, or as "proper" or "improper" grammar. You may even have heard certain words or phrases referred to as "good" or "bad" grammar, or even as "lazy" or "sloppy" grammar. For example, you may have heard that *I don't know nobody* is considered by some to be "bad grammar" or that such "double negatives" should be avoided. There are other words or phrases (such as *ain't* or *I seen it*) that are often put in the same category of "bad grammar," and that you may have been taught to avoid, in your writing, but also in your speech. This view of grammar, as a set of rules *prescribed* by some authority (maybe your teachers, parents, or even your friends) as the rules we should follow for social success, is called **prescriptive grammar.** As we'll see below, prescriptive grammar is different from **descriptive grammar,** though these two ways of approaching grammar also overlap in important ways.

Prescriptive grammar is very much a part of our cultural view of English, but where did this idea come from? What are some of the consequences of thinking of English grammar this way?

Prescriptive grammar

The view of English grammar as "good" or "bad" has its roots in seventeenth-century England, when speaking and writing "correctly" came to be considered a key to social success, and a variety of English spoken in London came to be considered "standard." This period saw the rise of English prescriptive grammar, rules that dictate how one *should* speak or write, according to the language authorities of the time. It was during this period that rules such as "don't end a sentence with a preposition" and "don't split infinitives" emerged, some of which were based on the grammar of Latin, the language of scholarship (and prestige) at the time.

One reason that language prescription, and the related notion of creating a "standard" language, arises is the belief that language variation can lead to misunderstanding. But interestingly, we often understand very well those whose language we claim is unclear or hard to understand based on our social perceptions of the speaker(s), those who don't "talk like us." Such concerns emerge as early as the fourteenth century. (Note that you can likely understand these excerpts even though they also look very different from the English you use!)

> Al the longage of the Northumres and speicialliche at York is so sharp slittynge and frontynge and vnshape, that we southern men may that longage vnnethe [= hardly] vnderstonde. (John de Trevisa, 1385)

> Oure language is also so dyuerse in it selfe that the commen maner of spekynge in Englysshe of some contre can skante [= scarcely] be vnderstondid in som other contre of the same lond. (Lydgate, 1530)

Dialects spoken in the North and West of England were stigmatized during this time, and Southern varieties of English, spoken in and around London by the upper classes, were perceived more favorably. In *The Arte of English Poesie* (1589), George Puttenham proposes that respected men should not "follow the speech of a craftes man or carter, or other of the inferior sort, though he be inhabitant or bred in the best towne ... for such persons doe abuse good speeches by strange accents or ill shapen soundes, and false ortographie."

We see these language attitudes reflected in literature as well. Chaucer often used different Middle English dialects to express certain (usually comic) aspects of character; a speaker of a stigmatized Northern dialect, for example, may end up hoodwinking the gentleman with the more prestigious Southern speech. Shakespeare, writing during the sixteenth century, also often used dialect to express different favorable or unfavorable aspects of character.

Other factors led to dialects of southern England becoming more highly valued. One of the earliest factors that set the process of standardizing English in motion was the printing press, brought to England in 1476 by the merchant William Caxton. Caxton set up shop in London, the center of commerce and education at the time, and printed far more books and distributed them far more widely than ever before. For practical reasons, Caxton printed books in the East Midland dialect, the dialect (or collection of dialects) of London's rising middle and upper classes, and the East Midland dialect became considered the "standard" dialect of English.

Latin, the language of the Christian church, was the language of scholarship in medieval England. As English inevitably began to compete with Latin as the language of commerce, literature, and scholarship, English was found sorely wanting and was considered corrupt. Between the fifteenth and the eighteenth centuries, scholars set out to "fix" and "improve" English, introducing spelling reforms, borrowing many Latin words into English, and attempting to codify its grammatical rules. Dictionaries also played a part in this process of standardization. Perhaps the most famous example is Samuel Johnson's *A Dictionary of the English Language*, completed in 1755. Although Johnson himself was aware of the futility of trying to fix meanings of words of a living language, his dictionary was nevertheless taken as authoritative, and others followed. In 1828, Noah Webster published *Webster's American Dictionary of the English Language*, and the *Oxford English Dictionary* first appeared in 1884 and continues to be the foremost authority on the English language today.

English grammarians attempted to establish a language academy, like those in France and Italy, which would codify and enforce this "improved" version of English. Scholars in the eighteenth century, which was often referred to as the Age of Reason, strove to find order and harmony in the natural (and divine, with Latin as the model of a perfect, divine language), and some extended this idea to grammar as well. Grammarians took it upon themselves to improve English by establishing the rules of English grammar and attempting to enforce them to prevent future change. John Dryden supported an academy, as did Daniel Defoe (author of *Robinson Crusoe*), and Jonathan Swift (author of *Gulliver's Travels*). Dryden's *Defence of the Epilogue*, written in 1672, criticizes supposed grammatical errors, stating (quite unapologetically), "From [Ben] Jonsons time to ours, it [English] has been in a continual declination." By the publication of Samuel Johnson's dictionary in 1755, the idea for an academy had died. (The idea for an English academy became fodder for political battles between Whigs and Tories and was criticized by others who thought an academy was too authoritarian. John Adams' proposal for an American academy met a similar fate.)

During this period, the idea arose that using the correct form of English was essential for social success. How-to books on English grammar began to appear and to be used in schools. Here is a quote from the preface to Joseph Aickin's *The English Grammar* (1693): "My Child: your Parents have desired me, to teach you the English-Tongue. For though you can speak English already; yet you are not an English Scholar, till you can read, write, and speak English truly."

Although people were certainly aware of language change and variation, people also believed that in order to be socially accepted and admired in the larger society, one had to adopt the linguistic practices of those who were accepted and admired. Thus emerged the "grammar anxiety" (related to "linguistic insecurity," see Labov, 1972 and subsequent work) we still see today and which has its source in two central ideas: that we must speak and write correctly for social acceptance and advancement, and that grammatical change and variation should be overcome and controlled.

By studying prescriptivism and the language attitudes that underpin it, we can gain insights not only into how English changed and varied over time but also into the sources of our current language attitudes. Curzan (2014, p. 24) proposes the following four categories of prescriptive rules, which reflect the themes we've discussed so far:

- *Standardizing prescriptivism*: rules/judgments that aim to promote and enforce standardization and "standard" usage.
- *Stylistic prescriptivism*: rules/judgments that aim to differentiate among (often fine) points of style within standard usage.
- *Restorative prescriptivism*: rules/judgments that aim to restore earlier, but now relatively obsolete, usage and/or turn to older forms to purify usage.
- *Politically responsive prescriptivism*: rules/judgments that aim to promote inclusive, nondiscriminatory, politically correct, and/or politically expedient usage.

You can probably think of examples that fit into each of these categories, though your examples might also vary, depending on the variety of English you speak, your educational background, and other factors. It's also important to note that prescriptivism is not uniformly negative and discriminatory; it also includes, for example, politically responsive prescriptivism that can promote positive social change, such as moves toward more inclusive, gender-neutral language (pronouns or names for professions, for example), or the addition of new words or phrases to replace terms that may be discriminatory or marginalizing.

Curzan's categories reflect the connection between prescriptivism and language standardization; in fact, prescriptivism is defined in terms of standard language. But, as mentioned above, what came to be considered "standard" English was not actually a specific dialect, but rather whatever language was associated with speakers with social prestige (the literate middle and upper classes in Southern England) at the time.

Although the idea of a unified, single correct form of English continues to be widely accepted today, what is considered standard still actually varies from speech community to speech community. Today, with English spoken around the world, what speakers in Birmingham, Alabama consider standard is not the same as what speakers in Bangor, Maine do, and what is considered Standard English in New Zealand or Jamaica is different from what is considered Standard English in Australia, the United Kingdom, or India.

Though no actual single standard English exists, the *idea* that there is a right/better and wrong/worse way to use English is very much entrenched in our social attitudes about language. *Standard Language Ideology* (SLI) underpins much of what we learn about language in school, and how we perceive members of different speech communities (see Cameron, 1995; Milroy and Milroy, 2012; Greenfield and Rowan, 2011 among others for more on SLI).

Lippi-Green defines SLI as:

> a bias toward an abstracted, idealized, homogeneous spoken language which is imposed and maintained by dominant bloc institutions and which names as its model the written language, but which is drawn primarily from the spoken language of the upper middle class. (Lippi-Green, 2012, p. 67)

The study of prescriptive grammar and SLI provides a key to better understanding the origins of many of our current language attitudes, in particular, why we feel so strongly about how others use language, and why maintaining our own language norms seems so important to us. Studying prescription also reveals important insights into language change, the history of the English language, and the foundations of SLI. Understanding prescriptivism leaves us in a better position to recognize and challenge ways in which SLI might be used to exclude and marginalize, in school, in the workplace, and even at home.

Descriptive grammar

As we mentioned in the introduction to this chapter, we can study language scientifically, in the same way that we study the circulatory system or the solar system, by examining data (in this case language data), constructing hypotheses that attempt to explain and describe these data, and testing those hypotheses against additional data. In so doing, we strive to construct a model of how language works, just as we might construct models of other systems. This inquiry-based approach to language became prominent in the United States in the 1950s when linguist Noam Chomsky revolutionized the study of language by posing the question we paraphrase here as "what does it mean to know a language?" That is, what does a language user need to know in order to produce and understand language? Chomsky's research and questions gave rise to modern linguistics, and research in linguistics has greatly advanced our understanding of the principles and operations common to all languages, despite how different they may seem on the surface. Linguistics, the scientific study of language, seeks to *describe* rather than *prescribe* the grammar of a language, the set of (often unconscious) rules and principles we use to produce and understand language. **Descriptive grammar** is therefore, in theory, quite different from prescriptive grammar and is based on how speakers actually use language (the "data" that linguists study), rather than how they *should* use language.

9

Both approaches to the study of grammar offer valuable insights; by studying descriptive grammar we gain a better understanding of how language as a dynamic system actually seems to work, and by studying prescriptive grammar we learn more about language history and the origins of social attitudes about language and language users. Descriptive and prescriptive grammar also overlap; as we saw above, if you use a variety of English that is considered "standard," the language you use is considered "prescriptively correct." To take a concrete example – "double negatives" such as *I don't know nobody* are often considered prescriptively incorrect (even ungrammatical) and nonstandard English. Alternatively, *I don't know anybody* is considered prescriptively correct (grammatical) and standard. These judgments are social; we stigmatize the speech of marginalized groups (speech communities in which this form of negation is systematically used) and attach prestige to the speech of speech communities with social power and authority (in which negation is expressed differently). From the point of view of descriptive grammar, however, both forms of negation are *grammatical* for the speech communities that use them, and both are interesting, worthy of study, and provide insights into how language (in this case English) works.

Although linguists strive to describe rather than prescribe language, neither approach to language and grammar is entirely objective, because none of us is without a language ideology and a set of norms we apply to language in our daily lives. Moreover, the language "data" that linguists study to gain insights into the descriptive grammar of a language comes from real people, whose languages are inextricably intertwined with culture. While we can't possibly include examples from every variety of American English, as we progress throughout the book we draw on data from a diverse range of speech communities in an attempt to provide a more inclusive picture of English, one that strives to decenter "standardized" Englishes.

The Components of Grammar

In this section, we provide a brief overview of the components of grammar as we'll approach them in this book. We will focus mostly on one component, *syntax*, or the rules and principles used to arrange words in sentences in patterns that can be recognized and understood as English. But as we'll see, the study of syntax overlaps with the study of *morphology*, the structure of words, and *semantics*, the study of meaning in language. Though we will not explore the sound system of language (the study of *phonetics and phonology*) in detail in the coming chapters, we briefly show here how the scientific study of grammar includes the study of this system.

Syntax

One of the things you may have encountered somewhere along the way is "parts of speech," the different categories that words fall into, such as noun, verb, or adjective. You might have learned that "a noun is a person, place, or thing," and "a verb is an action or a state." But these definitions don't capture what we actually know about syntactic categories or parts of speech (nor do they provide us with tools of analysis to study language in more depth). To illustrate, consider the following nwonsense sentence:

The flonkish warzile will blork one yerkon.

Are there any nouns or verbs in this sentence? If so, what are they? You may have identified *warzile* and *yerkon* as nouns, even though you don't know what these words mean (and whether each is a "person, place, or thing"). You may also have identified *blork* as the verb, again, even though you don't know whether it is an action or state. How did you do that? Though you may never have (consciously) learned what nouns and verbs are, as a speaker of a language you already know about syntactic categories and how to recognize them, even though you may not know the terminology, or *meta-language*, we use to talk about them.

You know, for example, that *warzile* is a noun because of its *syntax*, its position after *flonkish*, a word you may have analyzed as an adjective modifying *warzile*, and after *the*, a word that introduces nouns. You probably analyzed *blork* as a verb because it follows the subject *the flonkish warzile* and precedes the object, *one yerkon*. *Blork* is also preceded by *will* (a modal), a word that precedes other verbs (*will eat*). *Yerkon* itself is a noun because it follows *one*, a word that precedes nouns, and also because *one yerkon* follows the verb, a position in which we often find nouns (or more specifically *noun phrases* (NPs), but more on that later).

You may have noticed that *the* and *one* in the sentence above are actual English words, and they provide important clues to the categories of the words that follow them (nouns). These words express grammatical information (here, of number and in the case of *the*, definiteness) and differ from words that express lexical information, such as nouns and verbs. In other words, we know that certain *syntactic categories* are *functional*, and others are *lexical*. Lexical categories (noun, verb, adjective, and adverb) express the main content, or meaning in a sentence. Functional categories (pronoun, determiner, numeral, conjunction, auxiliary, and others) express grammatical information about definiteness, number, tense, gender, etc. (see Table 1.1). We will discuss the distinctions between lexical and functional categories in more detail in the coming chapters.

11

Table 1.1 Some examples of English syntactic categories.

Lexical categories	
Noun	eagle, friendship, mud, platypus, blog, fortune
Verb	encourage, forget, irritate, feel, canter, seem, text
Adjective	happy, malevolent, lovely, angry, tiny, eager
Adverb	quickly, lovingly, fast, still, now, soon
Functional categories	
Determiner	the, a, this, that, these, those, their, his, my
Numeral	one, five, ten, second, eighth
Quantifier	all, each, every, both, some
Pronoun	they, he, she, her, theirs, mine, yours
Preposition	without, in, on, over, behind, above, around
Conjunction	and, or, yet, for, but, so, nor
Degree word	very, so, quite, rather, too
Auxiliary verb	have, be, do
Modal	may, might, can, could, will, would, shall, should, must

Returning to our nonsense sentence, if we asked you to divide the sentence up into its two main parts, what would you do? You would probably do this in the following way:

The flonkish warzile / will blork one yerkon.

This suggests that you have intuitive knowledge of how words are grouped together in a sentence. We call those groups of words *phrases,* and the words that make them up are *constituents* of that phrase. What is the syntactic category (noun, verb, adjective, etc.) of each of these phrases?

The first phrase is a noun phrase (NP) because its main word, or *head,* is the noun *warzile.* The constituents of this NP are *the, flonkish,* and *warzile.* The other phrase is a *verb phrase* (VP), whose head is (*will*) *blork,* a verb, and whose other constituent is *one yerkon.* You might also have noticed that *one yerkon* is itself a phrase, an NP, which is a constituent of a larger VP.

You may also have observed that the first NP in the nonsense sentence is the *subject* of the clause, and that *one yerkon* is the *object* of the verb. You may also have labeled the VP the *predicate.* These are all *grammatical functions,* the functions of different phrases in the sentence.

That we can divide sentences up into parts that contain other parts tells us that sentence structure is not simply flat, made up of a linear strings of words, but *hierarchical,* with groups of words (phrases) that include other groups of words. Throughout the book, we will use tree diagrams (also called *phrase structure trees*) as a convenient way to illustrate hierarchical structure. Here we diagram our nonsense sentence as an example.

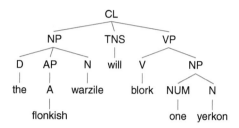

As this tree diagram shows, the largest syntactic unit, the clause (CL), includes, or *dominates*, the subject noun phrase, or NP, and the predicate verb phrase, or VP. Each of these phrases in turn dominates other constituents. Throughout the book, we will use tree diagrams to illustrate important concepts about phrase structure.

In this brief analysis of a nonsense sentence, we've discovered that our knowledge of syntax includes knowledge of syntactic categories (and the difference between lexical categories and functional ones), phrases, heads, constituents, and grammatical functions (subject, predicate, object). We have also discovered that phrase structure, which we can represent graphically in tree diagrams, is not "flat" (a linear string of words) but hierarchical. We therefore know much more about grammar than "a noun is a person, place, or thing" or that "a verb is an action or a state."

Morphology

You probably relied not only on your knowledge of syntax to identify the category of the words in the nonsense sentence; you likely also used your knowledge of word structure, or *morphology*. For example, you might have identified *flonkish* as an adjective, because it ends in *-ish*, an ending we find on other adjectives such as *pinkish* or *childish*. Here's another version of our nonsense sentence, with what may be some recognizable morphology:

The flonkish warziler will reblorkify one yerkoment.

You may recognize not just *-ish*, but the suffixes *-er* on *warziler*, *-ify* on *blorkify*, and *-ment* on *yerkoment*. These help us not only identify *flonkish* as an adjective but also *warziler* as a noun (like *driver* or *teacher*), *blorkify* as a verb (like *rectify* and *horrify*), and *yerkoment* as a noun (like *excitement* and *statement*). The prefix *re-* attaches to verbs (which may or may not end in *-ify*: *reword* and *reamplify*).

Affixation (in English, suffixation and prefixation) is one way we build words.

Table 1.2 Some English derivational affixes.

Nouns	-ity	serenity
	-ment	excitement
	-ion	transmission
	ex-	ex-president
Verbs	-ize	realize
	-ate	activate
	-ify	mystify
	en-	engage
	dis-	disengage
Adjectives	-ly	lovely
	-ish	boyish
	-ful	bashful
	non-	noncompliant
Adverbs	-ly	usually, quickly
	-wise	crosswise
	-like	crablike

Parts of words are called *morphemes*. *Affixes* are morphemes that attach to words or roots of words (and some languages have *infixes*, affixes that occur within words, or *circumfixes*, affixes that attach to the beginning and to the end of a word). There are two types of affixation, *inflectional* affixation and *derivational* affixation.

Derivational affixation
Derivational affixes derive a new word or dictionary entry. To take some real English examples, adding *re-* to the verb *seal* derives a new word, *reseal*, and adding yet another derivational affix, *-able*, gives us *resealable*. All are derived from the root verb *seal* by derivational affixation, and each has its own dictionary entry. We give some examples of common English derivational affixes and words they derive in Table 1.2.

Inflectional affixation
Inflectional affixes, on the other hand, don't create new words but attach to existing words, adding grammatical information. For example, the plural *-s* that we can add to nouns is an inflectional affix (rat → rats), as is the *-er* that can be attached to most adjectives (cold → colder). (Note that only *rat* and *cold*, but not *rats* and *colder* have dictionary entries.)

Here is a list of the possible inflectional affixes in English. As you can see, although there are many English derivational affixes, English has far fewer productive inflectional affixes – up to eight, to be exact!

14

nouns plural: *-s*, possessive *-s*
verbs: *-s, -ed, -ing, -en*
adjectives: *-er, -est*

As we'll see in the coming chapters, different varieties of English express inflectional information (person, number, tense, aspect, and other features) in different ways – sometimes morphologically with an affix, sometimes syntactically with no affix, and sometimes with both!

We illustrate once again with another version of our nonsense sentence, adding some inflectional affixes. Can you find them?

The furstiest warziles blorked six yerkons, while jeebling the strek's progue.

Analytic and synthetic languages
Languages vary in how many inflectional affixes they have, and some have none at all. Maybe you have studied a language like Latin or Russian, both of which have far more complex inflectional affixation than English. Navajo, Mohawk, and Spanish have more inflectional affixes than English does, and Old English had many more inflectional affixes than the language does today. Mandarin and Vietnamese, on the other hand, express inflectional relationships syntactically, with little to no inflectional morphology at all.

Here's an example sentence from Mandarin, where neither the verb "mǎi" nor the noun "shū" has any inflectional affixation. (The word "běn" is a counter word that occurs with numbers, labeled CL for "classifier" in the example.)

她 买 三 本 书
tā　　mǎi　sān　　běn　shū
she　buy　three　CL　book
"She buys three books"

And here's an example from Yup'ik, a language of Alaska, which has a high number of morphemes per word. This one word is both a word and a whole sentence.

kaipiallrulliniuk
kaig-pirar-llru-llini-u-k
be.hungry-really-PAST-apparently-INDICATIVE-they.two
"the two of them are apparently really hungry"
George Charles, speaker, cited in Mithun (1999, p. 38)

Table 1.3   Word formation rules.

Term	Formation method	Sample words
Coining	Inventing words not related to other words	bling, quiz, cheugy
Compounding	Two or more words behaving as one word	backlash, bailout, undertake, Zoombomb
Blending	Telescoping two words together	webinar, brunch, fancam
Clipping	Shortening words by omitting syllables	demo, lab, vax
Conversion	Assigning one word more than one syntactic category	father, tweet, email
Acronyms and abbreviations	Words from abbreviations	NFT, COVID, laser, radar
Eponyms	Words from names, including brand names	TikToked, kleenex, cardigan, sandwich

Languages that morphologically express a great deal of grammatical information are called *synthetic*, while those with few inflectional affixes (like English), or none at all (like Japanese or Vietnamese), are called *analytic*. Many languages, including English, employ some features of both and can be best understood as being somewhere on a continuum between analytic and synthetic.

Word formation rules

As we saw above, we can form new words through derivational affixation, deriving, for example, *blogger* by affixing the verb *blog* with *-er* to create a (new) noun. This is not the only way we create new words, however. A list of other word formation rules we use all the time is given in Table 1.3.

As you can probably see from the list in Table 1.3, we add new words to *lexical* categories (such as nouns, verbs, or adjectives) but not to *functional* categories. (We don't make up new determiners, pronouns, or conjunctions.) Lexical categories are therefore *open class* categories, accepting new members, but functional categories are *closed class* categories, and typically do not accept new members.

Semantics

We mentioned above that you might have learned meaning-based definitions of parts of speech, such as "a noun is a person, place or thing." We've also shown that you actually rely a good deal on syntactic and morphological evidence, rather than meaning, to identify syntactic categories. This is not to say, however, that our grammatical knowledge does not also include rules by which we construct and understand the meanings of words and sentences – it most certainly does. Here, we briefly explore our knowledge of meaning, or *semantics*, introducing some concepts we will return to later on. To begin, consider the following (rather famous) sentence attributed to linguist Noam Chomsky:

Colorless green ideas sleep furiously.

You probably recognize that this sentence is syntactically and morphologically grammatical (the words are all English words, arranged in English word order), but the sentence is still *anomalous* or nonsensical; ideas can't (literally) be green, nor can ideas sleep, much less furiously – you get the point. That we can recognize what is grammatical about this sentence (its syntax and its morphology) and ungrammatical (its meaning) tells us (a) that our grammatical knowledge includes knowledge of how to construct meaning from words and sentences and (b) that the component of grammar that governs meaning is in certain ways separate from other components of grammar. So, just as one can study syntax and morphology as separate (but interacting) components of grammar, one can also study semantics as a separate component of our knowledge of grammar, one which overlaps with syntax and morphology.

Though we've seen that semantic definitions of syntactic categories aren't always explanatory, syntactic categories do have semantic properties that we will investigate in later chapters. What, for example, is the difference between the following two nouns *furniture* and *couch*?

The furniture is really expensive.
The couch is really expensive.

You may say that to be a couch is also to be a piece of furniture, so *couch* entails, or includes, the meaning of *furniture*. You may also have noticed that in most varieties of English, *couch*, but not *furniture*, can be (morphologically) pluralized.

*The furnitures are really expensive.
The couches are really expensive.

This is because *furniture* in English is a *mass* noun, while *couch* is a *count* noun. Though not all varieties of English express plurality morphologically, they still have this semantic distinction. Other languages also share the distinction between mass and count but may differ in terms of nouns

17

that fall into each semantic class. For example, *furniture* in French is *les meubles*, a count noun. Mass and count are just two possible semantic features of nouns that we will explore in the coming chapters.

Adjectives also fall into different semantic classes, which we can illustrate here with a very simple example. We say:

small green chair

But not:

*green small chair

Why? It turns out that semantic classes of adjectives (size, color, origin, shape, age, etc.) occur in a certain order, and color adjectives usually do not precede size adjectives in English, but not necessarily in other languages.

Another semantic property we will discuss is *ambiguity*, which arises when words or sentences have more than one meaning. Consider this example:

Lee kissed the dog in the hallway.

Assuming the literal meanings of each word in this sentence, what are the two meanings? Who is in the hallway? Lee or the dog? It turns out that this sentence is ambiguous because it has two different structures, one in which the phrase *in the hallway* modifies the verb, and the other in which it modifies the noun *dog*. This is where tree diagrams come in handy; we can illustrate these two meanings with two different tree diagrams. In the first diagram below, the prepositional phrase (PP) *in the hallway* modifies the verb, *kissed*, and is a constituent of the VP.

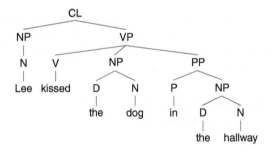

In the following diagram, however, the PP *in the hallway* is part of the NP and modifies the noun *dog*.

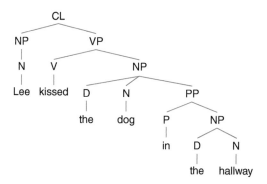

These diagrams illustrate *syntactic ambiguity*, that a sentence can be ambiguous because of its syntactic structure. Another kind of ambiguity is *lexical ambiguity*, or ambiguity based on a word with more than one meaning. Here's an example:

I grabbed the bat.

Here, the noun *bat* is ambiguous – it can mean "a nocturnal mammal with wings" or "a piece of sports equipment." Ambiguity in this case derives from the multiple meanings of a single word and can't be explained in structural terms (there is only one tree diagram for this sentence, where *bat* is a noun). We return to ambiguity later in the book.

Phonetics and phonology

Another essential component of grammar, one which we've said virtually nothing about so far, is *phonetics*, the inventory of sounds in our language, and *phonology*, the system of rules we use to combine those sounds, or phonemes, together to form syllables, words, and larger units.

Different phonetic inventories and phonological systems give rise to different *accents*, or pronunciations. A single language can be spoken with different accents; speakers of Scots English, for example, sound very different from speakers of Jamaican English. We may attach different social values to different accents; some tend to think of certain accents as more acceptable or more "standard" than others. Yet all accents are governed by systematic rules, and no accent, in linguistic terms, is better than another.

To explore accents a bit further, consider dialects that "drop *r*" such as varieties of English spoken in the United Kingdom, the southern United States, and New England. Speakers of these "r-less" dialects don't drop *r* just anywhere, they do so only under certain phonological conditions. For example, speakers drop *r* in a word when it follows a vowel and would therefore not pronounce the *r* in the following words:

heart, car, farm

But they would pronounce *r* in these words because *r* does not follow a vowel:

red, brick, scratch

The *r*-drop rule in words is even more complex; though you may be familiar with the phrase "pahk the cah in Hahvad Yahd," a stock phrase used to imitate this dialectical feature, real speakers of such varieties of English in fact retain a final *r* when the following word begins with a vowel. Speakers say "pahk the ca*r* in Hahvad Yahd." (A similar rule accounts for so-called *r-intrusion*, where some speakers add *r* to words that end in vowels before another word that begins with a vowel, as in *Mahther* (Martha) *is coming* or *That idear is a good one.*) This brief discussion of rules governing *r*-drop illustrates speakers' unconscious knowledge of a phonological rule, one that interacts with syntax.

Phonetics and phonology interact with other components of grammar as well. Adding a suffix to a word, for example, can change its pronunciation. Most speakers pronounce the final syllable of *serene* to rhyme with *keen* but then change this pronunciation when the affix *-ity* is attached, deriving *serenity* (and this same rule applies to other words, such as *divine/divinity*, *profane/profanity* and in other pairs such as *school/scholarly* and *provoke/provocative*). If we add the plural affix *-s* to words, their pronunciation can change as well. Consider the pronunciation of *-s* in *cats* and *desks*, which in words like *dogs* and *cans* is not pronounced as [s] but as [z] for most, because of a phonological rule (called *voicing assimilation*).

Summary

In this chapter, we provide a brief overview of some basic facts about language. One is that languages **change** over time and **vary** from place to place and from speech community to speech community. The language we call English is a dynamic system, and we can study the **grammar** of English from different perspectives. We can study the **prescriptive grammar** of English, rules of how one *should* speak (and write), according to some authority. We can also study the **descriptive grammar** of English, by exploring how speakers use language (in all contexts), to discover the principles and rules those speakers use to produce and understand language. Both approaches to grammar provide valuable insights into this language we call English, but each has different goals. Prescriptive grammar (mostly) strives to support **Standard Language Ideology**, and descriptive grammar (mostly) strives to explain how language works by investigating the interacting **components of grammar** of a language: **syntax, morphology, semantics**, and **phonetics** and **phonology**. No study of language, however, is completely objective, but our goal here is to provide you with tools to analyze the grammar of the language variety that you speak, tools which provide a foundation for you to study language in any way you choose, and to make your own informed decisions and choices about it. What we explore in the coming chapters will deepen your understanding of this uniquely human behavior, and, we hope, encourage you to continue to investigate it on your own!

Exercises

1. Changes in word meaning

Look up (in a comprehensive dictionary, such as the *Oxford English Dictionary* or *Merriam-Webster*) four words that you might consider slang or taboo. Discuss how the meanings of these words have changed over time. Are you aware of the origins of these words? What does this mean about language change?

2. Variation in word meaning

Look up four words in the online *Dictionary of American Regional English*, or DARE (DARE has a Quizzes link, where you can find word lists and try to match the meanings to words you likely don't know – it's a fun way to start this exercise!). What are the origins of those words and what do they mean? Who uses them?

3. Global English

Where is English spoken today around the world? Do some research on two or three different varieties of English spoken outside the United States and the United Kingdom. When, why, and how did English come to be spoken in the areas/regions you investigate? How many speakers are there, and what other languages are spoken? What is the status of English? Is it the dominant language of power or a minority language? Briefly discuss.

4. American varieties of English

Look up three varieties (you can also search under "dialects") of American English and discuss their origins and some of their linguistic features. Can you identify your own variety/dialect of English? If possible, explain the social attitudes toward the varieties you researched.

5. Pet peeves

Give at least two of your own grammar "pet peeves." Are there any words, phrases, or pronunciations that annoy you? For example, "It really bugs me when someone says 'nukeyuler' for nuclear" or "I think it sounds really weird when someone says, 'This car needs washed.'" Where do you think your feelings about such variations in usage come from? Briefly discuss.

6. "Error" correction

What aspects of your language have you been corrected for? Do you recall consciously making a change in your language use after being corrected? Do you now correct others for the same "errors?" Did it bother you to be corrected, and who are the language authorities in your life (has anyone ever corrected you on social media, at home, or at school)?

7. What's "grammaticality?"

Here are some examples of American English that may or may not be familiar to you, but all are common to some speech community. How would you label these sentences (think about before you read this chapter and after – have your ideas changed?). Would you label them as correct/incorrect or grammatical/ungrammatical or as something else? Who do you think uses these sentences (if you don't)? Check the *Yale Grammatical Diversity Project* website for more information (https://ygdp.yale.edu/phenomena/what-all#who-says-this)

(a) The car needs repaired.
(b) He liketa burn down the house one day cookin' french fries.
(c) I BIN started my paper Ma, so quit asking me.
(d) We usta could drive up that road.
(e) Your friend's fixin' to tell a story.
(f) Even in the small towns anymore, it's getting like that.
(g) They was just a-singing as loud as they could.
(h) My sister be working.
(i) Her mouth is steady runnin'.
(j) Where all did he go?

8.   Accents and other linguistic stereotypes

In this chapter, we discussed how we attach social values to different language varieties. These social values are reflected in many contexts, particularly in the media (movies and shows, video games, etc.). Find at least two examples of how language is used to express some aspect of character. How do accents or other aspects of language variation influence our social perceptions of a particular character?

9.   Standard English

Though many of us are familiar with the term "Standard English," upon close inspection, it is actually quite difficult to define. Look up at least three different definitions of Standard English (in dictionaries or in other resources – grammar and writing guides may include definitions, as might other education resources). How are they the same and/or different and what do they tell us about what the term Standard English means?

10.   Categories of prescriptive rules

Find two or three examples of each of the following kinds of prescriptive rules (from Curzan, 2014):

- *Standardizing prescriptivism*: rules/judgments that aim to promote and enforce standardization and "standard" usage.
- *Stylistic prescriptivism*: rules/judgments that aim to differentiate among (often fine) points of style within standard usage.
- *Restorative prescriptivism*: rules/judgments that aim to restore earlier, but now relatively obsolete, usage and/or turn to older forms to purify usage.
- *Politically responsive prescriptivism*: rules/judgments that aim to promote inclusive, nondiscriminatory, politically correct, and/or politically expedient usage.

A good place to start is Paul Brians' *Common Errors in English Usage* site, which includes a vast list of "errors" and explanations for why they are considered "non-standard" and incorrect. (There are other such sites if this one is unavailable.) Do you agree that the examples you cite are "errors"? Why or why not? Does what you find on this site support Standard Language Ideology? Why/why not?
https://brians.wsu.edu/common-errors/

2
Nouns

Introduction

Just what is a *noun* anyway? This is a term that you are probably all familiar with, and you certainly have intuitions about what a noun is. You may know the old adage that *a noun is a person, place, or thing*. And yes, this is somewhat accurate, but, as we'll find throughout this book, definitions that

Navigating English Grammar: A Guide to Analyzing Real Language, Second Edition.
Anne Lobeck and Kristin Denham.
© 2025 Anne Lobeck and Kristin Denham. Published 2025 by John Wiley & Sons Ltd.

rely on meaning alone don't always capture the kinds of knowledge we actually use to identify the syntactic category of a word. To illustrate, consider the following sentence. Is *talking* a noun or a verb?

Lee is *talking* about linguistics.
All that crazy *talking* is making me nervous.

In the first sentence, *talking* is a verb, and in the second, it is a noun. This shows that you cannot determine the category of a word in isolation; it depends on where it is in the sentence. And when *talking* is a noun, is it a person, place, or thing? How does the meaning of *talking* differ in each sentence? Does it?

Though defining a noun is based on what it means can be difficult, we're in luck; it turns out that we actually already know exactly what a noun is. As language users, we demonstrate all the time that we know what nouns are, and we use them perfectly accurately in the sentences we produce. So, though you may not be able to actually explain what a noun is, this is only because it's difficult to make our unconscious knowledge of language conscious, and that's what we're here to help you with! In this chapter, we will discuss intuitive knowledge of the semantics and morphology of nouns. In the next chapter, we turn to the syntax of nouns and the larger units that contain them, *noun phrases*.

Semantic Distinctions Among Nouns

There are many different types of nouns, based on distinctions in meaning, and languages may differ in the kinds of meaning distinctions nouns express. Some of these meaning distinctions provide us with some good evidence that the category Noun (or at least some way to express "nouniness") is something most if not all human languages share. Nouns are not something that linguists, grammarians, or schoolteachers invented. It is a real lexical distinction that we make in our minds – part of our unconscious knowledge of language.

In English, nouns express three basic semantic distinctions: *abstract/concrete*, *common/proper*, and *count/mass*. We discuss each in turn below. We will then discuss some other semantic types of nouns, *collective* and *generic* nouns.

Abstract and concrete

English and many other languages make distinctions between what we call *abstract* and *concrete* nouns. Abstract nouns are just that; they name things we can't touch or see – *love, anxiety, freedom*. Concrete nouns, on the other hand, are things we can see and touch – *mice, zucchini, umbrella, computer*. Though this seems like a simple distinction, sometimes it can get a little tricky. Is *territory* abstract or concrete? We may think of *territory* as something defined in terms of tangible, even visible, boundaries, but is that always the case? And what about *weather* or *homework*?

The reason that the difference between abstract and concrete nouns is not always easy to determine is that the distinction itself is oversimplified, and it's made to seem like a property of the nouns themselves, though it is more accurately a property of the things in the real world that the nouns refer to. Also, it's far more complex than we've made it here, with a simple binary distinction. For example, we might classify concrete nouns as those that name things that exist in three-dimensional space and are observable: people, animals, physical objects, things you can see and touch. Abstract nouns, on the other hand, might be divided into different kinds: for example, events and processes that exist in time (*weather, storm, sunset*) and other things that are not observable (*faith, belief, happiness*).

To make things even a bit more complicated, the classification of a noun can change depending on how that noun is used and what it's referring to in the real world. When *homework* refers to the idea of schoolwork that will be completed over time, it seems more abstract, but when it refers to an actual document that you submit for a class, it seems concrete:

I don't want to take that class because there will be a lot of *homework*. (abstract)
I know it's late, but here is my *homework*! (concrete)

Roughly, any noun that refers to an observable physical entity is "concrete;" everything else is "abstract," though semanticists may break down abstract nouns into different subtypes.

Common and proper

Another semantic distinction that English nouns express is the distinction between *common* and *proper* nouns. This is a distinction that is also reflected in our writing system; we capitalize proper nouns (though most other languages do not) but not common nouns. But what, exactly, is a proper noun?

Let's try a definition. A proper noun refers to a unique entity, what we call its *referent*. A common noun, on the other hand, has more than one referent. We can also think of the distinction between proper and common nouns in terms of sets; a proper noun picks out a member of a set, but there's only one member (referent) in that set – *Juneteenth, President of the United States, Eiffel Tower, Isabelle*. A common noun picks out a member of a set of more than one – *insanity, food, elf, seatbelt*. (Notice here that though we use the term *proper noun*, proper nouns are more accurately *noun phrases*, such as *The Oxford English Dictionary*. We'll take this up more later.)

Our actual intuitions about proper/common nouns are somewhat clouded by the convention of capitalization that is part of our written language. There is, in fact, a great deal of variation with respect to capitalization of proper nouns, especially in multiword proper nouns. For example, capitalization rules vary from publisher to publisher, according to their own "house style." Another book we wrote is cited in bibliographies in different ways, as *Linguistics for Everyone* in some places, but as *Linguistics for everyone* in others. And certainly there is variation across languages; in German, for example, the first letter of both common and proper nouns is capitalized (*das Buch*, "the book," *die Frau*, "the woman," *Deutschland*, "Germany"), which was also the standard in American English up until about 1800. And in some languages, even those that use the Roman alphabet like English and German, no capitalization is used at all.

As you might expect, just as we saw with concrete and abstract nouns, things can get a bit fuzzy when we delve deeper into the distinction between proper and common nouns. What about sentences such as the following; are the capitalized names proper nouns here?

I know two Gertrudes.
The Gertrude from down the street is from New York.

Do names pick out unique individuals? Linguists and philosophers have long debated about how to explain examples where a proper noun behaves like a common noun by taking an article like *the*, allowing pluralization, and not picking out a single entity. Some scholars claim that no sharp line can be drawn between proper and common, and that the difference is one of degree. Nonetheless, the distinction seems real and seems to exist to some extent (such as names being categorized as proper nouns) in most if not all languages.

Count and mass

The concept of countability is (in contrast to the other distinctions we've discussed) pretty straightforward: countable nouns denote discrete units, while uncountable nouns denote an unbounded mass. For example, the count noun *armadillo* is used to denote individual armadillos, but *information* cannot be used to denote individual "informations," so *information* is a mass noun (at least in English). In order to divide a mass into countable units, we have to use a special counting term such as a *piece* of information or an *item* of clothing.

A good test for a mass noun (such as *mud*) is that it cannot generally be pluralized (**muds*). (We use the inflectional affix -*s* throughout this chapter for illustration, but this affix is often absent in some varieties of English.) Another test is to see whether the noun can occur with certain words that express quantities, like numerals or quantifiers: *four, eight, another, both, each, every, many, few, several*, etc. Mass nouns, on the other hand, cannot occur with numerals or with those same quantifiers, and instead use a different set: *much* and *less*. Both mass and count can occur with *some, all,* and the determiner *the*. These tests are summarized below with examples.

count nouns occur with plural markers, numerals, and certain quantifiers: squirrels, *two* squirrels, *another* squirrel, *both* squirrels, *each* squirrel, *every* squirrel, *many* squirrels, *few* squirrels, *several* squirrels

mass nouns cannot occur with plural markers, numerals, or certain quantifiers:
*muds, *two muds, **another* mud, **both* mud(s), **each* mud, **every* mud, **many* muds, **few* muds, **several* mud(s)

And what about proper nouns? Are *Japan* and *Maya Angelou* mass or count? There is only one of each of them, so even though a proper noun can't be pluralized, it is still a count noun.

There is variation among speakers, too, in which words are used with mass nouns and which are used with count nouns. The words *much* and *less* (called *quantifiers*) are often used with mass nouns:

There isn't *much* water in the basement today.
I have *less* mud on my boots than you do.

Sometimes these words are used with count nouns as well:

You shouldn't put too *much* clothes in the dryer.
I have *less* classes than you.

Also, many count nouns can be quite easily used with a mass meaning. Consider the following nouns *chicken* and *water*:

We can't fit another chicken in the pot. (count)
No one can eat more chicken than Cary. (mass)

She longed to swim in the warm waters of the Gulf. (count)
She longed to swim in the warm water. (mass)

Although many (maybe all) languages seem to distinguish between mass and count nouns, they do so in different ways. For example, *furniture* is a mass noun in English, so it isn't pluralized: *furnitures*. However, as mentioned in Chapter 1, in French, it is a count noun and can be pluralized: *les meubles* "the furnitures." The same is true of the English mass noun *jewelry* and its French counterpart *les bijoux*, literally "the jewelries."

10 items or less? Fewer?

The use of *much* and *less* with count nouns has led to some arguments at the grocery store check-out line. According to some who subscribe to a more prescriptive code of language use, *less* should be used with mass nouns, and *fewer* with count nouns. But, this prescriptive rule is then violated by the "10 Items or Less" sign since *item* is a count noun. Some stores have changed their "10 Items or Less" signs to read "10 Items or Fewer," but this can still seem a bit, well, unnatural and stuffy. Some solve the presumed dilemma by using "Up to 10 items." In *Merriam-Webster's Collegiate Dictionary of English Usage* it is argued that certain uses of *less* with count nouns – like the check-out sign variety – are, in fact, entirely unremarkable and have been so for centuries. We would agree!

Collective nouns

Collective nouns are words used to define a group of objects, such as *team*, *pride* (of lions), and *jury*, and are actually count nouns. Unlike mass nouns, collective nouns can all be pluralized: *teams*, *prides*, *juries*.

One reason that such nouns are sometimes misclassified as mass nouns is that in some varieties of English, a collective noun can be treated syntactically like a singular noun, a single entity, and the verb that occurs with the noun is in this case singular:

The team *is* here.
The jury *has* arrived.
That committee *meets* every Tuesday.

These collective words act like mass nouns such as *mud* and *furniture*, occurring with singular verbs (*The mud is on my shoes.*). But unlike mass nouns, collective nouns can be pluralized, triggering plural verb agreement:

The teams *are* here.
The juries *have* arrived.
Those committees *meet* every Tuesday.

And to make matters even more interesting, there is variation in the treatment of some collective nouns; in some varieties of English, for example, collective nouns trigger plural agreement on the verb:

The team *are/*is* here.
The jury *have/*has* arrived.
The committee *are/*is* meeting every Tuesday.

Generic nouns

Generic nouns are another way that we can classify nouns in terms of their semantics.

Dogs are usually furry.
My neighbor is afraid of *cats*.

Most nouns have a generic meaning when they are used without a determiner or article (*the* or *a/an*). However, we can still understand nouns as generic even when they occur with articles.

A computer can be useful.
The computer has changed the way we communicate.

Neither of these examples refers to a particular computer, but to the generic idea of a computer. Most, if not all languages have generic nouns, though they differ in whether the noun must be introduced by an article (*the* or *a*) or not. In French and Spanish, articles are required: *les gens* "people" in French (*les* = plural), and *la gente* "people" in Spanish (*la* = singular). But in German, as in English, generic nouns can occur without articles: *Männer*, *Frauen*, and *Kindern* ("men," "women," and "children"). German (in contrast to English) tends to require an article more often with singular generic nouns, as in *Das Leben ist kurz* ("life is short"). Japanese, with no definite or indefinite articles, depends on context to determine whether a particular noun has a definite, indefinite, or generic reading.

Konpyuuta-wa benri   desu
computer   convenient   is
"The computer is convenient." / "A computer is convenient." / "The computer (previously mentioned) is convenient."

You can see throughout our discussion of the semantics of nouns that the meaning distinctions (*abstract/concrete*, *common/proper*, and *count/mass*) are all distinctions that are, on the one hand, fairly straightforward and follow

31

from the meanings of the labels. On the other hand, many of these distinctions can depend on your knowledge of the language, your knowledge of the world, and your own analysis of the data.

Noun classifiers

Some languages, including American Sign Language, Bengali, Korean, Mandarin, Swahili, and many others, use what are called "classifiers" – morphemes that occur with nouns and reflect some kind of meaning classification system, which often have to do with shape: one classifier for long, thin objects; another for small, round objects; another for social animals; another for humans; and so on. And some languages may not have an expansive classifier system, but they use classifiers with numerals and therefore have specific "counter" classifiers. The following examples from Mandarin illustrate this system, with a distinct counter (marked with "cl" in the gloss) for trees, animals, and long-wavy things (like a river).

三 棵树 (三棵樹)
sān kē shù
three cl[tree] tree
"three trees"

三 只 鸟 (三隻鳥)
sān zhī niǎo
three cl[animal] bird
"three birds"

三 条 河 (三條河)
sān tiáo hé
three cl[long-wavy] river
"three rivers"

Noun Morphology

We now turn to the morphology of English nouns – the different parts they can have, the ways we put those parts together, and the information those different parts convey. This morphological information is part of what we use to identify a word as a *noun*.

Recall from the discussion of morphology in Chapter 1 that one way we construct words in English is by *affixation*, attaching suffixes and prefixes to roots or words to form larger words. English also uses other ways to build words, by combining words (as in the compound *earache*) or by "clipping" part of a word (as in *dis* from *disrespect*) and so on. In this section, we'll discuss some of the ways we build nouns through affixation and other word formation rules.

Inflectional affixation

As you may recall from Chapter 1, there are two types of affixation, *inflectional* and *derivational*. Inflectional affixes express grammatical information. Two inflectional affixes can occur on nouns in English: plural -*s* and possessive -*s*, though they do not occur in all varieties of English. These affixes express grammatical information of, respectively, number and possessive (*genitive*) case.

We know these affixes are inflectional (rather than derivational) because when added to a noun they don't create a new word, or dictionary entry. So, *cat* is listed in the dictionary, but *cats* and *cat's* are not; the affixes add grammatical information, but these affixes do not create an entirely new word. A derivational affix, on the other hand, does create a new dictionary entry. For example, the word *cat* is listed in the dictionary, and if we add the derivational affix -*like* to the noun *cat*, we create another dictionary entry, the adjective *catlike* (also, as we saw in Chapter 1, an adverb).

Plurals
A morphological fact about most nouns (we'll return to the "most" part) is that they express number – they can be understood as singular or plural. As mentioned above, we can overtly pluralize an English noun by adding the morpheme -*s* (absent in some varieties of English, including African American English). But there are other ways to pluralize nouns, ways that we now think of as "irregular" plurals. But, each of these "irregular" plurals actually comes from a regular pattern in another language, either Old English (which was spoken around 450–1100 CE) or Latin or Greek.

Some Old English plurals:
internal vowel change: *goose/geese, tooth/teeth, mouse/mice, foot/feet*
no change at all: *deer/deer, sheep/sheep, fish/fish*
adding -*en* plurals: *oxen, brethren, children* (*brethren* and *children* are actually a combination of two Old English plural affixes: -*ru* and -*en*)

Some Latin plurals:
nouns ending in -*us* take -*i*: *syllabus/syllabi, stimulus/stimuli*
nouns ending in -*um* take -*a*: *medium/media, forum/fora, ovum/ova*
nouns ending in -*a* take -*ae*: *larva/larvae, alga/algae, antenna/antennae*

Many of these plurals are becoming obsolete and have been replaced by, for example, *syllabuses*, *forums*, and *antennas*.

Some Greek plurals:
nouns ending in -*on* take -*a*: *phenomenon/phenomena, criterion/criteria*
nouns ending in -*is* take -*es*: *hypothesis/hypotheses, parenthesis/parentheses*

Though the morpheme -*s* is a common way of marking plural, in the varieties of English that do so, there remain other ways to form plurals. Though most new nouns that come into the language can be pluralized with -*s*, sometimes, by analogy with other words in the categories shown above, a noun will take one of the "irregular" endings. For example, a moose is an animal native to North America, so moose certainly weren't around during the time when Old English was spoken. Nevertheless, its plural is typically *moose*, not *mooses*, by analogy with *sheep* or *deer*. Not that long ago (and still in some Northern dialects in England), more than one shoe was *shoon*, more than one egg was *eyren*, and more than one house was *housen*. And sometimes Latin plurals are used for nouns that look like they're from Latin, but really aren't, such as *octopi*. *Octopus* is originally Greek, with the plural *octopodes*. Generally, however, we now use the -*s* ending on new nouns (*blogs*, *faxes*, *tweets*, and *textmessages*).

Morphological marking of plurality has been gradually disappearing in English over the last 1000 years, and, as noted, many varieties of English do not use the -*s*. Though all languages have nouns, they don't necessarily all mark plurality morphologically. Some languages, such as Chinese, Malagasy, Lao, among many others, including varieties of English in the United States and around the world, use the same noun form for singular and plural; the plurality is usually made quite clear from the context or from other markers (for example, one dog, two dog). In addition to singular and plural, some languages mark dual numbers, with a distinct form for singular, dual, and plural. The Slavic language Slovene marks dual number, as shown in these forms for the noun "wolf": *volk* (one wolf), *volkova* (two wolves), and *volkovi* (wolves).

Possessives
Languages have different ways of marking *grammatical functions*. Some languages use morphological *case* to express these relationships; for example, in some case systems, the subject noun phrase morphologically expresses nominative case, and the direct object morphologically expresses accusative case, and so on. Case can be rather difficult to explain to English speakers, because in modern English, case is only morphologically expressed in

a few ways. Case shows up, for example, on pronouns, but not (except in the possessive, as we'll see below) on nouns or noun phrases.

She enjoyed talking to *him*.
she = nominative case, *him* = accusative case

He enjoyed talking to *her*.
he = nominative case, *her* = accusative case

One case that does show up on English noun phrases in many varieties of English is *possessive*, or *genitive* case, marked in some varieties of English by the affix -*s* on the possessor noun phrase. (In written form, an apostrophe, -'s is used; however, it's important to realize that this is a writing convention, and not part of the affix itself.) Below are some possessive noun phrases:

the dog's bowl
Fido's bowl
the dog we found by the bus stop's bowl

As you can see, the possessive -*s* inflectional affix is attached to the very rightmost edge of the *possessor*, a full noun phrase (we discuss noun phrases in more detail in the next chapter).

[The dog]'s bowl
NP

[Fido]'s bowl
NP

[The dog we found by the bus stop]'s bowl
NP

So we see that in those varieties that use the possessive inflectional affix, it does not attach to nouns but rather to noun phrases. (However, nowadays and for several centuries, in fact, an apostrophe plus -*s* shows up quite commonly in writing to mark plurals that are not possessive, as in *Mushroom's For Sale*.)

As mentioned above, some varieties of English do not use the inflectional affix to mark possession. Possession is clear, however, from the syntax of the phrase:

the dog bowl
Fido bowl
the dog we found by the bus stop bowl

And just as with plural marking, the inflectional marking of possessive has been gradually diminishing in English over the centuries.

English has another way of marking possession, with word order and prepositions, as in *the house of my friend*; this method of marking possession is common in a variety of languages. The prepositional phrase *of my friend* expresses the possessive relationship in the same way that the possessive affix *-s* does. English can even double-mark, as in *a friend of Lucy's*. Such double-marking raises some prescriptive eyebrows. Is it acceptable to simply have *a friend of Lucy*? *Lucy's friend*? *A friend of Lucy's*? These seem ok, no?

Derivational affixation

Recall that another way we build words is through derivational affixation. By attaching a derivational affix to a word or root we typically derive a new word, a new dictionary entry. As we saw above, by attaching *-like* to the noun *cat*, we derive the adjective *catlike*. There are also derivational affixes that derive nouns when attached to a root or word; we derive the noun *excitement*, for example, by attaching the affix *-ment* to the verb *excite*. A noun derived through derivational affixation is called a *nominalization*. A list of some of the derivational suffixes we use in English to form nouns is given in Table 2.1.

Notice that some of the derivational suffixes in the table attach to nouns to derive other nouns rather than words of another category. They do, however, derive new dictionary entries. For example, the noun *friend* is listed in the dictionary and so is the noun *friendship*, even though both are nouns.

Table 2.1   Some English noun suffixes and sample words.

Suffix	Sample words	Formation
-age	coverage, leakage	verb/noun + age = noun
-al	arrival, renewal	verb + al = noun
-ant	attractant, dispersant	verb + ant = noun
-ance/ence	endurance, divergence	verb + ance/ence = noun
-ee	employee, referee	verb + ee = noun
-ion	starvation, transmission	verb + ion = noun
-ism	Buddhism, classism	noun + ism = noun
-ist	mentalist, feminist	adjective + ist = noun
-ity	probability, fluidity, infertility	adjective + ity = noun
-ness	goodness, happiness	adjective + ness = noun
-ship	friendship, internship	noun + ship = noun

English has borrowed and continues to borrow affixes from other languages – primarily Latin and Greek – to create words via derivational affixation:

Latin:
-arium: *aquarium, herbarium, honorarium*
-tion: *nation, ration, fruition*

Greek:
-archy: *anarchy, monarchy, matriarchy*
-gram: *telegram, anagram, cardiogram*
-graph: *telegraph, phonograph, radiograph*
-logue/log: *catalog, travelogue, analog*
-phile/phobe: *audiophile, homophobe, arachnophobe*

And some words are *hybrids,* or English words derived using Latin and Greek morphemes, such as *television* (from Greek *telos* "far" and Latin *visio* "vision") and *mammography* (from Latin *mamma* "breast" and Greek *graphia* "writing").

Even though we may not know it consciously, we are quite good at analyzing the parts of words. We use our knowledge of affixes to determine a word's syntactic category, even when we do not know what the word means, as we saw in Chapter 1.

With great *glarkiness,* I ran to the *blarkiment.*
The *libidity* of the *snerkance* is what leads to *lorkage.*

All of the nonsense words are nouns, which we can determine because of their suffixes, as well as their placement in the sentence in relation to the other words (their syntax).

Other ways we form nouns

As we saw in Chapter 1, there are numerous ways other than affixation that we build words. Here are some examples of nouns brought into the language through some of the other common word formation processes. (You may want to refer to the list of word formation rules in Table 1.3 if you need to refresh your memory.) We form new nouns through acronyms and initialisms (COVID – *coronavirus,* ACLU = *American Civil Liberties Union*), through backformation (*crank, flab, grunge,* and *sleaze* from *cranky, flabby, grungy,* and *sleazy; diplomat* from *diplomatic; ideologue* from *ideology*), through blending (*permanent + frost = permafrost,* Brexit from *Britain + exit, mansplaining* from *man + explaining, web + seminar = webinar*), clipping (*demo* from *demonstration, condo* from *condominium, lab* from *laboratory*), coining (*bling, quiz*), eponyms (*kleenex, band-aid*), and conversion (*must* began as a verb, but in *that is a must,* it becomes a noun). (More frequently nouns convert to verbs rather than verbs becoming nouns: *mother, google, email*.) Another common word formation process is compounding (*backlash, bailout, Facebook*), which deserves a bit more discussion. We generally understand compounding to be the process of combining two or more words into a single new word. This raises the question, however, of what a word is. Some "words" that really seem to be single-word units are still written as two separate words with a space in between; *high school*, for example, or *ice cream*. There seems to be some evidence from psycholinguistic experiments and from stress patterns that such compound words are likely stored in our brains as single units and have therefore become *lexicalized*; they are filed in our mental dictionaries as a single word.

Summary

In this chapter, we've gone beyond the traditional definition of *noun* to explore some important aspects of the semantics and morphology of the syntactic category **Noun**. We've seen that defining a noun as a person, place, or thing, while somewhat useful, does not really capture our intuitive knowledge of this syntactic category. We've explored a different approach to the meaning, or semantics, of nouns, and how they fall into different semantic classes: **abstract/concrete, common/proper, count/mass.** Nouns can also be **collective,** referring to groups of things, or **generic,** referring to general classes of things. We then took a look at the morphology of nouns, and the kinds of morphological clues we use to identify a word as a noun. The plural **inflectional** affix -*s* tells us something is a noun, and the possessive -*s* tells us something is a noun or noun phrase. We form **nominalizations** through **derivational** affixation, and we also use our set of English word formation rules to create new nouns on a regular basis.

Exercises

1. Abstract and concrete

Determine whether the following boldface words are abstract or concrete:

(a) There's some **money** on the table.
(b) There's a lot of **money** in our bank account.
(c) We might not go if the **weather** is bad.
(d) That is some **weather** we had last week!
(e) My son's **art** is hanging in the living room.
(f) **Art** is an important component of culture.

2. Proper and common

Consider the following sentences:

There are three Mayas in my class.
Each of the Eiffel Towers in the painting is a different color.

How would you analyze the *Mayas* and *Eiffel Towers* in these contexts? Are they proper or common nouns, and why or why not? Do we need to consider revising our definition of a proper noun? What are some other examples that raise the same question?

3. Mass and count

Create two sentences for each of the following nouns, one of which uses the noun as a count noun and the other as a mass noun. Be prepared to provide evidence for its status as count or mass.

(a) turkey
(b) wine
(c) freedom
(d) light

4. Semantic features of nouns

Identify each of the following as count/mass, proper/common, abstract/concrete. Remember that each noun will have THREE different features, for example, *badgers* = count, common, concrete. Also, remember that some nouns can have different interpretations, and be mass or count, common or proper, abstract or concrete, depending on how you use them. For example in "Truth is beauty and beauty is truth," *truth* = mass, common, abstract, but in "We hold these truths to be self-evident," *truths* = count, common, abstract. If you find this to be the case with any of the following nouns, briefly explain the different interpretations and feature specifications.

(a) fun
(b) health
(c) wolf
(d) garden
(e) housework
(f) juice

5.   Noun formation

Come up with a list of relatively new nouns, including informal or slang terms, that have been formed through affixation and/or the word forma-tion rules discussed in this chapter (blending, clipping, compounding, etc.). Give the definition of each noun and analyze the morphological pro-cesses that derive each noun. Good places to look for new nouns are Word of the Year lists (major dictionaries have lists, as does the American Dialect Society).

6.   Practice

We offer here some text excerpts to use for practice. These excerpts are intended only to get you started; there may not be examples in these texts of everything listed here. We encourage you to explore texts of your own choosing to find additional examples.

(a)   Identify all the nouns in the excerpt.
(b)   Label the semantic features of each noun (count/mass, proper/ common, concrete/abstract).
(c)   Try to identify any collective or generic nouns (and briefly explain why you identified them this way).
(d)   Are there any possessive noun phrases in the excerpts?
(e)   Identify any nominalizations in the excerpts.
(f)   Look for nouns that are derived from the word formation rules (*clipping, blending, compounding, conversion,* etc.) discussed in the chapter.

The newspapers have been unspeakable. They say it was a pantomime, mounted by Trotsky himself to gain publicity. The police questioned every-one here, and poor Alejandro they held for two days, probably guessing his vulnerability. Keeping him awake, shoving a rifle butt into his shoulder, the police interrogated him about the so-called fake attack: if it had been real, they asked again and again, how could anyone have survived it? How could 70 bullets fill a room and every one miss its mark? (From *The Lacuna*, by Barbara Kingsolver.)

Around the beginning of this century, the Queen of Thailand was aboard a boat, floating along with her many courtiers, manservants, maids, feet-bathers, and food-tasters, when suddenly the stern hit a wave and the queen was thrown overboard into the turquoise waters of the Nippon-Kai, where, despite her pleas for help, she drowned, for not one person on that boat went to her aid. (From *White Teeth*, by Zadie Smith.)

Lydia packed her belongings from her dorm room, placed them in her car, and hugged Niecy. She drove to her granny's house, unloaded the boxes onto the back porch, and gave her the story she'd worked out with Niecy, that Lydia was staying with her roommate in Atlanta. Niecy's parents had a big house and did not mind company, but she did not want to bring all her junk to Niecy's house. Here was the number, in case of emergency. Lydia would see her granny in June. (From *The Love Songs of W.E.B. DuBois*, by Honorée Fanonne Jeffers.)

Noun Phrases

Introduction

In the previous chapter, we looked at the meanings (semantics) and internal structure (morphology) of nouns. We also touched a bit on noun phrases (NPs), or nouns that combine with other words to form larger syntactic units. In this chapter, we explore the syntactic structure of noun phrases in more detail. As we've often pointed out, though you might not think you

Navigating English Grammar: A Guide to Analyzing Real Language, Second Edition.
Anne Lobeck and Kristin Denham.
© 2025 Anne Lobeck and Kristin Denham. Published 2025 by John Wiley & Sons Ltd.

know what a noun phrase is, you actually do, even though you might not be familiar with the terminology we use to talk about them.

In the following sections, we discuss the different categories of words that occur with nouns in more detail. As we'll see, these words, together with the head noun, form the larger unit *NP*. We'll see how we can graphically represent the syntactic structure of the noun phrase using phrase structure tree diagrams.

Categories that Precede Nouns

In this section, we discuss the set of categories that precede the noun in the noun phrase. These include *determiners*, *quantifiers*, and *numerals*. (As we did in Chapter 2, we use morphological -*s* plural for illustration, though -*s* may be unpronounced depending on your variety of English.)

> *the* raccoon (*the* = determiner)
> *all* raccoons (*all* = quantifier)
> *ten* raccoons (*ten* = numeral)

You may have learned that all of these categories can be lumped together as *adjectives* (just like the word *furry* in *furry raccoon*). But, as you'll see as we discuss each of these categories in turn, they are quite different from adjectives and also different from each other. These categories provide us with important tools to identify nouns and noun phrases.

Determiners

As we mentioned briefly in Chapter 2, nouns can occur with a *determiner* (*the* or *a/an*), or they can occur without anything at all. So, although we can say that not all nouns must occur with a determiner, every determiner must occur with a noun.

> raccoons
> the raccoons
> *the

One way to define a noun, then, is to say that *a noun is a word that can occur with a determiner* (which we'll abbreviate as D). Together, the determiner and the noun form a larger unit, an *NP*, which can be expressed by the informal *phrase structure rule* below. Phrase structure rules are simply a notation that linguists use to describe the syntactic structure of groups of words, or phrases, each of which contains a *head*, here, N. Optional material is in parentheses.

NP → (D) N

This phrase structure rule for NP can be understood as "NP consists of an optional determiner and a (required, non-optional) head noun."

We can now diagram some simple NPs consistent with this phrase structure rule. Notice that a noun that occurs without D is still an NP (something we'll return to later):

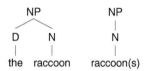

In English, determiners express definiteness, number, proximity, and distance. The category D can include the indefinite article *a/an*, the definite article *the*, the demonstratives *this/that, these/those/them*, as well as the possessive determiners *my, your, his, her, its, our, their/they*, and others. D is a *functional* rather than *lexical* category; we typically do not add new members to this category (so it is *closed*, rather than *open*) and words in this category have grammatical meanings. The category D is therefore very different from the category A, a lexical category to which we routinely add new members.

Let's unpack some of these terms so that we better understand what a determiner is. Determiners can be definite or indefinite. *Definiteness* is a way of expressing known or "old" information. So if I say to you *I saw the raccoon yesterday*, you would understand the NP *the raccoon* to mean the raccoon that we both know about (definiteness = known/old information). But if I were to say *I saw a raccoon yesterday*, I am not assuming that you know anything about this raccoon at all; here, the indefinite determiner *a* expresses new information or *indefiniteness*.

Determiners can also express number (in English, singular and plural). The indefinite article *a* is (obviously!) singular: *a raccoon/*a raccoons*. The definite article *the* is neutral in terms of number; it can occur with both plural nouns and singular nouns: *the raccoon/the/them raccoons*. *The* can also occur with mass nouns, which we've defined (in Chapter 2) as nouns that can't be counted, and thus are not pluralized: *the furniture/*the furnitures*.

A hundred? One hundred?

The indefinite articles *a* and *an* originated from the number *one*. *An* is actually the older form and was the unstressed form of the number, written *ān* in Old English. We can trace *one* back even further, to a word we think looked something like *oinos* in Proto-Indo-European, the ancestor of many languages of Europe and India. From *oinos* we get Latin *ūnus* (ancestor of Italian and Spanish *uno* and French *un*), Welsh *un*, Czech and Polish *jeden*, Russian *odin*, and Lithuanian *víenas*. In German, we find *ein*, in Dutch *een*, and in Swedish and Danish *en*. In these and many of languages, the word is used as both the numeral *one* and as the indefinite article.

English nowadays uses the original single form *an* only with words beginning with a vowel sound (not a vowel letter, as some people sometimes assume: it's *an hour* and *a useful tool*). Interestingly, the *n* has moved back and forth between words beginning with vowels for hundreds of years: *an uncle* would sometimes be written *a nuncle*, *an ox* as *a nox*, *an apron* used to be *a napron*, *nickname* came from an *ekename*, and so on.

Of course, both *a* and *an* can still be used to mean precisely one: *make a wish, a hundred dollars*.

Now take a look at another kind of determiner, demonstratives, which can include *this*, *that*, *these*, and *those/them* and other variations. Demonstratives express proximity. In the following sentence, the raccoon identified by *this* is closer (proximal) to the speaker than the other one, identified by *that* (distal). Proximal demonstratives are *this/these*, while distal demonstratives are *that/those/them*.

I like *this* raccoon better than *that* raccoon.

Demonstratives also express number – *this raccoon* but *these/them raccoons*. Demonstratives are also definite, expressing known information just like *the*. Consider the difference between, for example, *I saw a raccoon* versus *I saw that raccoon*. The second sentence, but not the first, refers to a raccoon that you have already discussed before.

Determiners can also be possessive: *my* in *my book* and *your* in *your book*. Possessive determiners are different from *possessive pronouns*: determiners occur with nouns (in D position in our phrase structure rule NP → (D) N) while pronouns replace full NPs. Sometimes, but not always, possessive determiners have forms that are distinct from possessive pronouns. The first example in each set is the possessive determiner, which occurs with a noun as part of the NP. The second example in each pair is the possessive pronoun.

my chicken
The chicken is *mine/mines*.

his/her chicken
The chicken is *his/hers/hisn/hern*

our chicken
The chicken is *ours/ourn*

your chicken
The chicken is *yourn/yours*

their/they chicken
The chicken is *theirs/theirn*

We can now diagram a few more different kinds of NPs, with demonstratives and possessive determiners.

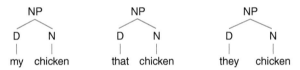

We now also have a few different ways to tell whether a word is a noun or not – we can see if it can be preceded by a (number of different kinds of) determiner, as expressed by our phrase structure rule below:

NP → (D) N

Noun phrases without determiners
Recall that we mentioned earlier that we would see how a single noun, such as *raccoons*, can be a noun phrase all by itself.

Raccoons like to wash their hands.

But how do we really know that the noun *raccoons* is just as much an NP as *the raccoon*? That is, what evidence is there that single nouns, such as *Lucinda*, *mud*, and *raccoons* are NPs, and not just single nouns?

We know that *Lucinda, mud,* and *raccoons* are noun phrases, just like the larger noun phrase *the raccoon,* because each can occur in NP positions. One such position is the subject position:

Lucinda/sat on the porch.
subject

Mud/is hard to get off your shoes.
subject

Raccoons/are interesting animals.
subject

If any single noun could occur in the subject position, we would expect sentences such as **Raccoon ran across the road* and **Mosquito is in my soup* to be grammatical, but they usually aren't (when they aren't being used as generic nouns). When we make these nouns into full NPs, however, the sentences are fine: *The raccoon ran across the road, A mosquito is in my soup.*

This is only one piece of evidence that sometimes what looks like single nouns are actually full NPs. We'll discuss more evidence for this claim later in the chapter.

Numerals

Numerals can also occur before nouns; they express – guess what? – number! There is much linguistic evidence that the functional category Numeral (which we'll abbreviate as NUM) is a category distinct from D (and also from the category A or Adjective). Numerals can introduce nouns, just like determiners: *one/four/six* … "I ate *fourteen* doughnuts." In fact, we can use numerals as a way to identify nouns, since only nouns occur in the position after NUM.

Numerals differ from most members of the category D (all except *a/an*) in being indefinite. To illustrate, consider the difference between the following sentences, where one includes the definite determiner *the.* (Recall that plural nouns in some varieties are not affixed with *-s,* as in *fourteen doughnut.* The noun *doughnut* here is nevertheless plural, just as is *doughnuts.*)

I ate *fourteen* doughnut(s).
I ate *the fourteen* doughnut(s)

Noun Phrases

In the first sentence, the indefinite NP *fourteen doughnut(s)* expresses new information, information that the speaker and hearer don't share. In the second sentence, however, the NP *the fourteen doughnut(s)* provides old information; we assume that the speaker and hearer both know which fourteen doughnuts are being referred to. So, we can make a noun phrase that includes a numeral definite by adding a definite determiner.

Numerals always follow the determiner if there is one, as you can easily see by the ungrammaticality of the following phrases (we include plural *-s* here for illustration):

I ate the fourteen doughnuts.
*I ate fourteen the doughnuts.

Those six dogs chased the coyote.
*Six those dogs chased the coyote.

The numerals we've talked about so far are called *cardinal: one, two, three, four,* and so on. Numerals can also be *ordinal: first, second, third, eighteenth,* etc. Ordinal numerals occur in the same position as cardinal numerals, after the determiner if there is one: "the *seventh* book," "*Second* Avenue."

Evidence from numerals in noun phrases suggests that our phrase structure rule for NP can be written as follows, where optional D is followed by optional NUM.

NP → (D) (NUM) N

With the addition of NUM to the noun phrase, we can now diagram NPs such as the following:

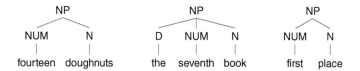

We can now also use NUM, like D, as a clue to whether a word is a noun or not. Only nouns occur in the position after a numeral and/or a determiner.

Quantifiers

The functional category Quantifier (which we will abbreviate as Q) may be one that you aren't familiar with since (like NUM) it isn't one of the traditional parts of speech you may have learned about. But just as we saw with determiners and numerals, quantifiers are a distinct functional category, with unique syntactic and semantic behavior.

Quantifiers include words such as *some, all, every, each, both, few, several, many, more, less,* and *much.* These words express quantity but in a different, more abstract way than numbers. Some quantifiers are definite, some are indefinite, and some are singular and others plural. The semantics of quantification is very complex, and a topic of much research in linguistics and other fields, including mathematics and philosophy. We won't get into the complexities of the semantics of quantifiers here; we'll stick to some basic semantic distinctions and will focus mostly on their syntax. With that in mind, consider the following examples.

all books
some books

All books means every single book there is, so *all* here is definite; both speaker and hearer understand exactly which set of books is being referred to. *Some books,* on the other hand, is indefinite; this phrase expresses new information that the speaker and hearer don't necessarily share. Both *all* and *some* are plural.

Now consider these examples:

each book, *every* book
many books, *few* books

Each and *every* are both definite (they express known information) but singular, in contrast to definite plural *all. Many* and *few* are indefinite and plural.

If you think about it, you can come up with differences among these quantifiers in terms of their meanings. *Many* seems to mean something like "a lot but less than all" but *few* seems to mean "fewer than expected." In contrast to numbers, quantifiers seem to express relative quantities in complex ways.

Another unique property of quantifiers is that they can take what's called *wide* or *narrow scope* over the members of the set of things they are quantifying. This scope difference can result in ambiguity, as in the following sentence:

Every person loves some person.

This sentence can either mean that every person (in the world) loves the same certain person, say, Pat; or it can mean that each person loves some other different person: Juno loves Kim, Kim loves Pat, and so on. You don't get that kind of ambiguity when quantifiers aren't involved. The following sentence is not ambiguous, for example:

The kids love Kim.

This sentence can only mean that there is some single person (namely, Kim) that the kids love.

We can now diagram some simple NPs with quantifiers.

The complex semantics of quantifiers highlights the importance of differentiating among the classes of words that precede nouns. Clearly, quantifiers differ from determiners and numerals, and the catch-all label of *adjective* for all these classes of words obscures important facts about our knowledge of language. Research on the syntactic and semantic properties of quantifiers has contributed much to the development of modern syntactic theory and has deepened our understanding of what it means to know a language. Quantifiers express relationships that are best captured by formal logic, also called predicate logic, a system also used in mathematics, philosophy, and computer science. Part of how we understand the meanings of words and sentences therefore involves unconscious knowledge of this complex system.

Order of D, NUM, and Q

We've seen that D and NUM occur in a certain order, namely, D first, then NUM. The order of D, NUM, and Q can be rather complicated, and describing the possible orders among the members of these categories might be difficult. One thing English speakers know is that NPs don't occur with two determiners:

*the that dog
*the these dogs

And even more specifically, NPs in English don't occur with more than one definite element. NPs can't, for example, occur with both a definite determiner and a definite quantifier.

*the every dog
*the all dogs

You may have come up with the examples *all the dogs* or *both my friends*, which seem to suggest that a definite quantifier *all* or *both* can be followed by a definite determiner. But these phrases are probably reductions of phrases such as *all of the dogs* and *both of my friends,* and thus not really examples of a definite quantifier and a definite determiner occurring together.

The above data suggests that at least in English, the first position before the head N in NP is reserved for definite elements. Numerals (which are indefinite, remember) and some indefinite quantifiers can occur with definite determiners.

| the | few/five | spectators |
| [definite] | [indefinite] | |

| the | most | points |
| [definite] | [indefinite] | |

| those | many | invitations |
| [definite] | [indefinite] | |

These examples suggest that in English, there can also be only one indefinite element per NP, and that indefinite elements seem to follow definite elements. We can express this informally as follows:

NP → (definite) (indefinite) N

(One counterexample to this order is *a few,* where the indefinite article *a* is followed by the indefinite quantifier *few*: *a few manatees.* This too is likely a reduction of "*a few of the manatees,*" so it may have a different syntactic structure.)

We will not dwell any further on the complex interaction between determiners, numerals, and quantifiers here. What we've shown is that these classes of words are distinct from each other, though they have in common that all three are functional categories that express grammatical information (definiteness, number, proximity, quantity) about the noun. D, NUM, and Q form larger NPs, together with head nouns, as diagrammed below.

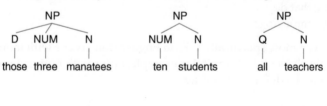

In a later section, we'll return to the functional categories D, NUM, Q, and the lexical category Adjective, a category that can modify nouns and also occur before the noun in NP.

Partitive, Measure, and Collective Noun Phrases

There are other kinds of NPs that indicate quantity and amount, aside from those we've discussed so far. *Partitive* NPs, for example, include quantifiers or numerals, and express the relationship of "a part to a whole." Partitives have the form *X of Y*.

    some of their suggestions
    many of those meetings
    three of my fingers
    all of their shoes

English also has partitive NPs that are built around measure words, such as *pound*, *feet*, and *quart*, as in the following examples (of a kind of partitive NP that we'll call a *measure* NP):

    one pound of flour
    three feet of wire
    a quart of Kim's cider
    two cartons of milk
    several boxes of those strawberries
    a piece of wood

Measure phrases can also modify adjectives, such as *long*, *high*, and *tall*, as in the following examples.

    The wire is *three feet* long.
    The grass is *ten inches* high.
    The road is *six miles* long.

Recall from Chapter 2 that measure nouns such as *pound*, *inch*, and *mile* are similar in certain ways to *collective nouns*, or nouns that name groups of things, such as *flock*, *gaggle*, *herd*, and *bunch*. Collective nouns also occur in *of* constructions, as you can see in the following examples:

    the flock of starlings
    a gaggle of geese

that herd of horses
one bouquet of roses

Partitive, measure, and collective NPs have very complex syntax, and we won't attempt to analyze them in any more detail here. Should you want to draw one of these complex NPs, you can use the convention below, a triangle. This convention still lets us express the important fact that these phrases are NPs, and as such, occur in positions where we find other NPs, but the triangle leaves the details of the internal structure of the NP aside.

| NP | NP | NP | NP |
| a gaggle of geese | some of those suggestions | ten feet | seven yards of silk |

Possessive Noun Phrases

So far, we've discussed the different functional categories that can precede N in NP, including D, NUM, and Q. We can also diagram a variety of different NPs. But now consider the following NPs. What is different about their syntactic structure? (The possessive morpheme -s is absent in some varieties of English.)

The student from Seattle('s) umbrella is bright red.
Lucy('s) umbrella is bright red.

The italicized phrases are all NPs, headed by the N *umbrella*. This head N in each NP is preceded not by a functional category D, NUM, or Q, but by a full NP (*the student from Seattle* and *Lucy*, respectively). Recall from our earlier discussion of inflectional affixes on nouns that in those varieties of English in which -s (in written form, -'s) shows up as the genitive or possessive case inflectional ending, it is attached to the NP *possessor*. The entire complex NP is called a *possessive* NP.

Possessive -s is one of the few morphological expressions of grammatical *case* that still exist in English. Recall from Chapter 2 that case inflection is expressed in English on subject and object pronouns (***They** saw Lucy/Lucy saw **them***). Subject pronouns express nominative case, and object pronouns express accusative case. Possessive case can show up morphologically as -s, as in *the student's umbrella*. Possessive case can also be expressed syntactically: *the student umbrella*.

NP or N: Pronoun substitution

We take a short detour here to talk about pronouns, because a better understanding of how pronouns work comes in handy in understanding and identifying possessive NPs and other NPs. Remember that earlier in this chapter we said that we would provide more evidence that single words, such as *dogs* or *Lucy*, are really NPs.

> *Dogs* make excellent pets.
> *Lucy* has a red umbrella.

Recall that one reason to analyze *dogs* and *Lucy* in these sentences as full NPs is that they occur in the same position that much bigger NPs occur in, namely, the subject position. We'll talk more about subjects later, but for now simply observe that much more complex NPs can occur in the same slot before the verb as *dogs* and *Lucy*.

> *Dogs that you find at shelters* make excellent pets.
> *The woman who moved to Seattle from Miami* has a red umbrella.

We could say, based on these data, that the subject of a sentence is either a noun *or* a (bigger) noun phrase. But this generalization wouldn't capture the fact that we can substitute or replace both what look like single nouns and full noun phrases with pronouns.

> *Dogs* make excellent pets.
> *Dogs that you find at shelters* make excellent pets.
> *They* make excellent pets. (*They* = *dogs/dogs that you find at shelters*)
> *Lucy* has a red umbrella.
> *The woman who moved to Seattle from Miami* has a red umbrella.
> *She* has a red umbrella. (*She* = *Lucy/the woman who moved to Seattle from Miami*)

We could say that the pronouns *they* and *she* simply replace either N or NP and be done with it. But notice that this isn't true; the pronoun *they* can't replace the noun *dogs* in our example, and the pronoun *she* can't replace the noun *woman*.

> *They that you find at shelters* make excellent pets.
> *The she who moved to Seattle from Miami* has a red umbrella.

We can explain what's going on here if we say that pronouns replace NPs rather than Ns. In fact, we can use *pronoun substitution* as a "test" to determine if we have an NP. That we can replace the NPs *dogs* and *Lucy* with pronouns is evidence that those words are actually NPs just like the larger NPs *dogs that you find at shelters* and *the woman who moved to Seattle from Miami.*

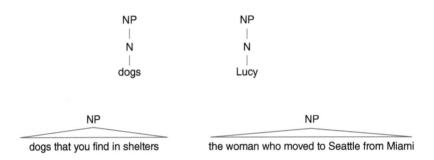

Singular *they*

Even before their more recent and widespread use as singular nonbinary pronouns, "they" and "them" have long been used as a gender-neutral way of referring to someone. The Oxford English Dictionary traces singular "they" back to 1375, where "they" appears in the medieval romance William and the Werewolf. The contemporary version of the Middle English is something like: "Each man hurried … till they drew near," where "they" refers to the singular "each man." It is now quite widespread for individuals to use *they* and *them* to refer to *themself*. A Pew research study in 2019 found that one in five Americans knows someone who uses a gender-neutral pronoun. These include not only the nonbinary or gender neutral "they" but also *xe/xem/xyr, ze/hir/hirs,* and *ey/em/eir,* as well as some "noun-self pronouns," in which an existing word is used as a pronoun (*kittenself, bunself*).

A table of English personal pronouns is given here for your reference (Table 3.1), though bear in mind that it is not exhaustive, especially in the plural categories.

Table 3.1 Some English personal pronouns.

Person[n]	Number	Subject (nominative case)	Object (accusative case)
1st	Singular	I	me
	Plural	we	us/we'uns
2nd	Singular	you	you
	Plural	you/y'all/yinz, …	you/youuns/y'all …
3rd	Singular	he/she/they/it	him/her/them/it
	Plural	they	them/they'uns

Modifiers of Nouns

So far, we've looked at the categories that can precede N in NP in English: Determiner, Numeral, and Quantifier, and the phrases that can introduce nouns, namely, possessive NPs. There are, of course, other kinds of words and phrases that can occur in *prenominal* (before the noun) position in NP. Here are a few examples:

an *unforgettable* experience
six *brick* columns
all *sleeping* dogs

You may have learned that all of the italicized words above are adjectives, but in fact, only the first one, *unforgettable*, is. What all these words have in common, however, is that they are what we call *modifiers* of nouns, adding additional information that helps us pick out what the noun refers to or "denotes." In the following section, we'll explore the distinctions among the italicized words in the above examples (it turns out that *brick* is a noun, and *sleeping* is a verb), and we'll also look more closely at the grammatical function of modification.

Adjectives that modify nouns

We'll start with *adjectives*, which are perhaps one of the most familiar modifiers of nouns. As you can see, the adjectives in the following examples provide additional descriptive information about the following noun.

the *huge* beast
an *incredible* story
those *delicious* cupcakes

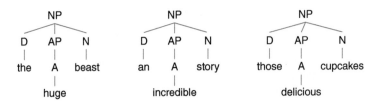

As the diagrams suggest, the adjectives in the above examples actually head adjective phrases, or AP, just as nouns head NPs. We'll discuss the phrase structure of adjective phrases in more detail in Chapter 7. For now, notice that adjectives can form a constituent with words that express degree (and are, in fact, called *degree words*, or DEG for short) such as *absolutely*, *rather*, and *very*.

> the *absolutely huge* beast
> a *rather incredible* story
> those *very delicious* cupcakes

And we can now provide a basic phrase structure rule for AP, where A can be optionally modified by DEG:

> AP → (DEG) A

We can diagram APs that include degree modifiers as follows:

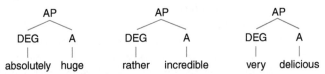

Adjective phrases add additional information to the noun, information that is different from the kinds of information expressed by determiners, numerals, or quantifiers. Recall that in English, these categories express definiteness, number, proximity, and/or quantity, different kinds of grammatical information. Determiners, numerals, and quantifiers are *functional* categories. Adjectives, on the other hand, are content words with lexical, rather than grammatical or functional meanings. The category Adjective is also an open rather than closed word class; as we discussed in Chapter 1, we add new adjectives to our vocabulary all the time. The category Adjective is therefore a *lexical* category, like the categories Noun and Verb.

To illustrate how adjectival modification works, consider the difference between the following two NPs:

> the child
> the ecstatic child

Noun Phrases

The first (definite) NP "picks out" a particular referent, namely, the child known to both the speaker and the hearer. The second (again, definite) NP also picks out a referent known to the speaker and the hearer, but in this case, the description of the referent is more limited; it's not just *the child*, but the one that also happens to be *ecstatic*. By adding additional information about the noun, the adjective phrase limits the denotation of the noun, and that limiting behavior is what modification is.

Adjective phrase modifiers are also distinct from D, NUM, and Q in position; they must follow any functional categories in NP:

The six *red* chairs (*the *red* six chairs / **red* the six chairs)
every *red* chair (**red* every chair)

Here is a brief summary of the properties of adjectives and how they are distinct from D, NUM, and Q:

- Adjective is a lexical category.
- Adjectives can be modified by degree words (such as *very*).
- APs must follow D, NUM, or Q in NP.

We can now diagram NPs that include AP modifiers:

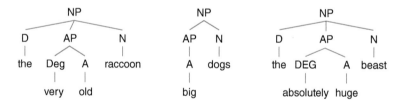

Nouns that modify nouns

It might seem odd that one noun can modify another noun, but in fact, this happens all the time in English. Here are some examples:

the poster
the *campus* poster
the *campus rally* poster
the *campus rally committee* poster
the *campus rally committee membership* poster

How do we know that the italicized words in each NP are nouns? Each of these words can occur in the position we've reserved for nouns, namely, after a determiner.

the poster
this campus
a rally
these committees
that membership

Adjectives can't occur in that position, so we know these words aren't adjectives:

*the incredible
*this huge
*a big
*these funny

We have another way to test whether a word is a noun or an adjective; as we've already seen, nouns can be modified by adjective phrases.

the *incredible* poster
this *beautiful* campus
a *large* rally
these *active* committees
this *exclusive* membership
incredible, beautiful, large, active, exclusive = AP

As noted above, adjectives aren't modified by adjectives, they're modified by degree words such as *very, quite, so, rather*, or adverbs that express degree, such as *absolutely* and *exceptionally*. We can illustrate this by modifying the adjectives in the above examples with degree words.

the *absolutely incredible* poster
this *exceptionally beautiful* campus
a *rather large* rally
these *quite active* committees
this *very exclusive* membership

Nouns can't be modified by degree words.

*the *rather* poster
*this *exceptionally* campus
*a *very* rally

And finally, there's evidence that our brains already know there's a distinction between noun modifiers and adjective phrase modifiers; if both modify a noun, they have to occur in a certain order. That is, the adjective phrase modifier has to precede the noun modifier.

the incredible campus poster
*the campus incredible poster

And also note that the phrase *the incredible campus poster* is ambiguous, because *incredible* can modify either *campus* or *poster*. This is exactly what we expect, because *incredible* is an adjective, and adjectives modify nouns!

So, using what we've learned about adjectives and nouns, we can apply certain tests to determine the category of a word, tests which show us that more traditional "catch all" descriptions of the words that precede nouns in the noun phrase are inaccurate, and blur certain important distinctions among categories.

Here's how we can diagram NPs with noun modifiers, and those that have both noun modifiers and AP modifiers:

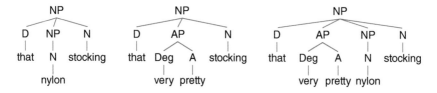

Verbs that modify nouns

Now that we've seen that not only adjectives but also nouns can modify other nouns, it might not surprise you to find that verbs can modify nouns too. Here are some examples:

the *crying* baby
three *laughing* students
the *honking* geese

Though you might want to call the italicized words adjectives, use what you know about adjectives to test whether these words are of the same category. Can you modify the italicized words with degree words such as *very*, *exceptionally*, and *rather*? Let's try it:

*the *very crying* baby
*three *exceptionally laughing* students
*the *rather honking* geese

Noun Phrases

You can see that these words can't be modified by degree words like adjectives can. We also know these words aren't noun modifiers, because they can't be modified by adjectives, which we'd expect if they were nouns. In the following examples, though the adjectives *loud*, *wild*, and *grey* can modify the nouns *baby*, *students*, and *geese*, respectively (as in *the loud, crying, baby*), these adjectives don't modify *crying*, *laughing*, and *honking*:

> *the *loud crying* baby
> *three *wild laughing* students
> *the *grey honking* geese

But *crying*, *laughing*, and *honking* can quite easily be modified by the class of words that modify verbs, namely, *adverbs*. Examples of adverbs include *loudly*, *wildly*, and *frantically*:

> the *loudly crying* baby
> three *wildly laughing* students
> the *frantically honking* geese

We can now diagram NPs with verb modifiers (which we diagram here as verb phrases or VPs). We include Adverb Phrase (AdvP) modifiers here for illustration – we return to these in Chapter 8.

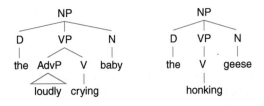

There are other ways to distinguish nouns, adjectives and verbs (and adverbs, for that matter) from each other, and we'll discuss them in later chapters. At this point, however, you have a basic set of syntactic tools to use to determine the category of a word. We've seen that adjectives, nouns, and verbs can modify nouns, and that:

- We can test whether something is an adjective by modifying it with a degree word (*very* hungry).
- We can test whether something is a noun by modifying it with an adjective (*fuzzy* squirrel).
- We can test whether something is a verb by modifying it with an adverb (*loudly* crying).

Summary

In this chapter, we have explored the basic internal structure of the **NP**, which we express with **phrase structure rules** and **tree diagrams**. We examined the grammatical properties of the functional categories that introduce nouns in English, **Determiner** (a category whose members include the **definite** and **indefinite articles, demonstratives,** and **possessive determiners**), **Numeral,** and **Quantifier**. We have discussed some other kinds of NPs, including **partitive, collective,** and **measure NPs,** and we also investigated how nouns can be introduced by **possessive NPs**. We have seen how we can use **pronoun substitution** as a test to distinguish NPs from single nouns, and in our discussion of **modification,** we've learned some other tests that we can use to distinguish the different categories of **modifiers** (adjective, noun, and verb) of nouns. We will build on these tools of analysis as we progress through chapters to come.

Exercises

1. Determiner, quantifier, numeral, or possessive NP

Label all the prenominal elements (including possessive determiners) in the following NPs. Use the abbreviations D, NUM, and Q. Are there any possessive NPs in these examples? If so, what is the possessive NP? (No need to further analyze the internal structure of the NP; just identify the entire phrase as a possessive NP.)

(a) these hedgehogs
(b) six hedgehogs
(c) my sister/my sister's hedgehogs
(d) all six hedgehogs
(e) my hedgehog
(f) many hedgehogs
(g) her hedgehogs
(h) them hedgehogs

2. Diagramming NPs

Diagram the NPs in (1) above. You may use a triangle for any possessive NPs.

3. Pronoun substitution

Here are some sentences, each with several NPs. Replace the NPs with pronouns (of your choice). You might also find that you can replace other phrases with *proforms* such as *here* or *then*, or *there*. What kinds of phrases do those proforms replace? Try to identify the category of the phrase substituted by the proform.

(a) Several pieces of paper blew across the highway during rush hour.
(b) That grocery store is never open on Sundays.
(c) At home, the kids like to play Monopoly.
(d) The leaves on the trees around the lake are turning yellow.
(e) Matilda walked to the park with her sister's best friend.

4. Noun, verb, or adjective?

Here are a number of NPs, each with a modifier. Use the tests discussed in the chapter to determine whether the italicized words are nouns, adjectives, or verbs (modifying nouns). Recall that adjectives can be modified by degree words, verbs by adverbs (in particular adverbs that express manner), and nouns by adjectives. Provide one piece of syntactic evidence to support your analysis of the category of each modifier.

(a) a *frisky* puppy
(b) a *brick* wall
(c) a *friendly* pony
(d) that *ticking* clock
(e) a *scathing* review
(f) a *dripping* faucet
(g) an *understated* dress
(h) a *howling* wind
(i) a *leather* saddle
(j) the *squealing* tires

Do words that modify nouns have to occur in a certain order? Can noun modifiers precede adjective modifiers or is it the other way around? What about verb modifiers of nouns? Can they precede or follow adjective modifiers? What kinds of evidence can we use to determine whether modifiers of nouns must occur in a certain order (or not)? Write down some examples and briefly explain.

5. Compounds and stress

Our focus in the text is on the syntax of lexical categories, but sometimes other components of grammar can help us identify categories. For example, phonological stress helps us distinguish a compound from a two-word phrase. Compare:

green house   greenhouse

The first phrase has stress on *house,* but in the second, a compound, stress is on *green.* The first is simply a house which happens to be green, while the second is a place to grow plants. These and other examples demonstrate how we unconsciously distinguish a compound word from one that is not. Using this *compound stress pattern,* identify which of the following are compounds and which are not. Which can be both?

rail fence   stone wall   ice cream   high school   bike trail

6. What's missing?

Consider the following sentences, paying attention to the italicized words.

I ordered two hamburgers but you ordered only *one.*
These books were pretty good but *those* were really boring.
Some legal documents are clear, but *most* are hard to follow.
Although *each* had a cell phone, the students didn't text during class.

In traditional grammar, *one, those, most,* and *each* are analyzed as pronouns when they occur in constructions such as these. What do you think about that categorization? Is there evidence for labeling them as such, or for labeling them otherwise (as NUM, D, or Q)?

7. Practice

We offer here some text excerpts to use for practice. These excerpts are intended only to get you started; there may not be examples in these texts of everything listed here. We encourage you to explore texts of your own choosing to find additional examples.

(a)   Identify all of the nouns in the following excerpts. If there are some you aren't sure about, apply at least two tests (morphological or syntactic) for nouns to try to figure out whether or not the word is indeed a noun.

(b) Use pronoun substitution to identify some NPs in the excerpts.
(c) Label the prenominal elements (D, NUM, Q) in the NPs you find in the excerpts.
(d) Label any modifiers of nouns (noun, adjective, verb) in the excerpts.
(e) Are there any possessive NPs in the excerpts? Label those as well.
(f) Practice diagramming some of the NPs in the excerpts.

After a quick cab ride from her apartment, the producer and director of *Stars on Mars* arrived at the Derry Street office. Her name was Rixey Bloomy and she was one of New York's hottest personalities. She was 36 years old and wore the most expensive leather trouser suit and zebra-skin ankle boots, and carried a matching furry handbag. Her hair was as bouncy as if she had just walked out of a shampoo commercial, her lips were plump and luscious (they had been plumped up by one of New York's top plastic surgeons), and her eyes were searingly blue. She looked suspiciously at Molly. (From *Molly Moon's Incredible Book of Hypnotism*, by Georgia Byng.)

The affluent, educated, liberated women of the First World, who can enjoy freedoms unavailable to any women ever before, do not feel as free as they want to. And they can no longer restrict to the subconscious their sense that this lack of freedom has something to do with apparently frivolous issues, things that really should not matter. Many are ashamed to admit that such trivial concerns – to do with physical appearance, bodies, faces, hair, clothes – matter so much. But in spite of shame, guilt, and denial, more and more women are wondering if it isn't that they are entirely neurotic and alone but rather that something important is indeed at stake that has to do with the relationship between female liberation and female beauty. (From *The Beauty Myth*, by Naomi Wolf.)

I dragged myself up onto her cabiny moose pillows and tried to soothe my deranged dear, rocking her, clutching her frowsy yellow head against my shoulder. Though she was older than me, Danae was spindly as a downy pre-woman. When she curled against me, I felt my heart surge and I became her shield against the world. Or maybe bulwark gives a more accurate picture. (From *The Sentence*, by Louise Erdrich.)

4

Verbs

Introduction

As we've mentioned before, identifying syntactic categories based on your intuitive knowledge of language is probably different from other approaches you have encountered when learning about so-called parts of speech. You may have learned, for example, that a verb is "what the subject is doing," or that the verb "expresses an action or a state." However, adjectives and nouns can also express states (the *happy* baby, an *annoyance*),

Navigating English Grammar: A Guide to Analyzing Real Language, Second Edition.
Anne Lobeck and Kristin Denham.
© 2025 Anne Lobeck and Kristin Denham. Published 2025 by John Wiley & Sons Ltd.

and nouns can also express actions (the *fight/battle/altercation*, a *kiss*). Moreover, you can probably easily figure out that *blenched* is a verb in the following sentence, even though you have no idea what all the words actually mean.

The zergots blenched six poffles.

One reason that you know that *blenched* is a verb here is because of its *form*, or morphology; *blenched* is affixed with *-ed*, a past tense ending on verbs expressed in some, but not all varieties of English. *Blenched* also occurs between the subject noun phrase, *the zergots*, and the object noun phrase, *six poffles*, in the position in which we find main verbs in English. So, as we've discussed already, a more effective way to analyze syntactic categories is by looking at morphology and syntax, in addition to meaning.

In this chapter, we will focus on the morphology of verbs, discussing in some detail the five possible different *forms* of English verbs. We'll see that there is quite a bit of variation among these forms in current varieties of American English, and that the forms of many English verbs have changed quite a bit over time (and continue to do so).

Main Verbs

We can divide up the (large) category Verb in several ways. We can distinguish among *auxiliary*, or "helping" verbs, including *have* and *be*; the class of *modals*, such as *may*, *might*, *can*, *could*, or *will*; and the class of *main verbs*, including words such as *eat*, *sleep*, *become*, *amuse*, *drive*, or *feel*. What we will call main verbs have lexical meanings, and like the other lexical categories we've discussed so far, Noun and Adjective, the lexical category Verb is an open class; we can add new members to it, and we do so all the time. We *blog*, *text*, and *IM* each other, we *downsize* and we *outsource*, *skype*, and *zoom*.

Main verbs can be pretty easy to spot; every clause must have a main verb, so if there's only one verb in a clause, it must be a main verb!

The zebra *chased* the lion.
   chased = main verb

Murray *became* a surgeon.
   became = main verb

We can define *main* verbs as the *required* verbal element in a verb string. Another way to put this is to say that the main verb is the *head* of the verb phrase, or VP. That means that any time you have a VP, you'll have (at least) a main verb. Some simple VPs are given below, each headed by a main verb followed by an NP. The phrase structure rule for these examples is:

VP → V (NP)

In these tree diagrams, *chased* and *became* are main verbs.

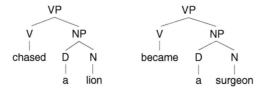

Main Verb Morphology

In this section, we discuss the ways we build main verbs through derivational affixation, and how we create new main verbs using different word formation rules. We also introduce the inflectional morphology of main verbs because it is inflectional morphology that gives us the five different forms of the verb. We discuss the forms of the verb in detail in later sections.

Derivational affixation and other ways we form verbs

As we saw in Chapter 2, we can build nouns through derivational affixation, creating nominalizations such as *excitement*, *friendship*, and *ugliness*. We can also build verbs through derivational affixation (both prefixation and suffixation). Some examples are given in Table 4.1.

As with nouns, we easily add new verbs to the language, using the word formation rules we discussed in earlier chapters. We *snapchat* each other (the verb *snapchat* is a conversion from the noun, the name of the platform, and

Table 4.1 Some English verb suffixes and prefixes.

Suffix	Sample words
-ize	regularize, maximize, realize
-ate	activate, punctuate, pontificate
-ify	mollify, horrify, unify
-en	tighten, deepen, thicken
en-	enroll, enchant, encase
dis-	disorganize, disinvite, disenchant
re-	rediscover, resend, renew

thus an eponym as well as a compound!). We *text* (a clipping of *textmessage*, also a conversion from noun to verb). You may also have *retweeted* or *googled* someone. Other examples of recently formed verbs include *TikToked* (eponym – "to be made a target on TikTok") *demonitize* (backformation of *de(monitization)* – "to remove ads from YouTube channel to deprive creator of revenue"), *screenshotted* (a conversion to a verb of the compound noun *screenshot*), *vax* or *vaxxed*, conversion to a verb of the clipped noun *vaccine/ vaccination*, and *greenwashing*, a misleading claim about the environmental-friendliness of a product or activity.

Inflectional affixation

As we've discussed earlier in the book, English has a maximum of eight inflectional affixes, a relatively small number compared to many other languages. We've also seen that these inflectional affixes are not always morphologically expressed in all varieties of English (plural *-s* and possessive *-s* for example). Four inflectional affixes can possibly show up on verbs: present tense *-s* (sometimes marking third person singular), past tense *-ed*, past participle *-ed* and *-en*, and present participle *-ing*. Consequently, there are only five possible basic morphological forms of the English verb; one without any tense affixes at all, what we call the *infinitival* form of the verb, and then four other possible forms.

Consider the following examples, which include the possible inflectional affixes on verbs in English.

Forms of the verb *walk*:

infinitive:	*to walk*
present tense:	*walks*
past tense:	*walked*
present participle:	*walking*
past participle:	*walked*

As we'll see, not all verbs express the morphological inflections illustrated above, and not all verbs follow the same pattern as *walk*. The past participle of *eat*, for example, can be *ate* or *eaten*, the past tense of *drink* can be *drank* or *drunk*, and the past tense of *walk* might be *walk* not *walked*. As you might by now expect, there is a lot of variation in the forms of the verb!

Infinitives
The most basic form of the verb is called the *infinitive*. The word *infinitive* comes from the Latin root meaning "in perpetuity, without end," which in terms of verb tense, means "without time." That is, the infinitival form of the verb has no inflection at all and expresses no tense (nor any agreement

inflection). In English, infinitives can be preceded by *to*, as in *to go, to walk,* and *to eat*.

> We arranged for a neighbor *to watch* the kids.
> Yusef tried *to be* on time.
> Elsie wondered how *to solve* the problem.
> They went to the mountains *to go* hiking.

English has a "two-word" infinitival verb form, *to run, to see,* etc. Other Indo-European languages (the family of which English is a member) have one-word infinitives. In Romance languages such as French, for example, "to say or to speak" is *dire*, and in Spanish *hablar*. In Germanic languages such as German and Icelandic, the infinitive can be preceded by the equivalent of "to," as in German *zu sagen*, and Icelandic *að tala*, "to speak."

Infinitival verbs in English can, under certain circumstances, show up without *to*. These *bare infinitives* follow modals (such as *should, could,* and *can*) in the following examples:

> Bo should *be* happy about their new job.
> That new biography could *appear* in stores any time.
> I can *smell* the flowers.
> *be, appear, smell* = bare infinitives

This generalization holds of double modal constructions too. Double modals occur in several different varieties of American English across the South Midland and Southern regions. In the following examples, the double modals *might could* and *might should* are followed by bare infinitival verbs, *go* and *talk*.

> We *might could* go to the movies tonight.
> I *might should* talk that over with my boss.
> *go* and *talk* = bare infinitives

Bare infinitives occur in other contexts as well. When verbs of perception like *see, feel, sense, hear,* or *watch* are followed by another verb in the next clause (the bracketed phrases below), that verb is a bare infinitive:

> We watched [Lee *dance* the flamenco].
> Jojo heard [the dog *bark* at the car].
> *dance* and *bark* = bare infinitives

Also, when a verb follows one of several verbs of causation or permission, such as *make, let,* or (main verb) *have*, that verb is the bare infinitive form:

> I made/let them *do* it.
> I had her *come* with me.
> *do* and *come* = bare infinitives

In some varieties of English, including African American English (AAE), the bare infinitive *be* also expresses habitual actions (or *habitual aspect,* which we discuss in the next chapter).

They *be* eating cookies.
(conveys that this is usually or always happening)

I *be* in my office by 7:30.
(conveys that this is typically or regularly the case)

As we saw with past tense and past participles, there is some overlap in forms of bare infinitives and other forms of the verb. For example, the bare infinitive can sometimes be hard to identify because it may be morphologically indistinguishable from the present tense form of the verb.

I/you/we/they *dance* the flamenco.
dance = present tense

I can *dance* the flamenco.
I saw Lee *dance* the flamenco.
dance = bare infinitive

One way to determine whether a verb is a bare infinitive or not is to simply remember that a modal (such as *can* above) is always followed by a bare infinitive, no matter how many other verbs are in the verb string. Another way to tell whether you have a bare infinitive or not is to replace the infinitive with another verb whose infinitival form is different from its present tense form. *Be* can be a good choice since it has more distinct forms than other verbs in most varieties of English, and the bare infinitival form of *be* is, well, *be*. So, if we can replace a verb such as *dance* with *be*, we know that *dance* is a bare infinitive.

I can *be* silly.
I saw Lee *be* silly.
be = bare infinitive

Another way to tell whether a verb is a bare infinitive or not is to check for morphological subject–verb agreement in varieties of English that express such agreement. For example, bare infinitives can't occur with present tense inflectional -*s*:

Lee *dances* the flamenco.
*I saw Lee *dances* the flamenco.

When we look at the present tense verbs in the next section, we'll learn more about this present tense affix -*s*. For now, simply note that subject–verb agreement inflection, when morphologically expressed, tells us that a verb is (you guessed it) inflected for tense, and thus not a bare infinitive!

Copula *be*

The English main verb *be,* like its equivalent in other languages, is somewhat exceptional. This verb is functional, rather than lexical (when you think about it, *be* doesn't really *mean* anything) and it is called a copular verb. The term "copula" comes from the Latin word that means "link," and the primary function of such words is to link the subject, *my friend* in the example below, with some kind of description, such as *a linguist:*

My friend is a linguist.

In fact, copular verbs like "be" are also called "linking verbs," a class of verbs we discuss in later chapters.

In English and in many other languages, the copula can be null (unpronounced), which we indicate with a null sign in these examples from a variety of English that can omit the copula, and Turkish, which can as well:

English (word order is Subject–Verb–Object, SVO, but the V here is Ø):

My friend Ø a linguist.

Turkish (word order is Subject–Object–Verb, SOV, but the V here is Ø):

Deniz mavi
sea   blue   Ø
"The sea is blue."

In some languages, including Hebrew, Russian, Hungarian, Arabic, Southern Quechua, and among others, a null copula occurs in the present tense, but in other tenses, the copular verb is there as a word.

Present tense

As we just mentioned above, *present tense* is expressed morphologically in some varieties of English by inflectional -s. This form of the verb can agree

73

with a variety of different subjects; it might agree with 3rd person singular subjects (*he/she/it/Lee/my housemate*):

He *runs* very fast.
It *rains* a lot here.

Lee *sleeps* late every day.
My housemate *collapses* on the couch after work.

In Smoky Mountain English (SME), -*s* marks agreement with 3rd person plural subjects that are NOT pronouns, such as *the cattle* in the example below. Note that in this example (from Montgomery and Hall, 2004), the 3rd person plural pronoun *they* is followed by a verb that is not affixed with -*s*, *feed*:

That's the way cattle *feeds*. They *feed* together.

The -*s* inflection in some varieties can also occur with 1st person singular subjects (*I, we*) in "historical present" contexts (when one is narrating a story, for example, as discussed in Green, 2002, p. 186).

I *thinks* to myself I'll just slide down there and see if he'd make me holler.
I tells you.

In a number of varieties of English, the verb expresses no overt tense inflection (or subject–verb agreement) at all. Nevertheless, each of the following sentences is in present tense:

I *sleep* late every day.   (*I* = 1st person singular)
You *work* too hard.   (*you* = 2nd person singular or plural)
He *run* very fast.   (*he* = 3rd person singular)
They *like* to dance.   (*they* = 3rd person singular or plural)

How do we know that *sleep, work, run*, and *like* here express present tense, even though they have no morphology that tells us that? Remember earlier in the chapter we said that when there is only one verb in a clause, we know that verb is the main verb (because every clause, in order to be a clause, has to have at least a verb, null or not, and a subject too, for that matter). Much research on English and other languages suggests that tense is another necessary component of independent clauses, whether expressed morphologically or not. It follows, then, that in an independent clause such as *I sleep late every day* the verb *sleep* is understood to be tensed, and more specifically to be in present tense.

Let's take a look at some of the evidence that every sentence must have tense. Suppose a teacher walks into a classroom and says *The exams to cover four chapters*. This utterance would be decidedly odd. But for the teacher to say *The exams cover four chapters* would make sense, and students would not bat an eye. The difference is that the first example is odd because it lacks tense; the verb *to cover* is an infinitive. But in the second example, the verb *cover* is understood to be in present tense. Independent clauses, then, need to be tensed, even if the verb may have no morphology marking it as such. What all of this means is that the absence of morphological inflection in English doesn't necessarily make English tense more confusing or ambiguous than in another language with more (or fewer) inflectional affixes. Rather, it simply makes English speakers rely on syntactic structure and context to interpret tense.

Past tense
One way that the past tense is morphologically expressed on the verb is with the affix *-ed*.

My housemate *collapsed* on the couch after work. (*-ed* affix)

This affix may be absent in some varieties of English, but the verb is still understood as being in past tense:

My housemate *collapse* on the couch after work.

Another way that English verbs express past tense is through *vowel mutation*, a vowel change rather than an affix. As we might by now expect, there is quite a bit of variation in vowel mutated forms across different varieties of English.

infinitive: *to sing, to drink*
present tense: *sing(s)/drink(s)*
past tense: *sang/sung, drank/drunk*

There are many verbs in which two forms, both the past tense *-ed* form and a vowel mutated form, are in use. Consider the following verbs, each of which has two forms currently in use. Are both forms possible for you? Do you use one form in one context and the other in a different context?

I *speeded/sped* up at the intersection.
I *lighted/lit* the fire.
I *dragged/drug* the log over to the campfire.
I *blowed/blew* out the candle.
I *catched/caught* a cold.

Can you think of other verbs that have more than one form in past tense? Though vowel mutation forms are often called *irregular*, they follow regular patterns that you may be familiar with. In fact, you can easily make up vowel mutation forms for past tense verbs on your own. For example, the mutated past tense of *fling* could be *flang*, and that of *slink* could be *slank* (by analogy with other words: *sing/sang*, *drink/drank*). Still other verbs form the past tense by both vowel mutation and affixation (of *-t* or *-ed*), as in *sleep/slept*, *keep/kept*, and *buy/bought*. So calling these verbs "irregular" depends on your perspective. They are irregular in the sense that new verbs we add to the language are typically affixed with *-ed* if affixed at all, but regular in the sense that they follow a recognizable pattern, one Present Day English has inherited from Old English.

The history of the past (tense)

English is a member of the Germanic language family, one of the branches of the (larger) Indo-European language family. All members of the Germanic language family share certain linguistic features, thereby distinguishing them from all of the other branches of Indo-European (such as the Romance, Celtic, and Slavic branches, for example). One of those distinctions is the way that Germanic languages form the past tense (or preterite) with a /d/ or /t/; consider Old English *fremede* "did," *bærnd* "burned," *lōcode* "looked," *cēpte* "kept." Not all verbs in Old English had the so-called dental (sounds made with the tongue right behind the teeth) past tense forms, though as the language developed this feature became more and more common. Consider the present-day forms of the verb form in the following Germanic languages, all of which have the /d/ or /t/ past tense ending: English, Frisian, Dutch, Low German, and German: *he worked, hy learde, hij werkte, he warkt, er werkte.*

As we have already noted above, there is quite a bit of variation in the morphological form of both present and past tense verbs in English. This is not surprising, given that language constantly changes over time, and that different speech communities may adopt one pattern versus another. Consider, for example, the following sentences, each of which has two possible forms for the past tense verb. Do you prefer one or the other in your own speech?

I *dreamed/dreamt* about you last night.
The frog *leaped/leapt* from the lilypad.
They *burned/burnt* the toast.

For the most part, the -*t* forms are decreasing; that is, the -*ed* form is the more recent one, with speakers gradually adding more verbs into this "regular" category. In other cases, however, we have taken a regular -*ed* past tense form and created a new form, modeled on a pattern with vowel mutation. For example, consider the following:

I *sneaked/snuck* into the hallway.
The girls *dived/dove* into the pool.
They *lighted/lit* the candles.

In all of these examples, the -*ed* form is the older form, and the mutated forms (*snuck, dove, lit*) are the more recent innovations.

What about future tense?
We've discussed present and past tense forms of the verb in English, and you may be wondering, what about future tense? Is there a verb form for that? Future tense is expressed morphologically on verbs in many languages; for example, in French, the first person plural future tense form of the verb *partir*, "to leave" is *partirons:*

Nous *partirons* en vacances en janvier.
"We will go on vacation in January."

But in English, future tense is syntactic: it is formed by adding a word, such as modal *will* to the verb string.

We *will* go on vacation in January.

As we'll see in Chapter 5, modals (*will/would, shall/should, can/could, may/ might/must,* and others) can be interpreted as past, present, or future (among other complex meanings) depending on context:

You *should* clean your room this minute!
    should = present tense

You *should* clean your room tomorrow.
    should = future tense

As you can see in the above two examples, English also uses adverbial phrases such as the adverbial NPs *tomorrow* and *this minute* to express tense.

Future tense is also expressed by verb strings with *going to/gonna,* and *gon.* (The example below is from DeBose, 2015):

We *are going to/gonna/gon* have a party.

77

Another more specific way of expressing futurity is by using *fixin' to*, a feature of Southern American English, with the variant *finna* in AAE (Rickford, 1999; Green, 2002). According to Green and others, *fixin to/finna* is distinct from *going to/gonna/gon* in meaning "imminent future," which can be paraphrased as "about to."

I'm *fixin to* go to town.
I don't know about you but I'm *finna* leave. (Green, 2002, p. 70)

The formation of the future tense in English is therefore a syntactic process typical of analytic languages more generally. That English can also express present and past tense morphologically demonstrates that the language is a mixed system, both analytic (expressing grammatical features by adding separate words) and synthetic (expressing grammatical features through inflectional affixes).

Present and past participles
So far, we've looked at the infinitival, past tense, and present tense forms of the verb. As the labels indicate, an *infinitive* does not convey time, or tense, and *past* and *present tense* forms do, either morphologically or semantically. We're now going to look more closely at the *verb string*, or sequences of verbs in a sentence. As we'll see, the *participial* forms of English verbs follow an auxiliary verb (which may be unpronounced or null), a form of *have* or *be*. These participial main verbs themselves do not express tense, but they occur with an auxiliary verb that expresses that tense information, or tense can be interpreted from context.

The *present participle* form, which is the *-ing* form of the verb, can occur after a form of the auxiliary verb *be*, thereby expressing what is called **progressive aspect**, which we'll return to in Chapter 5. (We follow Green's (2002) analysis of auxiliaries in AAE as syntactically null in certain cases.)

She is *competing* in a marathon today.
They are *riding* their bicycle to class.
The giraffe is *running* away from the Land Rover.
They were *sleeping* late that day.
I ain't *going* to that meeting.
He Ø *eating* dinner.   Ø = *is*

As we briefly mentioned above, in AAE and other varieties of English, the present participle can also follow infinitival *be*, to indicate habitual aspect, which we also discuss in more detail in Chapter 5. The following sentence has the habitual meaning of "they are working all the time."

They be *working*.

And as we'll also discuss more in Chapter 5, present participles can occur in longer strings that include more than a single auxiliary verb (and in AAE the tensed auxiliary *have* can be null).

She/they might have been *working*.
She/they ∅ been *working*.   ∅ = *have*

In some varieties of Southern American English, as well as some varieties of British and Scots English, present participles can show up prefixed with *a-*:

He was just *a-singing*.

Turning now to *past participles*, as we have already mentioned above, they have a variety of forms, depending on whether the form of the verb undergoes affixation or vowel mutation, both, or neither! The past participle can occur following a form of the auxiliary *have* (which in some cases may be null), as in the following examples:

(have) walked
    put
    eaten/ate/aten/ate
    sang/sung
    drank/dranken/drunk/drunken
    blowed/blown/blew

As with present participles, past participles can occur in longer strings. Here, auxiliary *be* is a past participle (*been*), following (either null or pronounced) auxiliary *have*:

They might have *been* working.
They have/had *been* working.
They ∅ *been* working.   ∅ = *have*

Suppletion

Though we assume that the forms of a particular verb will all be (in some way) related to each other, some verb forms seem to be completely unrelated to the infinitival form of the verb. For example, the past tense (and sometimes also the past participle) of *to go* is *went* (*I went to school/I should have went to school*). This kind of irregularity is called *suppletion*: one form of the verb has no obvious phonological similarity to another. There are historical roots to these suppletive verb forms, however, and they aren't entirely random. The variation we have in the current conjugation of *go/went*, for example, is due to the fact that it is from two distinct Old English verbs, *ëodan* and *wendan* (related to the verb *wend*: *I wended my way home*). It's hardly surprising that children produce *goed* before they learn suppletive *went*!

Suppletion is not confined to verbs, of course; consider the comparative and superlative forms of the adjectives *good* and *bad*. These are also examples of suppletive forms: *good/better/best, bad/worse/worst*. As we might expect, children acquire the basic form of the adjective and produce forms like *gooder* and *goodest, badder* and *baddest* until they conform to the more idiosyncratic *better/best, worse/worst*.

Perhaps the most obvious example of suppletion in English is illustrated by forms of the verb *be*. (We discuss negative forms of *be* such as *ain't/weren't* in Chapter 6.)

Forms of *be*	*to be (infinitive)*	
	am/is/are/was/were	present/past tense
	being	present participle
	been	past participle

The notoriously irregular forms of *be* have an interesting history. In Old English, the verb *beon* was used in the present tense, and the past tense and present participle forms derived from a different verb, *wesan*. These two distinct verbs led to the familiar, but irregular pattern we have today. In fact, in most languages, the verb that means "to be" is irregular. There is quite a bit of variation in English *be,* some of which we discussed above: in terms of subject–verb agreement (*they was/were working*); in the use of infinitival *be* (*he be working*); and forms of *be* in negative sentences (*I weren't working*) for example. As we mentioned above in the box on main verb *be* and copular verbs, in English and in many languages, there is variation in whether *be* shows up at all: *My sister ∅ a doctor* versus *My sister is a doctor.* We discuss main verb *be* more in Chapter 6.

Summary

We have seen that main verbs in English can be defined as the head of the verb phrase or VP. Main verbs can have up to five different **forms**, though for some verbs, these forms overlap because of the lack of distinct morphological inflection in English. In varieties of English in which inflection is morphologically expressed, the **present tense** affix is -s, and the **past tense** affix is -ed or -t (*walked, kept*). **Present participles** are affixed with -*ing* (is *walking/eating*), and **past participles** with -ed or -*en* (have *walked/eaten/aten*). The form of the verb can also be indicated by **vowel mutation** (*sing, sang, eat,* and *ate)* rather than affixation, or by both affixation and vowel mutation (*buy, bought,* and *boughten*). Still others are indicated by **suppletion** (*go, went*). The **infinitival** form of the verb has no inflectional morphology at all and can be introduced by *to* (or not, in the case of *bare* **infinitives**, which occur, for example, after modals: *can walk*). **Future tense** in English is often expressed syntactically, with the addition of adverbial phrases such as *today/ tomorrow,* modals such as *shall/will,* and phrases such as *going to/gonna/gon* and *fixin to/finna*. Though present, past, and future tense are not consistently morphologically expressed on verbs in English, speakers nevertheless interpret independent clauses as tensed based on context and other clues.

Exercises

1. Forms of main verbs

Label the form of each boldface **MAIN** verb in the following sentences as infinitive, present tense, past tense, present participle, or past participle. Keep in mind that some of the sentences may not match your own verb form – discuss these with your classmates!

(a) Ferdinand has been **eating** dandelions.
(b) Lee ain't **taking** calculus this term.
(c) A mosquito has just **bit** me!
(d) I **says** to him that he better not be late.
(e) Have you **seen** the movie?
(f) Yes, I **seen** it yesterday.
(g) Lee will **love** that gift.
(h) They **want** to go home.
(i) We done already **finished** that.
(j) The orange tree had **froze** during the snowstorm.
(k) They **come** late yesterday.
(l) She hopes **to see** the movie tomorrow.
(m) The kids **creeped** into the empty house.
(n) Elisabeth **lived** in Chicago.
(o) I've already **ate**.
(p) The students expected **to stay** after class.
(q) I should have **went** to that meeting.
(r) Last year he **run** in the race.

2. Suppletion, vowel mutation, affixation, or?

Determine the form of each of the following bolded verbs and if that verb is formed through suppletion, vowel mutation, affixation, or some combination (or none at all!).

    (a)   I should have **put** more than six cucumbers in the salad.
    (b)   They had already **boughten** new umbrellas.
    (c)   We **dragged** the hose from the front yard.
    (d)   We **drug** the boxes out of the garage.
    (e)   They **be** taking exams.
    (f)   They **clumb** up the water tower.
    (g)   We only **went** to work on Tuesdays.

3. Participles in other places

We've seen in this chapter that English verbs can occur in a sequence, or *string*. Present participles typically follow some form of auxiliary *be*, and past participles typically follow some form of auxiliary *have*.

    is walking   *has walked*

As we progress throughout the book, however, we'll find that past and present participles show up in other contexts as well (some of which we already introduced in Chapter 3 in the section on *Modifiers of Nouns*). See if you can identify the past and present participles in each of the following sentences. Also see if you can informally explain the function of each participle.

    (a)   A helicopter passed overhead, flying low.
    (b)   She ran for the car, the rain pelting her face.
    (c)   The whistling wind blew through the cracks in the walls.
    (d)   The haunted house stood on the corner, amid tangled weeds and encircled by an overgrown hedge.
    (e)   I've never seen such a boring movie!
    (f)   Two garbage cans, tipped over by the wind, blocked the driveway.
    (g)   The only thing left after the picnic was a half-eaten apple.

4. Verb search

Find a text excerpt three or four sentences long. For each sentence, identify the main verb of each clause. Label the form of each main verb.

5. Variation in English

Conduct some research on a variety of English in or outside of the United States that is different from your own, focusing on verb strings. Label the form of each verb in the string. Are they the same or different from forms you would use?

6. Practice

We offer here some text excerpts to use for practice. These excerpts are intended only to get you started; there may not be examples in these texts of everything listed here. We encourage you to explore texts of your own choosing to find additional examples.

(a) Identify all of the main verbs.
(b) Identify the form of each main verb.
(c) Are there any verbs that modify nouns? If so, what are their forms?
(d) Which, if any, words are difficult to analyze? Do your best to explain why.

No wonder we are stretched top to bottom from both ends of our being. No wonder the soul can't decide where to wedge itself. Of course, there are those who aren't troubled by these things, for instance, my mother. As I said, she has decided to get her law degree. She moved down here to live with Grandma Zosie and Grandma Mary and go to night school. During the day, she works as a checker in a big discount food warehouse. For this, I guess she has learned to question nothing. She knows that prices change constantly and yet are precisely fixed. Every evening, I run the city lake while she walks the curved shore in startling peace. We meet at the bridge. There, her profile held simple against the sky, it seems to me that my mother is held equally by sky and earth, home and city. Some days with her I feel the perfect suspension, the balance. Other days I know how small a thing it takes to throw us off. (From *The Antelope Wife*, by Louise Erdrich.)

If things ever get that bad, Sandi thought she would sell her charm bracelet with the windmill that always got caught on her clothing. She would even cut her hair and sell it – a maid back home had told her that girls with good hair could always do that. She had no idea who would buy it. She had not seen hair for sale in the big department stores Mami sometimes took them through on outings "to see this new country." But Sandi would make the needed sacrifices. Tonight, she thought, with the rich Fannings, she would present herself as the daughter willing to make these sacrifices. Maybe they would adopt her and give her an allowance like other American girls got, which Sandi would then pass on to her real family. Provided she could see them periodically, that would not be a bad life being an only child in a fine, rich childless American family. (From *How the Garcia Girls Lost Their Accents*, by Julia Alvarez.)

The third BL [Black Language] feature in Obama's "Nah, we straight" is a well-studied variation of what leading sociolinguist John R. Rickford called BL's "showcase variable," the copula. As sociolinguists have shown, BL has a more complex verbal system than any White American variety of English. While speakers of White American varieties only have two ways of representing the copula, BL speakers have three. Depending on context and meaning, in BL, you can say "We are straight," "We're straight," or "We Ø straight." Black folks shift among these variants, all of which have the same literal meaning, but differ in social meaning. But Black folks don't be just leaving the copula out randomly – copula absence follows a well-documented set of linguistic constraints (From *Interview with Geneva Smitherman*, by Samy Alim).

Introduction

At this point, you are familiar with different possible morphological forms of the main verb: *infinitive, past tense, present tense, present participle,* and *past participle.* You also know that English verbs overall show little inflectional morphology, and that we sometimes identify verbs based on syntax, or their order in the verb string (*is walking/have walked*). We have explored ways in which English expresses future tense syntactically, by adding

Navigating English Grammar: A Guide to Analyzing Real Language, Second Edition.
Anne Lobeck and Kristin Denham.
© 2025 Anne Lobeck and Kristin Denham. Published 2025 by John Wiley & Sons Ltd.

modals (*will* for example) to the verb string, and/or by adding verb forms such as *going to/gonna/gon,* and *fixin to/finna.*

In this chapter, we take a closer look at the syntax and semantics of the verb string or *verb phrase* (VP), and how sequences of verbs (auxiliary, modal, and main verbs) in English express not only tense but also *aspect.* Aspect is semantically complex, and to simplify things we will focus on three recognizable aspects in English: *perfect, progressive,* and *habitual* aspects. We conclude the chapter with a brief discussion of *passive voice.* Passive voice, like aspect, affects the syntax of the verb string or VP.

Auxiliary Verbs

In Chapter 4, we spent some time exploring the morphology of main verbs, the verb that is the lexical head of the VP. We mentioned another class of verbs, *auxiliary verbs,* a functional category, which includes *have* and *be.* Auxiliary verbs are also sometimes called "helping verbs" (the word *auxiliary* means "helping" in Latin) because they only occur with main verbs, and never alone. As with other functional categories, the class of auxiliary verbs is a closed class; we typically don't add new members to this class of verbs.

Think about how difficult it is to explain what the verbs *have* and *be* mean in the sentences repeated as follows:

> Kim *has/had walked* to the store.
> Kim *is/was walking* to the store.

It's easier to describe their *function* – together with the main verb they form a sequence of verbs, a verb string, that expresses important grammatical (as well as lexical) information. We return to this grammatical information, namely, *tense* and *aspect,* after we briefly discuss the morphology of auxiliary *have* and *be.*

Auxiliary *have*

Recall that main verbs have five forms: infinitive, present, past, present participle, and past participle. Auxiliary *have,* on the other hand, is a little more restricted. (We leave aside for the moment variation in subject–verb agreement, and conditions under which *have* can be null for some speakers, as discussed in Chapter 4.)

> ... might like *to have* played the drums
>   = infinitive, with *to*

> ... might *have* played the drums
>   = bare infinitive

... *have/has* played the drums
    = present tense

... *had* played the drums
    = past tense

As you can see from this set of phrases, the auxiliary verb *have* has only three forms: infinitive (*to* and bare), present tense, and past tense. Auxiliary *have* doesn't have present or past participle forms (for reasons we don't need to go into here).

Auxiliary *be*

Now, let's look at auxiliary *be*. This auxiliary verb differs from *have* in showing up in all five forms (and like *have*, can under certain conditions be null):

... might like *to be* playing the drums
    = infinitive with *to*

... might *be* playing the drums
    = bare infinitive

... *am/is/are* playing the drums
    = present tense

... *was/were* playing the drums
    = past tense

... has *been* playing the drums
    = past participle

Auxiliary *be* can also show up as a present participle, namely, in passive sentences such as the following. (We discuss passive verb strings in a later section of this chapter.)

The drums were *being* played.
    = present participle

Like main verbs, auxiliary *have* and *be* have different tensed and participial forms, but as "helping" verbs they never occur alone. There is, however, a main verb *have*, and a main verb *be*, that differ from these auxiliary verbs. We turn briefly to each of these main verbs below.

Main verb *have*

It's important not to confuse auxiliary *have* with main verb *have*. Main verb *have* has a lexical meaning, something like "to possess," or "to experience."

As with other main verbs, subject–verb agreement patterns vary across different varieties of English.

> I *have* six dollars in my bank account.
> The people up the street *has/have* a nice dog.
> Lawrence *had* a bad day.
> My sister *has/have* two kids.

In all of the above examples, *have* is the only verb in the clause, and is therefore the main verb. It is also interpreted as tensed regardless of its form. Main verb *have* can also occur untensed, as an infinitive:

> They don't want *to have* dinner with us tonight.

And as we might expect, main verb *have* can occur in longer verb strings, together with (null and pronounced) auxiliaries *have* and *be* and modals:

> I have *had* up to one thousand dollars in my bank account.
> > *had* = past participle

> The people up the street might *have* a party tomorrow.
> > *have* = bare infinitive

> Lawrence was *having* a bad day.
> > *having* = present participle

> They ∅ *having* a bad day.
> > *having* = present participle (∅ = *is*)

In these examples of verb strings, main verb *have* can show up in all the same forms as any other main verb: as an infinitive (*(to) have*), as present tense (*have/has*), or past tense (*had*), as a past participle (*had*), and as a present participle (*having*).

Main verb *be*

As noted in Chapter 4, *be* can also be a main verb. We can tell it's the main verb in the examples below because it's the only verb in the sentence. It's hard to explain what *be* means here; recall that main verb *be* is a function verb, called a "copular" verb because it simply connects the subject to some kind of description (see box in Chapter 4).

> My sister *is* happy.
> They *were* in a good mood.
> Sally Ride *was* a famous astronaut.

As with any verb, there is variation in subject–verb agreement patterns with main verb *be*. And as we've mentioned before, main verb *be* can be null under certain conditions (examples here are from Lumbee, Appalachian, and African American Englishes).

The child *be* happy.
They *is/Ø* happy.
They/she *was* happy.
The child *bes* happy.
The child *were* happy.
There *weren't* even a sprig of fire in his place!
The fire *were* plumb out.

And like any other main verb, main verb *be* can combine with auxiliary verbs and modals in longer verb strings:

The child might *be* happy.
  be = infinitive

The child has/had *been* happy.
  been = past participle

The child Ø *been* happy.
  been = past participle (Ø = *have*)

The child might have been *being* naughty.
  being = present participle

Like other main verbs, main verb *be* has an infinitival form, as well as present tense (*am, is, are*), past tense (*was, were*), past participle (*been*), and present participle (*being*) forms. Some of these forms look unrelated to each other but recall from Chapter 4 that the forms of *be* are examples of *suppletion,* in this case with forms that are derived historically from two different verbs. Main verb *be* is exceptional in English in being a functional, rather than lexical verb. It is different from other main verbs in other ways as well, which we discuss more in Chapter 6.

Modals

You may have already observed that we can add yet another verb to the English verb string in addition to auxiliary *have* and *be*.

Lorenzo *may* have been eating sushi.
The professor *should* be discussing the exam tomorrow.

As you may recall from Chapter 4, words such as *may* and *should* are called *modals*, verbs that have properties that distinguish them from both main verbs and auxiliary *have* and *be*. Some of the words that fall into this class, the category *Modal*, are given below:

> *can, could, may, might, must, will, would, shall, should*

Some other words and phrases are labeled as *semi-modals,* because they behave like modal auxiliary verbs but also like main verbs:

> semi-modals: *need, dare, had better, ought, used to*

The category Modal is a closed class; we don't add new modals to the language, at least in any productive way. Modals are also function words but differ from auxiliary *have* and *be* in having quite complex meanings. For example, modals (*must, would,* and *should*) express necessity and desire, as well as prediction and obligation:

> Eli *must* get a new car. (necessity/obligation)
> I *would* like to go to Thailand. (hope/desire)
> You *should* learn to play the cello. (prediction/obligation)

Modals also differ from *have* and *be* in having invariant forms; in other words, modals don't show subject–verb agreement, nor do they have participial forms.

> I *can* take a morphology class.
> He *can* take a morphology class.
> They *can* take a morphology class.

As you can see from the above examples, modals don't express morphological tense inflection (with *-s* or *-ed*). But they are still interpreted as tensed, though the tense they express depends on context, not form.

> I can take that morphology class now.
> I could take that morphology class now.

> I can take that morphology class next year.
> I could take that morphology class next year.

It isn't really accurate to say that *can* is the present tense form of the modal and *could* is the past tense form. In the following sentence, *could* can express past tense, present tense, or future tense, depending on context:

> Eli could not leave for Toronto. (yesterday/today/tomorrow)

And *must* in the sentence below expresses either present tense or future tense, again, depending on context.

Eli *must leave* for Toronto. (now/tomorrow)

In all of these sentences, the modal is followed by a bare infinitival verb. This again suggests that the modal, not the main verb, expresses tense, but that tense interpretation (as past, present, or future) depends on context.

Semi-modals

There are a few words that are often classified as *semi-modals* because they share some characteristics of main verbs and some of modal verbs. For example, like the modal *can*, the semi-modal *dare* can occur in questions:

Can I drive to school today?
Dare I drive to school today?

Dare can occur to the left of *not* in the same position as modal *can*:

You *can* not drive to school today.
You *dare* not drive to school today.

But *dare* can also pattern like a main verb. For example, we can form questions in sentences with main verbs using auxiliary *do:*

I drove to school yesterday.
Did I drive to school yesterday?

I dared drive to school yesterday.
Did I dare drive to school yesterday?

And *dare* can also pattern with main verbs in negative sentences.

I *did* not drive to school today.
I *did* not dare drive to school today.

We discuss these properties of modals (and the properties of auxiliary *do*) in more detail in Chapter 6, but for now, simply note that depending on the variety of English you speak, *dare* and *need* (and possibly some other verbs as well) might be included in your list of modals.

Verb Strings with Auxiliaries and Modals

Modals have the distinction of always occurring first in the verb string, before *have* and/or *be*, and therefore also occurring before the main verb. We repeat some examples below. We have also seen that when the modal is followed by the main verb, the main verb is a bare infinitive.

Lorenzo may *eat* sushi. (*may* = modal, *eat* = bare infinitive)

The forms of the verbs that follow modals, and auxiliary *have* and *be*, are listed below, based on the examples we've discussed so far.

modal + infinitive
have + past participle
be + present participle

These basic patterns help us label the forms of the words in the verb string. In the following sentence, the modal *may* is followed by an infinitive, *have*. Auxiliary *have* is followed by a past participle *been*, and auxiliary *been* is followed by a present participle *eating*:

Lorenzo *may have been eating* sushi.
may + *have* (infinitive)
have + *been* (past participle)
been + *eating* (present participle)

We can extend the pattern to verb strings with null auxiliaries; as we've noted, in African American English null auxiliary *be* is followed by a present participle, and the null auxiliary *have* is followed by a past participle.

The child ∅ *walking* to school.
∅ = is + *walking* (present participle)

The child ∅ *been walking* to school.
∅ = have + *been* (past participle) + *walking* (present participle)

You might now (after some practice of course) be able to label the forms of the verb in each verb string that follows these patterns. You can also identify auxiliaries, modals, and main verbs. Another important fact about verb strings in English is that the first verb expresses tense (regardless of its form, and regardless of whether it is pronounced or null), whether that verb is an auxiliary, a modal, or a main verb.

Aspect

Now that you have some understanding of tense and the verb string, consider the following two sentences. (In this discussion we assume for illustration verbal morphology that may not be expressed in all varieties of English.)

Kim walks. (present tense)
Kim walked. (past tense)

In the first sentence, the main verb *walk* is in present tense (*walks*), and in the second, past tense (*walked*). In the first sentence, the event (Kim's walking) is happening right now, and in the second, the event happened in the past (and is over). Pretty simple, right? Now consider these pairs of sentences.

Kim is walking.
Kim has walked.

Kim was walking.
Kim had walked.

Each of these four sentences also includes a tensed verb, in this case, an auxiliary verb in present tense (*is/has*) or in past tense (*was/had*). But something else is going on. How does each pair differ from the "simple" present *Kim walks* and past *Kim walked*?

As you might have noticed, the difference among these four sentences can't really be described in terms of a simple difference in tense. The first sentence (*Kim is walking*) can be interpreted as happening right now, with auxiliary *is* in present tense. But in the second sentence (*Kim has walked*), auxiliary *has* is also in present tense, but we understand this event of walking to be completed, and past. And what's the difference between the last two sentences then? In both, the auxiliary is in past tense, but there is a difference in how the action (*was walking/had walked*) is interpreted. This difference is called *aspect*.

English has different aspects that are reflected in the order and forms of verbs in the verb string. One is *perfect aspect*, and another is *progressive aspect*. Another is *habitual aspect*, which can be, but isn't always, expressed by a particular verb string. Below, we discuss each of these aspects in turn.

Progressive aspect

Progressive aspect is also called *durative* aspect; progressive aspect expresses an ongoing action or event (in the present, past, or in the future). The progressive aspect is fairly easy to identify; it is indicated by a (sometimes null) form of auxiliary *be* and a present participle.

meaning: duration
form: auxiliary *be* + present participle
examples: *is/ ∅ walking, was/were eating*, etc.

When the event is ongoing in the present, it is in *present progressive*, when ongoing in the past it's in *past progressive*, and when ongoing in the future it's in (you guessed it!) *future progressive*.

Kim *is/ ∅ walking* to school.
= present progressive

Kim *was walking* to school.
= past progressive

Kim *will be walking* to school.
= future progressive

Perfect aspect

Perfect aspect is expressed by (again, sometimes null) auxiliary *have* and the past participle of the verb.

meaning: completion
form: *have* + past participle
examples: *have/has/∅ walked, had walked, have/has/∅ eaten*, etc.

When the auxiliary is in present tense, the sentence is in the *present perfect* aspect, and when *have* is in past tense, the sentence is *past perfect*. Adding modal *will* to the string gives us *future perfect*.

Kim *has/∅ walked* to school.
= present perfect   (∅ = *have*)

Kim *had walked* to school.
= past perfect

Kim *will have walked* to school.
= future perfect

As you might expect, we can put progressive and perfect aspects together to form *perfect progressive* aspect. The verb string in this case includes both auxiliary (pronounced or null) *have*, auxiliary *be*, plus the main verb.

Kim *has/∅ been walking* to school.
= present perfect progressive   (∅ = *have*)

Kim *had been walking* to school.
= past perfect progressive

And if we add a modal to express future, we form *future perfect*, the *future progressive*, and the *future perfect progressive*:

Kim *will have walked* to school.
  = future perfect

Kim *will be walking* to school.
  = future progressive

Kim *will have been walking* to school.
  = future perfect progressive

Aspectual markers *BIN* and *done*

Linguist Lisa Green (2002, pp. 45–47) provides a detailed analysis of the aspectual markers *be*, *BIN*, and *done* of African American English, showing that although they appear similar in form to auxiliary verbs in what are considered by some to be "standardized" Englishes, in AAE these words have quite different meanings.

The auxiliary BIN (respelled from *been* to emphasize its distinct function and capitalized to indicate that it receives stress) is used to indicate that a state or habit was ongoing in the past:

She BIN eating.

BIN used with the past tense main verb indicates a completed action in the remote past:

She BIN ate.

Done plus a past tense main verb conveys what is called the "resultant state" aspect:

She done ate.

Done is used as an aspectual marker in other varieties as well, including Appalachian English, where it also suggests completion or a resulting state, though in a different way from in AAE: *He done gone* (meaning something like "he has already gone"). (The word *done* may have been borrowed from the West African language Wolof word *doon*, rather than being derived from *do*.)

Habitual aspect

Let's look now at yet another aspect, *habitual aspect*, which is expressed in a variety of ways. Some examples are given below.

Birds sing.
People talk.
Professional athletes thrive on competition.

As you can see from these sentences, the main verb is in present tense, but the semantic interpretation here is of something that happens regularly or habitually. These sentences are also called *generic sentences,* because they address what we might consider typical behavior of a group, species, or individual (what we might also call a *generalization,* usually expressed by a *generic noun,* which we discussed in Chapter 2). We can add the adverb *usually* or *always* to each of these sentences, consistent with the habitual interpretation.

Birds always sing.
People usually talk.
Professional athletes usually thrive on competition.

There are many ways to express habitual aspect, but the point here is that in some varieties of English, this aspect, unlike the progressive and perfect aspects, is not necessarily dependent on a particular verb string, nor on a particular form of the verb. Here are some other ways to express habitual aspect:

We *used to* go to Europe every summer.
We *would* climb mountains every day.
I *like to* eat cereal for breakfast.

As we mentioned in Chapter 4, in some varieties of English (including but not limited to AAE and varieties of Chicano English) habitual aspect is syntactically expressed by the verb string: infinitival (or "invariant") *be* marks habitual aspect:

We *be playing* basketball.
My mom *be* at work.

These sentences are ungrammatical if interpreted as other than habitual; *my mom be at work,* for example, does not mean "my mom is at work right now," but rather (something similar to) "my mom is usually at work," or, "it is generally the case that my mom is at work."

96

Passive Voice and the Passive Verb String

We conclude this chapter by introducing one more variation in the English verb string. This variation does not stem from aspect, but rather from *passive voice*. Technically, *voice* is a grammatical way in which the subject and object (the *direct object,* to be more exact, but we return to this in Chapter 6) of the verb are arranged in the clause.

> The cat chased the rat.
> = active voice

In *passive voice*, the subject and object, *the cat* and *the rat,* respectively, change position:

> The rat was chased by the cat.
> = passive voice

In addition to the change of position of subject and object, there are several other things to notice here. One is that when we shift from active to passive, we do not change the tense of the clause: *chased* is in past tense, and so is its passive counterpart, *was chased*, as indicated by the past tense form of the auxiliary *was*. But the syntax of the verb string changes: we add a form of auxiliary *be* in the passive, and the main verb is in its *past participle* form.

> *was chased*
> = *be* + past participle

Recall that in our earlier discussion of progressive aspect, auxiliary *be* is followed by a *present participle:*

> *was chasing*
> = *be* + present participle

Passive voice therefore results in a verb string that differs syntactically from the pattern we expect to find in verb strings in active voice.

> passive verb string:
> (some form of) *be* + past participle.

One way to identify a passive sentence, then, is to look for a verb string that includes some form of *be* + past participle. This is particularly useful because other ways to identify passive voice may not be obvious. For example, the *by*-phrase (*by the cat*) can be omitted:

> The rat was chased by the cat.
> The rat was chased.

Here are some more examples of sentences in passive voice. What are their active counterparts?

The fly was caught (by the spider).
The window is cracked (by the wind).
The pharmacist was sent the prescription (by the doctor).

Passive voice provides us with a way to highlight or foreground the object, rather than the subject of the sentence, and in some cases, eliminate the subject altogether! Here's an example you may be familiar with:

Mistakes were made.

Examples we've shown so far include only a simple passive verb string. But passive voice can be a part of longer verb strings that contain other modals and auxiliaries and are combinations of progressive and perfect aspectual combinations. Consider, for example, the following active sentences and see if you can change them into their passive counterparts. Remember, to form passives of these active sentences, the object becomes the subject, and then a form of *be* is added, and the main verb occurs in its past participle form.

active: The cat was chasing the squirrel up the tree.
passive: The squirrel was *being chased* by the cat up the tree.

active: The cat has chased the squirrel up the tree.
passive: The squirrel has *been chased* by the cat up the tree.

active: The cat might have chased the squirrel up the tree.
passive: The squirrel might have *been chased* by the cat up the tree.

active: The cat might have been chasing the squirrel up the tree.
passive: The squirrel might have *been being chased* by the cat up the tree.

Even though these passive verb strings look long and complicated, you can still identify the pattern that makes them passive:

be + past participle

As you can see, speakers are actually performing quite a complex operation when they produce passive sentences, one that they can do quite effortlessly and unconsciously. We return to passive voice in Chapter 6.

Summary

In this chapter, we have explored some of the syntactic, morphological, and semantic differences between **auxiliary verbs** *have* and *be*, and **modals** (including **semi-modals**), and how these functional verb classes differ from the lexical category (main) **Verb**. We have discussed in some detail different verb sequences or **verb strings** made up of auxiliaries, modals, and main verbs, identifying some of the patterns that occur in these strings, or VPs. We have also seen that these verb strings can express different **tenses** and **aspects,** such as **perfect aspect** and **progressive aspect.** We also explored **habitual aspect**, which can be, but is not always, expressed by a particular form of the verb or verb string. We concluded the chapter with a short discussion of yet another verb string pattern, one that expresses **passive voice.**

Exercises

1.   Auxiliary verb forms

Label the form of each bolded auxiliary verb as *infinitival, present tense, past tense, present participle,* or *past participle.* Remember that subject-verb agreement patterns in English vary, so some of these sentences may not be familiar to you, but you still should be able to label the form of the auxiliary verb based on its position in the verb string.

(a)   The wind **had** broken the window.
(b)   Her mouth **is** steady runnin'.
(c)   That intense wind might **have** broken the window.
(d)   They have **been** doing homework for hours.
(e)   Not one senator **was** running for office again.
(f)   The trees **have** been planted in the yard.
(g)   The bears **is** getting into the garbage.
(h)   Those students **were** getting on the bus.
(i)   Our cat **has** not budged from the couch all day.
(j)   They **is** talking about that party.
(k)   The moon **were** shining bright.
(l)   The next installment is **being** published tomorrow.
(m)   Classes might **be** delayed because of the weather.
(n)   They **was** just a-singing as loud as they could.

2. Modal tense and meaning

What tense would you assign to each of the following modals and semi-modals? And what meaning does each modal convey? Permission, necessity, obligation? Something else? Provide a context for each sentence to illustrate.

    (a) No one but you **can** know about this!
    (b) The package might **should** be arriving soon.
    (c) I think you **might** want to hide that candy.
    (d) That golfer **must** practice a lot.
    (e) You **need** not be so polite.
    (f) The children **ought to** pick up their toys.

3. Verb strings – forms

Label the form of each bolded main verb in each verb string below.

    (a) The family had never **seen** the Grand Canyon.
    (b) My dog is/Ø **chasing** his tail.
    (c) Dogs **chase** their tails.
    (d) I ain't **seen** nothing of him.
    (e) We might be **vacationing** in Hawaii this winter.
    (f) The director has **made** a new movie.
    (g) They was **eating** some pizza for dinner.
    (h) Students should **turn** in their final papers.
    (i) That's not what I was **a-wanting** to hear.
    (j) Swallows used **to roost** in our barn.
    (k) Liza can **eat** more hotdogs than anyone else.
    (l) Some students will have **attended** the concert.
    (m) The children be **playing** in the park.
    (n) They haven't ever **ran** that far before.

4. Verb strings – tense and aspect

Label any verb strings in the sentences in (3) that are in *perfect* or *progressive* aspect. If you can, also label the tense of the verb string (*past/present/future* perfect or progressive). Are any of the sentences in *habitual* aspect? Remember that not all verb strings express aspect, so some sentences may have no labels at all. You may not all have the same answers, so discuss why!

5. More aspect practice

Write out sentences that illustrate each of the following aspects. Use different main verbs for each sentence. Draw your examples from any variety of English you choose.

(a) present perfect aspect
(b) past perfect progressive aspect
(c) habitual aspect
(d) past perfect aspect
(e) present perfect progressive aspect
(f) future perfect aspect
(g) future perfect progressive aspect

6. Passive voice

Here is a list of active sentences, some of which include more than one verb in the verb string. Change each active sentence to passive. Pay particular attention to the tense of each active verb string – the passive verb string should be in the same tense!

If you can form two different passives for one sentence, try to explain why.

(a) The hiker spotted a grizzly bear in Yellowstone Park.
(b) Athletes should eat yogurt and bananas for breakfast.
(c) The people next door have invited the entire neighborhood to the party.
(d) My sister may be buying a new car from Germany.
(e) Beowulf had been hunting Grendel for a long time.

7. Practice

We offer here some text excerpts to use for practice. These excerpts are intended only to get you started; there may not be examples in these texts of everything listed here. We encourage you to explore texts of your own choosing to find additional examples.

(a) Identify the main, auxiliary, and modal verbs.
(b) Label the forms of each verb in each verb string.
(c) Identify any examples of tense and (perfect, progressive, or habitual) aspect.
(d) Identify any passive verb strings. If the *by*-phrase is missing, what information is left out?

The strength of a concept rests in its ability to organize information. What at first appears to be a disorganized body of knowledge is made comprehensible and useful when a unifying framework is developed. Scientific inquiry is often presented as a jumble of disorganized but interrelated procedures. Teacher and teacher candidates are regularly encouraged to use inquiry processes in demonstrations, lessons, and labs, but there is little organizational pattern provided to relate inquiry to these approaches. (From "Levels of Inquiry: Hierarchies of Pedagogical Practices and Inquiry Processes," by Carl J. Wenning, 2005.)

They had come with buckets, scrub brooms, rakes, scythes, and mattocks. Men had been chopping weeds all morning, so that a schoolyard already existed, ready for games. It was bordered on one side by the most beautiful bank of wild white roses you can possibly imagine, and by the thick green forest on the other. Behind the school, they had gathered rocks to hold two washtubs over fires to heat water brought from the spring nearby and were busily cleaning all the desks. The windows had already been washed. The empty floors had been swept and were now being scrubbed by the men. Windows and doors stood open to let in the hot August sun and to air out the two classrooms. Memorable Jones sat to the side on a large "table rock," scowling and smoking his pipe. I dared not approach him – I could not have done so then if my life depended on it! (From *On Agate Hill*, by Lee Smith.)

Aunt June's bedroom closet was carpeted, the inside of a closet if you can believe, and big enough for the three of us. We'd sit in the dark with stripes of lift coming sideways through slits in the door, me and Maggot and the twenty-one pairs of shoes, hearing Emmy's ER stories. Some guy's cut-off leg that got buried with the wrong body. Also, Aunt June stories. Guys at Jonesville High that had wanted to screw her but got kicked to the curb, even after one or more of them begged her to marry him. Same thing, different guys, in nursing school. We kept waiting for the part about what happened to Emmy's parents and why she's living with Aunt June, if the lady was so hot to get away from the would-be husbands and babies. No mention. Emmy had other concerns, like her secret stash under some loose carpet. The first time she went digging around, I saw the light-striped face of Maggot looking at me like, What the hell? And up she comes with flattened packs of cigarettes and gum. Asking did we want gum. We said okay. (From *Demon Copperhead*, by Barbara Kingsolver.)

6

The Clause

Introduction

You can now label the forms of each verb in the verb string, and you know which verbs are auxiliary verbs and modals, and which are main, or lexical, verbs. You also know that the verb string can express different kinds of information, such as tense and aspect, and that the verb string takes a

Navigating English Grammar: A Guide to Analyzing Real Language, Second Edition.
Anne Lobeck and Kristin Denham.
© 2025 Anne Lobeck and Kristin Denham. Published 2025 by John Wiley & Sons Ltd.

different form in the passive voice. In this chapter, we continue our discussion of the English verb string and discuss some important syntactic differences between tensed auxiliary verbs and modals, on the one hand, and main verbs on the other. This closer investigation of the syntax of the verb string in English will in turn uncover more about the structure of the *independent clause*, and its component parts, the subject NP, the predicate VP, and the Tense position.

The Independent Clause

In the previous chapters, we have discussed the basic syntactic structure of noun phrases and verb phrases in English, which we represent as NP and VP. These two phrases form the basic building blocks of the clause (CL); in fact, we can define a *clause* as a syntactic unit, a subject (NP) and a predicate (VP). We can represent this using phrase structure rules:

CL → NP VP

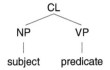

We can diagram simple tensed clauses such as these:

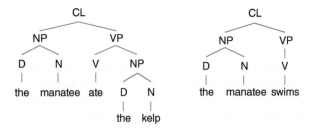

Each of these clauses is an *independent clause*, a clause that is not part of another phrase or clause. If we *embed* a clause inside another phrase, it becomes a *subordinate clause* (also called an *embedded* or *dependent* clause). For example, we can turn each of the clauses above into subordinate clauses by embedding them in a larger (independent) clause:

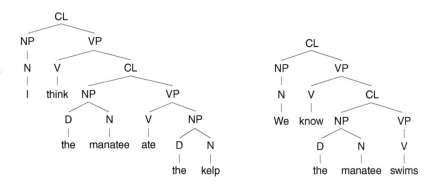

We discuss subordination in detail in Chapter 10. In this chapter, we focus on the syntactic structure of independent clauses. We'll start with subjects.

The subject position

According to the phrase structure rule for clause:

CL → NP VP

every clause must have a subject (and a predicate, for that matter). Although subjects are sometimes defined as "the doer of the action," this semantic definition only works some of the time. For example, if we say that the subject is the doer of the action, or what linguists call an "agent," we have to assume that, in the following sentence, *the ivy* is an agent. But clearly, a plant isn't an agent with any kind of conscious volition.

The ivy climbed the trellis.

Contrast the "ivy" sentence with the sentence below where the subject *is* an agent:

The boy climbed the trellis.

And what about these sentences? Are the subjects of these sentences "doers" of an action?

The ice melted.
The glass shattered.
Mary broke her leg.
The teacher received a letter.

It is difficult, if possible at all, to describe the subjects of these sentences as doers of any action. We can, however, define each of the italicized NPs as the **syntactic** subject of the clause; each of these NPs occurs in the **subject position**:

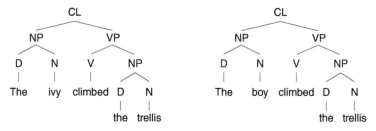

Rather than defining subjects in terms of their meaning (as agents or doers), we can define subjects as phrases occupying a certain syntactic position. In the following section, we'll explore the notion of *subject* in more detail, investigating the difference between the *syntactic subject* and the *logical subject* of a clause.

Subjects of passive sentences
Consider these active and passive sentence pairs. Remember from Chapter 5 that in passive sentences, the object occurs in the subject position, and the subject occurs in a *by*-phrase at the end of the clause.

> *The sun* melted *the ice.*
> *The ice* was melted by *the sun.*

In the active sentence, *the sun* is the syntactic subject, and also the logical or semantic subject; it is the thing that is melting the ice. *The ice* is the object of the verb *melt*. In the passive sentence, however, *the ice* is in the subject position and is therefore the syntactic subject; but note that it is not also the logical subject – in the passive sentence *the sun* is still melting the ice, even though the word order has changed. This kind of evidence suggests that the *subject position* in the clause may be occupied by a phrase that may not also be the logical or semantic subject. In fact, a phrase in the subject position can have no meaning at all, as we'll see in the following section.

Pleonastic subjects
English is one of a number of languages that requires *something* to be in the subject position, even when that something means nothing at all. Consider the sentences below. What occupies the *subject position* (and is therefore the syntactic subject) in each clause?

> There was a fire last night.
> There were three linguists standing in the boat.

> It rains in Spain.
> It is obvious that the team will win.

If you answered *there* and *it*, you're right, even though you probably also want to say that something else is the logical subject of each of these independent clauses (*a fire, three linguists, Spain, the team* perhaps). Ignoring certain details, the basic phrase structure trees for clauses with *there/it* subjects are the following:

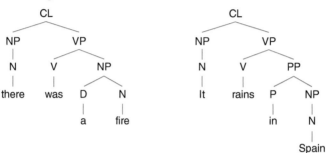

Why might it be difficult to consider *there* and *it* as subjects here? Neither word really means anything, though both words, in other contexts, can be meaningful. Let's first distinguish the meaningful meanings from the meaningless ones.

There in the above sentence is what we call "existential" or "pleonastic" *there*, distinct from "locative" *there*, which refers to a location. Existential *there* can be paraphrased as "there exists" and does not indicate location. Contrast existential *there* above with locative *there* in the following sentences:

> *There* is that pesky cat!
> I put it over *there*.
> She was standing *there*, by the dock.

In these examples, *there* refers to a location or place. Although locative *there* can occur in the subject position just like existential *there*, it is different from existential *there* in being able to occur in other positions as well (over *there*, standing *there*).

Locative *there* can also be stressed or emphatic, as indicated by the capitalization in the following examples:

> THERE is that pesky cat!
> I put it over THERE.
> She was standing THERE, by the dock.

Existential *there*, on the other hand, can't be stressed. If we stress existential *there*, it becomes locative, and as a result sounds quite odd, if not ungrammatical in the following sentences:

> THERE was a fire last night.
> THERE are three linguists standing in the boat.

Now consider sentences with *it* in the syntactic subject position:

It rains in Spain.
It is obvious that the team will win.

In these examples, *it* is the syntactic subject of each clause – it occupies the subject position. But *it*, like *there*, doesn't really mean anything in these sentences.

These "meaningless" subjects occur in similar forms across varieties of English. In African American English, *it* and *dey* (and *they got*, see Labov et al., 1968; Rickford, 1999) are used to indicate that something exists. Once again, these proforms are non-referential and occur in the subject position (Green, 2002, pp. 80–82):

It's some coffee in the kitchen.
Dey some coffee in the kitchen.
They got some hungry women here.

And in Southern Appalachian and Smoky Mountain English *they* can express that something exists (Montgomery and Hall, 2004):

They is something bad wrong with her.

Like existential *there/dey/they*, *it* in the above sentences is different from the indefinite pronoun *it* that actually does refer to something, as illustrated in the exchange below:

Do you like the weather in Seattle?
No, I don't like *it*. (*it = the weather in Seattle*)

The pronoun *it* here, unlike in the above sentences, is *referential*; it refers to something, namely, the weather in Seattle. Here are some more examples, where the pronoun *it* refers to some previously mentioned thing or topic, a *referent*.

I saw *it* lying on the ground.
We know *it* to be true.
I put *it* over there.

For each sentence, you can imagine a situation or thing that *it* refers to (you may recall from Chapter 3 that what a pronoun refers to is called its *antecedent*). The non-referential *it*, on the other hand, refers to nothing at all. Like meaningless existential *there/dey/they*, *it* is a pleonastic pronoun or proform that fills the syntactic subject position.

What this discussion of different kinds of subjects tells us is that we can consistently identify the *syntactic subject* of a clause: it is the NP in the subject *position*, the NP in the phrase structure rule CL→ NP VP. When we try to identify the subject of a clause in terms of its meaning rather than its position, we run into snags when we consider non-agentive subjects, the subjects of passive sentences, and sentences with pleonastic subjects. We will therefore use the term "subject" to refer to *syntactic* subject here and throughout the rest of this book.

Null subject languages

We mentioned above that English is a language in which the subject position must be filled (with something, even a pleonastic something), but that this is not necessarily a requirement in all languages. What does that mean, exactly? How could a clause possibly lack a subject? There are many other languages, called *null subject languages*, that do not require lexical subjects. Italian and Spanish are such languages, and sentences such as the following are completely grammatical.

Isabella non vuole mangiare. (subject pronounced)
Isabella not want to eat
"Isabella does not want to eat."

Non vuole mangiare. (subject unpronounced)
not want to eat
"[She/he/it] does not want to eat."

Interestingly, null subject languages appear to lack pleonastic subjects like English *it* and *there/dey/they* because null subject languages also lack the requirement that the subject must be expressed or pronounced. When an Italian speaker says, "It's raining," they simply say "Piove!"

Linguists consider subjects to be a linguistic universal – all languages have them. "Null subject" languages, such as Spanish and Italian, are not counterexamples to this claim; they do have subjects, but those subjects are not necessarily pronounced. There is a great deal of syntactic evidence that null subjects are null in the same way that auxiliary "have" and "be" are null – they are syntactically present, but simply silent!

109

The complement position

So far, we've assumed that the clause can be divided into roughly two parts, the subject and the predicate. In the preceding section, we defined the subject of the clause syntactically, and we can do the same for the predicate: it is the VP in the phrase structure rule CL→NP VP. Predicates can also be semantically defined, but we'll put that aside here, and focus instead on the syntactic structure of the VP in independent clauses.

As we've noted above, VPs can include NP complements:

The manatee ate *the kelp.*
The sun melted *the ice.*
The boy climbed *the trellis.*
The teacher received *a letter.*

The main verbs in each of these sentences (*ate, melt, climb, receive*) take an NP object, or what is called a **direct object.** We can loosely describe the verbs that take a direct object as "action" verbs, and the direct object as the receiver of that action. Verbs that take direct objects are called **transitive** verbs.

Clearly, not all verbs in English are transitive (and, as a result, not all take direct objects). Consider, for example, the following sentences:

The manatee swims.
The ice melted.
The glass shattered.
The temperature climbed.

Here, *swim, melt, shatter,* and *climb* take no object at all; these are **intransitive** verbs.

And what about the verbs in the following sentences? Do they take direct object NPs?

The girl seemed *happy/sad.*
She became *upset about the issue.*

What about the verb *believe?*

They believe *the witness.*
They believe *in you.*
They believe (*that*) *the moon is made of green cheese.*

Your answer should be *not necessarily* – as these examples illustrate, different kinds of verbs take different kinds of phrases after them, phrases that "complete" the VP. We call these phrases **complements**, or phrases whose grammatical function is to "complete" another phrase.

Whereas transitive verbs take direct object NP complements, "linking" verbs such as *seem* and *become* take adjective phrase or AP complements (*happy/sad/upset about the issue*). And yet another verb, *believe*, can take either a direct object NP complement (*the witness*), a prepositional phrase (PP) complement (*in you*), or a clause (CL) complement (*the moon is made of green cheese*).

We will return to different kinds of complements as we progress throughout the book. For now, simply note that the position to the immediate right of the head of a phrase (XP below) is the **complement position**. X of that XP can be any head, including N, V, a preposition P, an adjective A, or an adverb Adv. A verb such as *seem* will take an AP complement (*happy/sad/upset*) but a transitive verb such as *melt* or *eat* will take an NP complement, and so on.

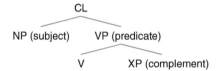

Let's explore this notion of *complement* a bit further. Note that in a general sense, we can say that verbs "take" or even "require" certain complements.

Consider the verb *like*. It can't stand alone; it takes/requires a direct object NP. This means that *like* is a transitive verb.

They like [pizza]
        NP
*They like

Some verbs require more than one complement. Consider *put* for example:

She put [the bike] [in the garage].
        NP   PP
*She put [the bike].
        NP
*She put [in the garage].
        PP

This set of sentences tells us that the verb *put* requires two complements: a direct object NP *the bike*, but also a PP of location (a "locative" PP) *in the garage*.

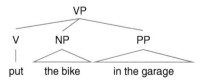

111

We can account for verbs that take more than one complement by revising our phrase structure rule for VP as follows (again, where the variable X means a phrase of any category):

VP → V (XP) (XP)   X = any category (N, V, A, P, Adv, CL)

According to this phrase structure rule, a verb can take up to two complements, or it can occur with no complements at all (the parentheses, remember, indicate that a phrase is optional). Depending on the verb, complements can be of any category: NP, VP, AP, AdvP, PP, or CL. A few examples of possible complements are given below.

In discussions of word order "typology," a language's word order is described in terms of Subject (S), Verb (V), and Object (O). The Object, however, may be better described as the complement, since it can refer to not just direct objects, but other kinds of complements like those listed just above.

To conclude this brief introduction to the complement position, let's take one more look at direct objects, a complement type we are already somewhat familiar with. As we've noted, direct objects are complements of transitive (action) verbs. In the following sentence, *a cockroach* is the complement of the transitive verb *chased*.

Will chased *a cockroach*.

Interestingly, Passive appears to operate only on direct object complements but not on NP complements that are not direct objects, such as the NP complement of a linking verb *become;* the NP complement of a linking verb is called a **subjective complement.** We'll return to subjective complements in more detail in Chapter 7.

Will chased a cockroach. → A cockroach was chased by Will.
Will became a cockroach. → *A cockroach was become by Will.

Not only do different verbs (and other heads of phrases, such as adjectives and prepositions) take different kinds of complements, but complements differ from each other in ways that may not be obvious only from their syntax. Even though both *chase* and *become* take NP complements (and even the very same NP, *a cockroach*) those NP complements mean quite different things: in the first sentence *the cockroach* is a separate entity that is being acted upon, and in the second it is a description, and more specifically, a description of the NP subject of the clause, *Will.*

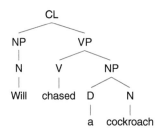
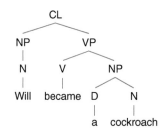

Though the NP complements in these clauses occupy exactly the same position, only the direct object of *chase* (but not the NP subjective complement of the linking verb *become*) can undergo Passive. Another way to put this is that Passive applies only to a certain kind of complement, namely, a direct object NP. We can use Passive, then, as a test or diagnostic to determine whether an NP is a direct object or not.

We will return to complements in subsequent chapters, to explore their syntax (and when relevant their semantics) in more detail. In the following section, we turn to yet another structural component of the independent clause that we'll consider in this chapter, the Tense (TNS) position.

The Tense position

So far, we have analyzed the phrase structure of the clause as:

CL → NP VP

But as we noted above, this phrase structure rule allows only for clauses with a single verb, namely, the V head of VP. But we know that clauses often include verb *strings*, such as the examples below.

Rue *is playing* chess.
   has been playing chess.
   will have been playing chess.

Recall that the tensed auxiliary or modal is always the *first* verb in the verb string. There is quite a bit of evidence that in English, the tensed auxiliary verb or modal occupies not V, but an entirely different position, what we'll call the Tense or TNS position. In this section, we'll briefly review the evidence for this position, which leads us to revise our phrase structure rule for the clause as follows:

CL → NP (TNS) VP

This TNS position is required in independent clauses (every independent clause must be tensed) but optional in subordinate clauses. We discuss subordinate clauses in more detail in Chapter 10. For now, we will focus on independent clauses, which *must* include a TNS position, for reasons we outline below.

Subject–auxiliary inversion

In English, we form *yes/no* questions in the way illustrated in the following statement–question pairs. Notice what happens to the tensed auxiliary verb or modal when a statement is turned into a question.

Rue *is* playing chess.
Is Rue playing chess?

Rue *has* been playing chess.
Has Rue *been playing* chess?

Rue *will* have been playing chess.
Will Rue *have been* playing chess?

As these sentences illustrate, to form a *yes/no* question in English, it looks like we simply move the tensed auxiliary verb or modal (*is, has,* or *will,* in these examples) to sentence-initial position.

But in sentences with only a main verb, we don't move that main verb (the head of VP) to sentence-initial position:

Rue *plays* chess.
*Plays Rue chess?

You might have determined that to form a question here, you use auxiliary *do*: *Did/do Rue play chess?* That's true, but we'll leave *do* aside for the moment. What's important here is that in clauses with verb strings, the tensed auxiliary or modal, but not the main verb, moves to sentence-initial position to form a *yes/no* question in English. We call this operation *Subject–auxiliary inversion* or SAI.

Note that as we might expect, SAI operates on clauses with pleonastic subjects (which provides us with some additional evidence that these pleonastic subjects occupy the subject position):

There *are* three linguists *standing* in the boat.
Are there three linguists *standing* in the boat?

It *is raining* in Spain.
Is it *raining* in Spain?

How do we explain the evidence that only the first verb in the verb string, but not the main verb itself, inverts with the syntactic subject to form a question? Linguists propose that this is because the first verb in the string occupies a completely different position than the main verb, what we are labeling here as the TNS position. The main verb, on the other hand, occupies V, the head of VP position.

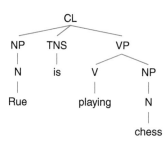

SAI operates on TNS, but not V, the head of VP. It follows that only words that occupy TNS (namely, tensed auxiliaries and modals) invert with the subject in *yes/no* questions in English, but the main verb, in V, does not.

Tag question formation
Here's another bit of evidence for these two separate positions, TNS and V. Consider the following sentences:

My friends *are* playing chess, *aren't they?*
Rue Ø playing chess, *ain't she?*
Juno can play chess, *can't they?*
There are three linguists in the room, *aren't there?*
It is raining in Bellingham, *isn't it?*

This kind of question is called a *tag question,* a question tacked on to the end of the clause. We form tags in a variety of different ways in English and in other languages, but what is relevant to us here is that one way to form a tag question is to add a form of a tensed auxiliary or modal onto the end of the clause. (Note that even if the auxiliary in the clause is null, a full form of the auxiliary shows up in the tag.) The subject NP is also repeated or copied at the end of the clause but in the form of a pronoun or proform. And finally, tags are usually opposite in *polarity* with the independent clause: if the clause is affirmative, the tag is negative, and vice versa:

My friends *aren't* playing chess, *are they?*
Rue Ø not playing chess, *is she?*

115

Juno cannot play chess, *can they?*
There aren't three linguists in the room, *are there?*
It isn't raining in Bellingham, *is it?*

Returning to our focus here, namely, evidence for the TNS position, we can say that tag question formation appears to operate on words that occupy a specific position in the clause, namely, on the auxiliary or modal in TNS. Tag question formation, like SAI, does not operate on V; if it did, we'd expect main verbs to occur in tags, but they don't:

Juno plays chess.
*Juno plays chess, playn't they?

Once again, note that we can form tag questions in clauses with tensed main verbs and no other auxiliaries by adding *do*. (We will return to auxiliary *do* later in the chapter, so we put an explanation for this aside for now.)

Juno plays chess, *doesn't/don't they?*

To summarize briefly, we've explored two ways to form questions in English, SAI and tag question formation. Both of these syntactic processes appear to operate (only) on the tensed auxiliary verb or modal in the verb string, but not on the main verb. We explain this distinction by proposing that the tensed auxiliary or modal occupies a different syntactic position, TNS, and that the main verb occupies V, the head of VP. SAI and tag question formation operate only on TNS, but not on V.

Negation
Yet more evidence for the TNS position comes from negation. In English, one way to negate sentences is by inserting *not*.

Rue is playing chess.
→Rue is *not/ain't* playing chess.
Rue can play chess.
→Rue can *not/can't* play chess.
There are three linguists in the room.
→There are *not/aren't/ain't* three linguists in the room.
It is raining in Bellingham.
→It is *not/isn't/ain't* raining in Bellingham.

Negated auxiliaries (as we've already seen in the tag questions in the previous section) show up in various forms, in particular when *not* is reduced or contracted to *n't*. There is also quite a bit of variation in subject–verb agreement, as we've seen in previous chapters:

I/they/we *ain't* eating.   She *haven't* ate.   I *hain't* seen nothing of him.

In Lumbee English and other varieties, the form *weren't* is the form in the past tense in negative clauses:

I/you/he/she/they/we *weren't* eating

And in many varieties *ain't* is the present tense negative form, regardless of the subject:

I/you/he/she/we/you/they *ain't* leaving soon.

What's important here is the position of *not* or *n't*; as you can see from all of the above examples, regardless of the form of the tensed auxiliary, *not* or *n't* occurs to the *right* of the tensed auxiliary or modal, but to the *left* of the main verb.

Rue is *not* playing chess.
Rue *ain't/isn't* playing chess
*Rue is playing *not* chess.

And as we might by now expect, *not* occurs to the right of a modal in the verb string:

Rue will *not* be playing chess.

We can explain this syntactic difference between tensed auxiliaries/ modals, *not*, and main verbs by proposing that *not* occurs *between* TNS and V, as illustrated in the following tree diagram (where we assume that *not* is inserted under NEG):

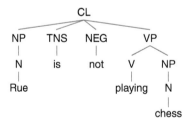

If we assume this structure of negative clauses, it follows that the tensed auxiliary or modal in a verb string in TNS will always occur to the left of *not*, but the main verb will always occur to the right of *not*. Once again, we have good evidence that TNS is a position distinct from V.

Semi-modals

Do the following examples sound natural to you or do they sound archaic or from a variety of English different from your own?

> I mustn't be late tonight.
> Might you be able to loan me your car?
> He shall be arriving tomorrow, shan't he?

And what about the semi-modals discussed in Chapter 5: *ought*, *dare*, and *need*? Can these modals do all the things other modals do in your dialect?

> You ought not say that.
> You oughtn't say that.
> You ought (to) say that, oughtn't you?
> We needn't tell anyone about that.
> Need we tell anyone about that?
> I dare not say.
> I daren't say.
> Dare I say?

If some of these sound a bit old-fashioned to you, that's an indicator that they may be on their way out of your variety as modals – or have never even been there. While these may be disappearing, there is also innovation in the auxiliary system in tag questions. For example, there are a lot of examples of "invariant tags," such as *ayah* in Maine, *eh/ay* in Canadian English, and *innit* in the English of urban teenagers in London. *Innit* also shows up in some varieties of Native American English.

> We need to decide what to do about that now, innit? (don't we?)
> Now I can start calling you that, INNIT? (can't I?)
> I'll show young Miss Hanna round to all the shops, innit? (won't I?)

These are called invariant because the same form is used regardless of the subject. Invariant tags are common in other languages: Spanish has "¿verdad?" and "¿no?," German has "nicht wahr?" and "oder?" and French has "n'est-ce pas?"

Diagramming Verb Strings

We're now in a position to diagram some clauses with longer verb strings. We have established that clauses include a position, namely, TNS, specifically reserved for the tensed auxiliary or modal. The main verb occurs as the head of VP. We've also assumed that VP can include optional complements, of any category.

CL → NP (TNS) VP
VP → V (XP) (XP)   X = N, V, A, Adv, P, CL

We can now diagram two-word verb strings (which may include a null auxiliary) such as the following:

Rue is playing chess.
Rue should play chess.
Rue Ø playing chess.

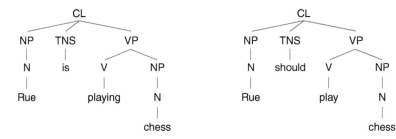

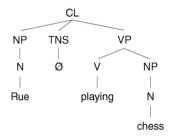

But what about longer strings? Given our phrase structure rule for VP, it is possible for V to take a VP complement. This allows us to diagram other verbs in the verb string as follows:

Rue has been playing chess.
Rue might have been playing chess.

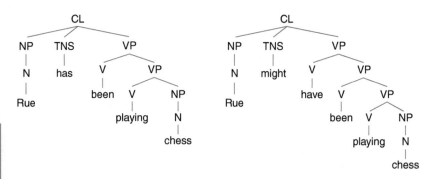

Note that in these trees, VP can be headed by an auxiliary verb (*have, been*). These auxiliaries are not tensed (*have* is an infinitive, and *been* is a present participle), and we therefore diagram them as occupying the V position rather than the TNS position.

And finally, as we saw previously, NEG occurs between TNS and V, and this remains the case, even with longer verb strings or null TNS:

Rue is *not* playing chess.
Rue might *not* have been playing chess.
Rue Ø *not* playing chess.

In the following section, we turn to the unanswered question: what about auxiliary *do*? When do we use this auxiliary *do* and why? These questions allow us to explore the structure of the English verb system in yet more detail, and to tackle some more theoretical questions about how it works.

Do Insertion

Now that we have a way of diagramming clauses with auxiliaries in TNS, consider clauses such as the following, where there is no auxiliary in TNS at all:

She *walk(s)* to school.   She *walk(ed)* to school.   They *walk* to school.

In these clauses, the main verb expresses present tense or past tense (with or without inflectional morphology). It might even express future tense: *She walks to school tomorrow for the first time.* How do we diagram clauses with only main verbs? Is there a TNS position?

These independent clauses (and all independent clauses for that matter) are certainly tensed, but there is nothing overt in the TNS position. We can propose here that these clauses, like others with tensed auxiliaries or modals, include a TNS position, but that this position is simply specified for *tense features* [present] or [past] or [future].

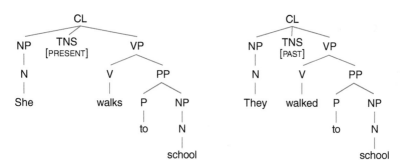

You may recall from the discussion so far that under some circumstances, auxiliary *do* shows up in yes/no questions, tag questions, and in negation, exactly those contexts which require an auxiliary or modal.

Rue plays chess.
Does Rue play chess?   (Subject–auxiliary inversion)
Rue plays chess, *don't they?*   (tag question formation)
Rue *does not/doesn't/don't* play chess.   (negation)

We refer to *do* as a *pleonastic* auxiliary, a "dummy" auxiliary that stands in for a tensed auxiliary when none is available. This pleonastic auxiliary *do* therefore occurs only in clauses in which TNS is specified as [past] or [present], in clauses with only a tensed main verb. More precisely, *do* is inserted into TNS in such clauses to form yes/no questions, tag questions, and negative sentences.

Because *do* is inserted into TNS, it's perhaps not surprising that when this happens, *do* expresses tense (like other auxiliary verbs and modals in that position), and the main verb becomes a bare infinitive. We can see this below when *do* is inserted as a result of SAI:

Rue plays chess.   *Does* Rue play chess?
plays = present tense   *does* = present tense   *play* = infinitive

Rue played chess.	*Did* Rue play chess?	
played = past tense	*did* = past tense	*play* = infinitive

The conditions under which *do* Insertion applies here tell us quite a bit about the syntax of the verb string. The evidence we have discussed here suggests that *do* is inserted in exactly those contexts in which some operation applies to the TNS position (SAI, tag question formation, or negation), when that position is not otherwise filled with a tensed auxiliary or modal. And as a result, *do*, rather than the main verb, expresses tense, just as in other verb strings with tensed auxiliaries or modals.

Main verb *be* raising

One interesting exception to the pattern of *do* Insertion discussed above comes from main verb *be*. Consider examples like the following (from Green, 2002, p. 48):

Your phone bill *is*/Ø high.
Your phone bill *be* high. (habitual *be*)

Since *be* (whether tensed or infinitival, and whether null or pronounced) is the only verb in these sentences, it appears to be the main verb. When we form a *yes/no* question, however, *do* Insertion does not apply in the first sentence, but it does in the second:

Is your phone bill high?
Do your phone bill be high? (habitual *be*)

The same pattern emerges with tag questions and negation; the tensed form of *be* seems to behave like an auxiliary verb, occurring in the tag question, and to the left of *not*. Infinitival *be* behaves like other main verbs: *do* Insertion applies in both tag questions and negation:

Your phone bill is/Ø high, isn't/ain't it?
Your phone bill be high, don't it?

These patterns suggest that infinitival *be* appears to pattern more like other main verbs with respect to *do* Insertion. Tensed main verb *be,* on the other hand, seems to pattern like a tensed auxiliary verb (and *do* Insertion therefore does not apply in questions and negation).

Linguists explain the behavior of tensed main verb *be* by proposing that this main verb (and *only* this main verb, in American English) undergoes a process that infinitival *be* and other main verbs do not; tensed main verb *be* moves, or **raises,** from its original position in V, to TNS. The form of *be,* then, in the following examples (whether showing tense or null), raises from V to TNS.

Your phone bill is/ø high.
They were chess players.
Juno was president.

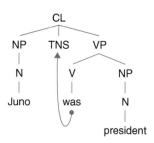

Because tensed main verb *be* then occupies TNS, it undergoes all the operations that apply to other tensed auxiliaries and modals in that position, namely, SAI and tag question formation. Tensed main verb *be* also occurs to the left of *not,* which is what we expect if it occupies (after raising) TNS rather than V. Infinitival *be,* on the other hand, does not raise, and *do* Insertion applies as expected.

We conclude this chapter, then, with a brief excursion into linguistic *theory,* taking a deeper look at *why* English verbs seem to behave the way they do. In order to understand the syntactic properties of the English verb string, we need to make some hypotheses, and here we have proposed both *do* Insertion and Main verb *be* raising to explain certain interesting syntactic patterns.

Summary

In this chapter, we have investigated the structure of the clause, and more specifically, the structure of the **independent clause.** We have explored the difference between the *syntactic* and *logical* **subject** of the clause and defined the subject of the clause as the phrase that occupies the **subject position.** We have also briefly discussed the **predicate** or VP, and how verbs (and other heads) can occur with different kinds of **complements.** One type of complement is the **direct object,** the complement of an action or **transitive verb. Intransitive verbs,** on the other hand, take no complement at all. We provided evidence here for the **Tense (TNS) position** in the clause, from **SAI, tag question formation**, and **negation.** Proposing that clauses include a TNS position allows us to explain a range of syntactic properties of the verb string, including the conditions under which *do* **Insertion** and **Main verb** *be* **raising** occur (and do not occur). Our investigation of the clause and the syntax of the verb string has led us beyond a simple description of the English verb system to some surprising explanations for what at first appear to be a range of seemingly unrelated phenomena.

Exercises

1. Finding subjects with SAI and tag questions

How can SAI and tag question formation help us identify the syntactic subjects in the following sentences? With SAI, the tensed auxiliary or modal inverts with the subject NP, and in tag question formation the subject is repeated as a pronoun in the tag. Apply SAI and tag question formation to each of the following sentences. What are the syntactic subjects of each sentence?

(a) The small dog wearing a pink coat is barking like crazy!
(b) There is a lot of traffic heading west.
(c) Lou has to keep wearing that old sweater.
(d) My family will try to host the dinner here.
(e) It is really cold outside.
(f) The two children on our block have learned to ride bicycles.
(g) Four students who met on a trip to Japan are getting together tomorrow.
(h) The extensive report was written by the journalist.

2. Which *there* is *there*?

Existential *there* (or whatever proform is used this way in your variety of English) is inserted only under certain conditions and is distinct from locative *there*. Label each of the following uses of *there* as existential or locative. How do you know which is which? What are some of the differences between the two types of *there*?

(a) I think it would be fun to go to Antarctica because I've never been there.
(b) Maurice looked for his coat in the closet but it wasn't there.
(c) There are only two more cookies left in the jar.
(d) Only there can you find a real bargain.
(e) There seems to be a problem.
(f) There is only one way to do that, my way!

3.   Pleonastic *it*

We have discussed how the subject position can be filled with pleonastic *it*, in examples such as the following:

(a)   It is wrong to kill animals.
(b)   It seems cold today.
(c)   It is quite possible that Meryl Streep will win another Oscar.

Now, consider the following uses of *it*.

(a)   You shouldn't pet that dog because he doesn't like it.
(b)   I put my phone somewhere, but now I can't find it.
(c)   It could be in the refrigerator, but I'm not sure.

How do these uses of referential *it* differ from pleonastic *it*? Test your hypothesis by analyzing the following sentences. Which *it* is it? Briefly explain.

(a)   It might be nice tomorrow, and we can go for a walk.
(b)   The movie just came out and I haven't seen it.
(c)   It could be said that for some people, pit bulls are good pets.
(d)   Oh, just get over it.
(e)   You won't believe it, but I just got offered the job!
(f)   Leo had heard about the Mona Lisa but he'd never seen it.

4.   Complements

In the following clauses, identify the complement of each italicized verb (some verbs might be intransitive and take no complement at all!). Don't worry about whether you can identify the category of the complement (as NP, VP, AP, etc.) – just try to identify which phrase(s) are complements. Which complements are direct objects? How do you know? Does Passive apply?

(a)   The fountain in the square *broke* again.
(b)   The loggers *removed* a lot of trees on the mountainside.
(c)   Several bystanders *videotaped* the incident.
(d)   The advertisement *suggests* that the product works very well.
(e)   Ole *believes* in ghosts.
(f)   The children *seem* very excited about the picnic.
(g)   Everyone in the auditorium *clapped*.

5. Which *do* is it?

We discussed a very specific form of auxiliary *do* in the chapter, namely, pleonastic *do*, which is inserted in specific syntactic contexts. But *do* can also be a main verb. Which of the following sentences include main verb *do*, and which include pleonastic *do*? Which include both? How do you know?

(a) You never *do* anything I ask.
(b) *Do* you always have to be so stubborn?
(c) Maisie likes cookies, *don't* she?
(d) *Did* you go to the store?
(e) I told you I *didn't do* it!
(f) Maisie says she's going to *do* something about that.
(g) Let's *do* the dishes together!

6. More verb raising

We discussed Main verb *be* raising at the end of the chapter, a verb raising rule that is widespread across varieties of American and other Englishes. You may be familiar with another main verb raising rule, Main verb *have* raising, that still exists in varieties of British English, for some Canadian English speakers, and is certainly familiar to many of us from reading older literature, including nursery rhymes!

(a) *Have* you any wool?
(b) I *haven't* any money.
(c) *Have* you a cold?
(d) You *haven't* a dollar, *have* you?

What are the equivalents of these sentences in your variety of English? Do you use Main verb *have* raising or *do* Insertion to form questions and negative sentences with *have*? Give examples!

7. Diagramming clauses

Diagram the following independent clauses. Remember to draw each with a TNS position, either specified for tense features [present], [past], or [future] or filled with an auxiliary or modal (which may be null).

(a) Six students toured the gallery.
(b) They could have been viewing the paintings.
(c) My friend paints.
(d) That person Ø asking a question.

(e) Some artists are opening a gallery.
(f) There might have been an auction.
(g) Tourists will need directions.
(h) They should take the train.
(i) Tourists have been taking the bus.
(j) The paintings were being sold.

8. Practice

We offer here some text excerpts to use for practice. These excerpts are intended only to get you started; there may not be examples in these texts of everything listed here. We encourage you to explore texts of your own choosing to find additional examples.

(a) Find the syntactic subjects of two or three of the clauses in the excerpts. Are any of the subjects pleonastic?
(b) Find and label any syntactic subjects of clauses that are in the passive voice.
(c) Find examples of transitive verbs that take direct object complements.
(d) Diagram a few clauses of your choice. What occurs in the TNS position?

At first, she could not determine if this was a boy or a girl, though Edward said the boys were shorn of their long hair; this child's hair seemed long, though it was too tangled with weeds to be certain. The cook was in the laundry helping the new maid iron the linens, but she did not disturb them. Edward's household staff was accustomed to the needs of a bachelor who spent more than ten months of the year away on expeditions. Hattie was in no hurry to make changes; she wanted the cook and maids to feel comfortable with her. In the summer, when he was not away on an expedition, Edward hired two or three Indian boys to help with the weeding and mowing. She wanted the child to see she meant no harm, so she proceeded to measure the grassy arcade created by the lilacs. While she paced off the length of the lawn, she kept watch from the corner of her eye for any sign of the child. She wondered what the school fed the Indian children. Did they feed the children the tribal foods they were accustomed to? She paced off the width of the grassy area and noted the measurements on one of the note cards she carried in her pocket, a habit left over from her days of scholarly research into early church history. During her mother's last illness, the orchid house and garden were neglected, but the acres of lemon and orange trees were tended by Edward to occupy himself. He did not talk about those difficult years, so Hattie did not press him, but she saw evidence of some sort of breakdown in the neglect of the orchid house. (From *Gardens in the Dunes*, by Leslie Marmon Silko.)

Every invitation was successful. They were all disengaged and all happy. The preparatory interest of this dinner, however, was not yet over. A circumstance rather unlucky occurred. The two eldest little Knightleys were engaged to pay their grandpapa and aunt a visit of some weeks in the spring, and their papa now proposed bringing them and staying one whole day at Hartfield – which one day would be the very day of this party. His professional engagement did not allow of his being put off, but both father and daughter were disturbed by its happening so. (From *Emma*, by Jane Austen.)

This water is cool and clean as anything I have ever tasted: it tastes of my father leaving, of him never having been there, of having nothing after he was gone. I dip it again and lift it level with the sunlight. I drink six measures of water and wish, for now, that this place without shame or secrets could be my home. Then the woman pulls me back to where I am safe on the grass and goes down alone. The bucket floats on its side for a moment before it sinks and swallows, making a grateful sound, a glug, before it's torn away and lifted. (From *Foster*, by Claire Keegan.)

7

Adjectives

Introduction

So far, we have discussed the categories NP and VP in some detail, paying particular attention to the English verb system, and the basic structure of the clause (CL). In this and the next chapter, we explore two lexical categories in English, Adjective and Adverb. In Chapter 9, we discuss the category Preposition, whose classification as a lexical category is a bit fuzzy;

Navigating English Grammar: A Guide to Analyzing Real Language, Second Edition.
Anne Lobeck and Kristin Denham.
© 2025 Anne Lobeck and Kristin Denham. Published 2025 by John Wiley & Sons Ltd.

prepositions actually share certain features with functional categories. Here, we discuss the syntax of adjectives in some detail, examining the different positions in which we find adjective phrases (APs), and how they function in those positions (as modifiers and as complements). We begin, however, with the semantics and morphology of adjectives.

Adjective Semantics

The semantics of adjectives are (as you might expect) quite complex. In general, adjectives (and more specifically, adjective phrases) are *modifiers*, or phrases that describe nouns, as we mentioned above. Another interesting property of adjectives is that they fall into a number of different semantic classes. Here are a few, though there are more!

value/opinion:	wonderful, attractive, worse
size:	tiny, enormous, minute
age/temperature:	old, warm, chilly
shape:	oblong, twisted, round
color:	blue, red, fuchsia
origin:	Athabaskan, local, Northwestern
material:	solid, wooden, digital

English is a language with a preferred semantic order of adjectives; adjectives in certain classes precede those in other classes. The general schema for English follows the order in the list above. For example, size adjectives typically precede color adjectives, which precede material adjectives (there is some variability in possible orders, as you may find as you examine different examples):

the big brown wooden table
    size color   material

*the brown wooden big table
    color   material size

*the wooden brown big table
    material color   size

Speakers pick up on the order unconsciously, but speakers of other languages may find that this order may be different from the preferred order of adjectives in their language(s). That adjectives of certain semantic classes occur in certain orders illustrates how semantics (meaning) interacts with syntax (word order).

Another fact about adjectives to note, which again illustrates the overlap of semantics and syntax, is that adjectives can "iterate," or occur in

130

(potentially long) strings, provided that they occur in the right semantic sequence. Here are some more examples:

the nasty, little, twisted, green, Northwestern slug
    value size shape   color origin

the cute, slimy slug
    value value

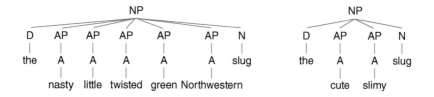

In traditional grammar, determiners, quantifiers, and even numerals are often classified as "adjectives." Recall from Chapter 2, however, that these categories are distinct from the category Adjective. One distinction is that they never iterate (in English, anyway!).

*all some trees
 Q   Q

*six   ten trees
 NUM NUM

*the this tree
 D   D

Adjectives of origin present some interesting questions (again, about semantics and syntax). To illustrate, consider the following examples.

the French teacher
the Japanese interpreter

Each of these examples is ambiguous, as the French teacher could be either the teacher from France (who may or may not teach the French language) or the teacher of the French language (who may or may not be from France); and the Japanese interpreter could be either the interpreter who is from Japan (who may or may not be an interpreter of the Japanese language) or the interpreter of the Japanese language (who may or may not be from Japan).

What is the source of this ambiguity? When we understand *French* or *Japanese* as labels for someone from someplace, we understand these words as adjectives, modifying the nouns *teacher* and *interpreter*, respectively. When we understand these words as the names of languages, we are interpreting them as nouns.

We can diagram noun phrases with adjectives of origin, and with noun (language name) modifiers, as follows. These phrases are syntactically ambiguous because each has two different syntactic structures.

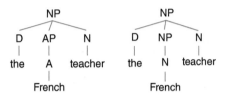

There are many such ambiguous examples, because in English we often use the same words for the people from a place and a language they speak (*Swedish, Chinese, Finnish, Navajo*). But often these terms are distinct; *Kenyan*, for example, can refer to someone from Kenya, but there is no corresponding *Kenyan* language. In Kenya, some 69 languages are spoken, most commonly Swahili and Kikuyu.

Adjective Morphology

Derivational affixation and other ways we form adjectives

Because the category Adjective is an open, lexical word class, we add new members to this class on a regular basis. One way we form new adjectives is by attaching different derivational affixes to root words (Table 7.1).

Table 7.1   English adjective affixes and sample words.

Affix	Sample words
-ish	pinkish, bullish, warmish
-ful	harmful, careful, soulful
-y	messy, lucky, dirty
-ly	lovely, friendly, portly
-like	doglike, catlike, birdlike
-ous	dangerous, monstrous, fabulous
-able	breakable, readable, thinkable
-less	sugarless, cordless, timeless
un-	unhappy, unbreakable, unfriendly
dis-	dishonest, disinterested, disengaged

We also use word formation rules to create adjectives. *Narcissistic* and *Victorian* are *eponymous* adjectives, adjectives derived from proper names, but also using adjectival affixes: *-ic* and *(i)an*. We also derive adjectives through compounding:

Our weekend was *trouble-free*.
It's easy to come up with a *gender-neutral* pronoun.
Many suitcases on the plane are *overweight*.

We can also coin brand new adjectives (*gnarly, cheugy, cringey*) or derive adjectives from clipping (*rad* from *radical*).

The meanings of existing adjectives also change over time, and they sometimes mean different things in different varieties of English. In many current varieties of English, *sweet* and *sick* mean "good" (*I got a sweet deal, That concert was sick*). By the time you read this book, the meanings of these adjectives may have shifted yet again!

Participial adjectives

As we discussed briefly in Chapter 3, adjectives can also be *participial*, formed from present participles such as *exciting* and *thrilling*, affixed with *-ing*, or past participles such as *annoyed*, *bored*, and *disgusted*, typically affixed with *-ed*.

The movie became *exciting/thrilling* toward the end.
Juno seems *annoyed/bored/disgusted*.

the *exciting/thrilling* movie
the *annoyed/bored/disgusted* person

We have some good evidence that these participles are adjectives here, not verbs. Recall from Chapter 3 that like other adjectives, these participial adjectives can be modified by a degree word such as *very*, *so*, *too*, or *rather*.

The movie became *so exciting/thrilling* toward the end.
Juno seems *very annoyed/bored/disgusted*.

Participial verbs, on the other hand, can't be modified by degree words:

The movie is *thrilling* me.
*The movie is *very thrilling* me.

Juno was *annoying* me.
*Juno was *very annoying* me.

There is more syntactic evidence for analyzing participles such as *exciting* or *bored* in such cases as adjectives rather than as verbs. We discuss this evidence in later sections.

Inflectional affixation: comparative and superlative adjectives

Adjectives in English take only two inflectional affixes: the comparative and superlative affixes *-er/-est*. Comparative and superlative adjectives can also be indicated by word order, using the words *more/most* and *less/least*. We'll illustrate here with *more/most*.

Generally, shorter adjectives (including most monosyllabic adjectives), words of Anglo-Saxon origin, and shorter words borrowed from French (e.g., *noble*) use the suffixes *-er/-est*.

big	bigger	biggest
small	smaller	smallest
large	larger	largest
soft	softer	softest
old	older	oldest
hot	hotter	hottest
noble	nobler	noblest

But adjectives with two syllables tend to vary in whether they take *-er/-est* or *more/most*. Some take either form; for example, *commoner* and *more common*. Two-syllable adjectives that end in the sound [i], most often spelled with *y* (but not *-ly*), generally take *-er/-est*, for example:

pretty: prettier, prettiest   ? more pretty, most pretty
happy: happier, happiest   ? more happy, most happy

Two-syllable adjectives that don't end in the sound [i] take either *-er/-est* or *more/most*.

shallow: shallower, shallowest   *or* more shallow, most shallow
friendly: friendlier, friendliest   *or* more friendly, most friendly

Longer adjectives, especially those derived from Greek and Latin, and most adjectives with three or more syllables, generally occur with *more* and *most*,

more/most expensive, more/most satisfying, more/most satisfactory
*expensiver, *satisfyinger, *satisfactorier

though there is variation. In Appalachian English, for example three-syllable words often do occur with -est (example from Montgomery and Hall, 2004):

All my family thought that was the *wonderfullest* thing ever was.

Though now many varieties tend to use either *more/most* or -er/-est, it was common in earlier stages of the language to use both. Shakespeare, writing in Early Modern English, used double comparatives and superlatives. One example is from Shakespeare's description of Julius Caesar's murder by his friends as *the most unkindest cut of all*.

That's a big-ass pile of wood! It was a cold-ass winter!

Siddiqi (2011) calls the -ass suffix an intensifier (what we are calling a degree word), much like *very*; however, unlike other degree words -ass is a bound morpheme. The -ass suffix can be attached to an adjective (*big, cold*) and typically seems to occur before the noun it modifies (in prenominal position).

The winter was very cold.
*The winter was cold-ass.
It was a cold-ass winter.

It also seems to work better with certain adjectives than others (Pullum, 2011); it's a bit odd to say *uncomfortable-ass* or *picturesque-ass*. Maybe it has to do with the word's length, its other affixes, or its level of formality.

Another adjectival suffix -ish can now occur not just as a suffix but as a stand-alone word, meaning something like "sort of," "somewhat."

Are you coming at 7:00?
....*ish*

Adjective Syntax

In this section, we first discuss the internal structure of the adjective phrase. We then turn to the positions in which APs themselves can occur in the clause.

Modifiers of adjectives

As you know by now, adjectives themselves can be modified by a category of words called degree words, such as *very, so, too, rather,* or *quite.* We use the label DEG for members of this category.

a *tall* student	a ***very*** *tall* student
six *grey* kittens	six ***completely*** *grey* kittens
these four *young* children	these four ***rather*** *young* children
some *delightful* novels	some ***quite*** *delightful* novels

You might be tempted to think that adjectives can be modified by other adjectives because we often hear and say phrases such as the following: "that *pretty/real exciting* movie." But *pretty* and *real,* both of which can function elsewhere as adjectives, are functioning here as degree words; they are actually synonyms for *very.* Here's where they show up as adjectives:

Sunsets are *pretty.*
The gemstone was *real.*

Not surprisingly, adjectives *pretty* and *real* can be modified by degree words:

Sunsets are *so pretty.*
The gift was a *very real* surprise.

We include in the class of degree words a certain set of adverbs, which we'll call *degree adverbs.* This set of words includes examples such as those below:

That *amazingly/fantastically/awesomely* exciting movie.

We discuss adverbs in the next chapter, but for now, simply notice that the meanings of the degree adverbs above are similar to the meanings of *very, so,* or *quite.* When we use them as (non-degree) adverbs, these words have lexical meanings.

She plays the piano *amazingly/fantastically/awesomely.*
(She plays the piano in an *amazing/fantastic/awesome* manner.)

Together, an optional degree word and a (head) adjective form a larger adjective phrase, or AP, as expressed by the phrase structure rule below:

AP → (DEG) A

We can draw examples of AP like this:

We can draw NPs now, with AP modifiers:

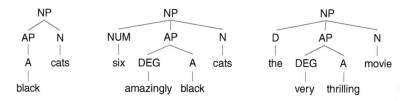

Certain other adverbs can modify adjectives; these adverbs do not necessarily express degree.

The publication was **readily** *available.*
The **openly** *vicious* attack
She seemed **silently** *furious.*

When adverbs do not express degree, we will diagram them simply as adverb phrase modifiers of adjectives (we will discuss these in more detail in the next chapter):

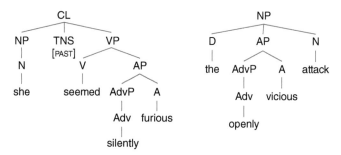

The degree word test for adjective phrases
We can use the evidence that adjectives are modified by degree words as a test for adjective-hood. We can call this test the "degree word test." To test whether a word is an adjective, see if it can be modified by DEG (*very, so, too, rather, quite,* etc.),

very/so/too tall

This test allows us, in general, to distinguish adjectives from other categories, in particular those that introduce nouns in the noun phrase, such as DET, NUM, and Q. None of these functional categories can be modified by degree words. This provides us with evidence that these categories are distinct from adjectives.

*very *the* dogs   (DEG + DET + N)
*quite *six* dogs   (DEG + NUM + N)
*so *some* dogs   (DEG + Q + N)

Degree words also can't modify nouns:

I bought a *dog*.
*I bought a *very dog*.

And although many verbs can be modified by adverbs such as *quickly, slowly, loudly*, verbs can't be modified by degree words.

She *quickly/loudly laughed* at the joke.
*She *very laughed* at the joke.

And as we saw above, participial adjectives can be distinguished from participial verbs using the degree word test:

the *very exciting/thrilling* movie
      adjective

*The scary movie was *very thrilling* the children.
      verb

Adjectives that can be modified by degree words are typically *gradable adjectives*, such as *hot/cold, rich/poor*, and *happy/sad*. Other adjectives, however, cannot be measured in terms of degree; these adjectives are called *complementary adjectives*, such as *dead/alive, legal/illegal, infinite*, and *pregnant*. So technically speaking, phrases such as "very dead" or "very pregnant" are semantically anomalous (nonsense), because you either are or you aren't dead or pregnant. Nevertheless, we do often use degree words for emphasis with such adjectives. Origin adjectives are also adjectives that we don't think of as being modified by degree. Yet we do sometimes use degree modifiers with such adjectives, when we want to suggest that someone has a lot of the qualities that we associate with being, say, *French* or *Northwestern*:

The movie was *very French*.
This dish has a *rather* Northwestern flavor.

Adjective phrase positions

In this section, we turn to some of the positions in which adjective phrases themselves occur, namely, in noun phrases as modifiers, and in verb phrases as complements of the verb.

Adjective phrases as prenominal and postnominal modifiers of nouns
As the examples we have discussed so far show, one common position in which we find adjectives in English, or more specifically, AP modifiers, is before the noun in NP. We call this position *prenominal* position.

the *wicked* witch

In English, adjective phrase modifiers of nouns typically precede rather than follow the noun:

*the witch *wicked*
a *good* soup
*a soup *good*

these *sad* movies
*these movies *sad*

a *big* house
*a house *big*

Sometimes, however, adjective phrases can occur in *postnominal* position, when they modify indefinite pronouns such as *something, nothing, anything, everything,* or similar terms, which are, in fact, ungrammatical with prenominal AP modifiers.

something *wicked*	**wicked* something
nothing *good*	**good* nothing
anything *sad*	**sad* anything
everything *big*	**big* everything

139

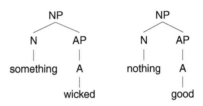

There is another small group of fixed expressions in which the AP follows, rather than precedes the noun; these phrases come to English from French, a language in which adjectival modifiers generally occur in postnominal position.

president *elect*, heir *apparent*, attorney *general*

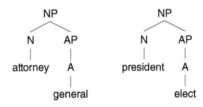

Attorneys general? Attorney generals?

Which plural sounds better to you in each of these pairs?

two attorneys general   two attorney generals
four heirs apparent   four heir apparents

The terms *attorney general* and *heir apparent* are derived from French, a language in which adjectives often follow the noun they modify. However, English speakers have English, not French, intuitions about morphological rules, and so many speakers treat *attorney general* just like, say, *military general*, where *military* modifies *general* (not the other way around). The fact that both options for pluralization of such phrases exist can be accounted for by proposing that the second set of plurals conforms to speakers' descriptive rules of English, but that the first set of plurals are exceptions, and have to be consciously learned, in the same way as many other prescriptive rules.

We can now elaborate our phrase structure rule for NP from Chapter 3 to include adjectival modifiers (optional in prenominal and postnominal position).

NP → (DET) (Q) (NUM) (AP) N (AP)

Although this may look complicated, it is simply a way of illustrating all of the modifiers that can occur with a noun inside an NP. The only required element is the N itself.

We'll now turn to yet another position that adjective phrases occur in, a position that is not within NP at all.

Adjective phrases as subjective complements
We have already talked about *grammatical functions*, the grammatical roles that phrases play in the sentence. The grammatical functions you are familiar with so far include *subject, predicate,* and *complement*. Phrases can also function as *modifiers*, as we saw above.

Returning for a moment to phrases that function as *complements*, recall the discussion of direct objects from Chapter 6. In the following example, the direct object NP *the kelp* is a complement of the (transitive) verb *eat* that selects it to complete the verb phrase, as illustrated here.

The manatee ate the kelp.

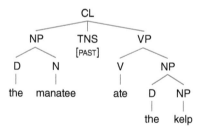

As we introduced in Chapter 6, there are many other kinds of complements (because there are many different classes of verbs, and not all, of course, are transitive). In fact, adjective phrases can function as complements, as illustrated by the following sentences.

Brutus seems *tall*.
The cat became *very upset*.

The italicized adjective phrases above, together with the main verb (*seems* and *became*), make up or "complete" the VP.

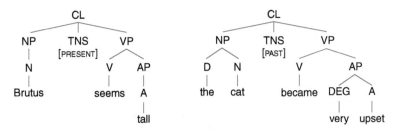

AP complements occur in what we will refer to as *predicate position*, as part of VP, rather than as part of NP. In traditional grammar, APs in this position are called *predicate adjectives*.

AP complements occur with a certain set of verbs, called *linking verbs*. These verbs do not express actions but connect ("link") the subject noun phrase to a phrase that describes it. Linking verbs include *remain, seem, appear, grow, be,* and *become,* among some others. *Sense verbs* are also linking verbs: *taste, smell, feel,* and *look,* for example. We call the complements of linking verbs *subjective complements,* because, together with the verb, they form a predicate that describes the subject:

Juno becomes/is/seems/remained/appears/grew *very happy.*
The soup tasted/smells/looks *weird.*
The dog's coat feels *rough.*

APs in predicate position describe the subject that the verb links them to. Linking verbs are therefore semantically very different from action/transitive verbs such as *play, kick, eat,* or *throw.* The meaning of linking verbs is much harder to define because these verbs don't express actions. (Try explaining what *seem* means, for example, and compare it to how you might describe what the action verb *kick* means.)

Other subjective complements: NP and PP
Adjective phrases are not the only phrases that can be subjective complements. Both noun phrases and prepositional phrases (which we discuss in Chapter 9) can be subjective complements. Some examples are given below:

My sister is *a lawyer.*
           NP subjective complement

The scientist became *a celebrity.*
           NP subjective complement

Jill seemed *out of sorts*.
        PP subjective complement

He is *over the hill*.
       PP subjective complement

In each of these examples, the NP or PP occurs in predicate position, as the complement of a linking verb. These NP and PP subjective complements describe the subject, just as the AP subjective complements do in the other examples we've discussed. Notice in particular that the PP subjective complements are idiomatic (nonliteral) in interpretation and can be paraphrased as APs:

Jill seemed *depressed*.
        AP subjective complement

He is *old*.
       AP subjective complement

Interestingly, PP subjective complements can also be modified by degree words, which is what we expect if they actually have adjectival interpretations:

Jill seemed *very out of sorts*.
        AP subjective complement

We can diagram NP and PP subjective complements as follows.

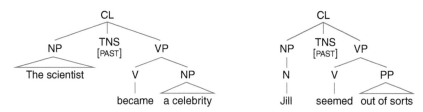

Direct objects versus subjective complements
We take a detour here from adjectives specifically to revisit NP subjective complements. You now know about two different kinds of NP complements, subjective complements and direct objects. You've also seen that subjective complements, like direct objects, can be NPs. This means that syntactically, a direct object can look very similar to an NP subjective complement; they are both NPs that occur to the right of the verb:

Yost remained *a good friend*.
        NP subjective complement

Yost visited *a good friend*.
       NP direct object

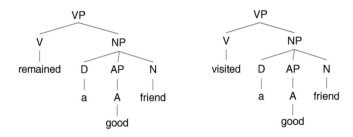

Remember, though, that NP direct objects are complements of transitive verbs and are therefore distinct in this way from NP subjective complements, which are complements of linking verbs. A subjective complement describes the subject, and it is more accurately defined as part of the predicate, rather than as a phrase that takes the action of the verb (a direct object).

We also have a very good syntactic test for direct objects: Passive. As you know, passive sentences are derived from active ones by moving the direct object to the left into the subject position, and moving the subject to the right, as illustrated below.

> *Yost* visited *a good friend.*
> *A good friend* was visited by *Yost.*

As we might expect, since Passive applies only to direct object NPs, we won't be able to passivize an NP subjective complement. As the following example illustrates, this prediction is exactly right; Passive fails with subjective complements:

> *Yost* remained *my good friend.*
> **My good friend* was remained by *Yost.*

Passive therefore provides us with evidence that although both direct objects and subjective complements occupy the same position to the right of the verb, and though both are NPs, they are distinct in terms of the verbs that take them as complements, and also distinct in their semantic and syntactic functions.

The seem *test for adjective phrases*

Since most APs can occur following linking verbs, a good test for identifying them, at least most of the time, is to see if they can follow a linking verb. The verb *seem* is a particularly good choice, because unlike other linking verbs, *seem* typically takes an AP subjective complement, but not an NP subjective complement.

Adjectives

Edna seems *ecstatic.*
　　　　AP subjective complement

*Edna seems *a doctor.*
　　　　NP subjective complement

Seem can also, as we might expect, occur with PP subjective complements, because these function very much like AP subjective complements:

Edna seems *under the weather/sick.*
　　　　PP/AP subjective complement

Seem can also be followed by an infinitival phrase as in *Edna seems to like basketball.* (This isn't relevant to the discussion here, though we will return to infinitival clause complements such as these in Chapter 10.) We can therefore now test whether a phrase is an AP or not by checking to see whether it can occur as the complement of *seem.*

Let's return to the participial adjectives we discussed in previous sections. As we might expect, participial adjectives can occur after *seem*:

Edna seems *excited/bored.*
The movie seemed *thrilling.*

But participial verbs can't occur in this position, which is also exactly what we expect:

*The horse seems *galloping.*
*The tourist seems *laughing.*

We can also use the *seem* test to identify the category of words that modify nouns. We know that adjectives can modify nouns:

the *high* fence
The fence seems *high.*

We also know that nouns can modify nouns:

the *wire* fence

And as expected, noun modifiers of nouns fail the *seem* test:

*The fence seems *wire.*

We now have two very good tests for adjective phrases, the *seem* test and the degree word test. We will continue to use these two tests in the following chapters, as we move on to discuss Adverbs and Prepositions.

Summary

This concludes our discussion of the semantics, morphology, and syntax of adjectives and adjective phrases. We've seen how adjectives fall into different **semantic classes** and occur in a general semantic order before the noun they modify. We have explored the **derivational** and **inflectional morphology** of adjectives, and how we add new adjectives to the language quite regularly using different word formation rules. We have discussed in some detail **participial adjectives**, adjectives which have participial forms, but which function as adjectives rather than as verbs. We discussed how **gradable adjectives** can themselves be modified by **degree words** such as *very/so/too*, providing us with a way to construct a test for adjectives (that are not **complementary adjectives**), which we called the **degree word test**. We have revisited the concept of grammatical function in this chapter as well, expanding our knowledge of **complements**, and how they differ from **modifiers**. We saw how adjective phrases can occur either before or after the noun they modify, in **prenominal** or **postnominal** position, respectively. Adjective phrases can also be **subjective complements**, occurring in **predicate position** in the verb phrase, after a special class of verbs, called **linking verbs**. We can construct a fairly reliable test for adjective phrases in this position, the *seem* **test**. We have also seen that Passive, an operation that in English applies to direct objects, provides us with a means to distinguish direct objects from other types of NP complements, such as NP subjective complements.

Exercises

1. Color terms

In the text, we've assumed color terms are adjectives. However, can color terms sometimes be analyzed as nouns? Consider the following examples.

> We painted the wall dark *brown.*
> *Blue* is my favorite color.
> The couch is a deep *purple.*

Are *brown, blue,* and *purple* adjectives or nouns here? Provide evidence to support your answer. Remember to use the tests for adjective phrases we discussed in this chapter, and to consider the grammatical functions of the APs as complements and modifiers.

2. Adjectives or nouns

Here are some sentences that include words that may be adjectives or nouns, depending on how we interpret them. Label each as an adjective or noun, and briefly explain why you analyzed each the way you did. Some might be both!

(a) My first language is *Japanese*.
(b) The presentation was given by an *Oneida* speaker.
(c) Our *Swahili* teacher also speaks Kikuyu.
(d) The *Bantu* language Zulu is spoken by more than 9 million people in South Africa.
(e) She is a *Finnish* interpreter.

3. Adjective phrase positions

Each sentence below contains at least one adjective phrase, in prenominal, postnominal, or predicate position (as a subjective complement). Label the position of each AP. There may be more than one AP in each sentence so be sure to label all of them!

(a) Experts claim that crows are attracted to shiny objects.
(b) Her whereabouts to this day remain unknown.
(c) The two small ceramic teapots are cracked but usable.
(d) Nothing good will come of this!
(e) The candidates all seem surprisingly confident about the upcoming election.
(f) Lorna got sick because she ate something bad.
(g) Stranger things have happened, but this seems entirely unprecedented!

4. Distinguishing direct objects from subjective complements

We've seen that when NPs follow verbs, they can be either direct objects, like those in (a) and (b) below, or subjective complements, like those in (c) and (d).

(a) Kim met *the famous physicist*.
(b) Students often write *term papers* for their classes.
(c) Kim became *a famous physicist*.
(d) Kim and Ziggy remained *friends*.

Recall that only direct objects, not subjective complements, can undergo Passive, as we see by the grammaticality of the sentences in (e) and (f) compared to those in (g) and (h):

(e) *The famous physicist* was met by Kim.
(f) *Term papers* are written by students for their classes.
(g) **A famous physicist* was become by Kim.
(h) **Friends* were remained by Kim and Ziggy.

Using Passive as a test, determine whether the italic phrases below are direct objects or subjective complements. Another hint is to determine whether the verb is a linking verb or an action verb.

(a) The dog's barking disturbed *the children*.
(b) The dedicated student became *president*.
(c) Cary visited *the dentist*.
(d) The police arrested *the suspect*.
(e) My aunt became *a famous tennis player*.
(f) Bo seemed *in a good mood*.
(g) The bread tastes *delicious*.
(h) Many psychics seem *out of touch*.
(i) The child put *the toy* in the box.
(j) That breeze feels *lovely*.
(k) The child kicked *the soccer ball*.

5. The good, the bad, and the ugly

It is common in English to encounter constructions in which what appears to be an adjective is introduced by a determiner.

The rich usually drive expensive cars.
A doctor cares for *the sick*.

Are the words *rich* and *sick* here adjectives or nouns, and on what do you base your hypothesis? (Think, for example, about modification; how do you modify these words?) What are some other examples of constructions like this?

Try to come up with examples of this construction using the following adjectives. Explain why you find your examples grammatical or ungrammatical, based on your analysis.

good, green, young, new, short, happy, interesting, fuzzy

6. Practice

Here are some text excerpts to use for practice finding adjectives. We have provided a few suggestions about what to look for. Remember that there may not be examples in these texts of everything listed here. We encourage you to explore texts of your own choosing to find additional examples.

(a) Find all the adjectives. Be sure not to include nouns or verbs modifying other nouns. If you need to, use the degree word test or the *seem* test to help you.

(b) Label the semantic class of a few of the adjectives you find.

(c) Analyze the morphology of some of the adjectives you find. Identify some different derivational and/or inflectional affixes that occur on adjectives.

(d) Label the function of each adjective phrase as a *modifier* or as a *subjective complement*. Are there any PP or NP subjective complements in the excerpt?

(e) Label the position of each adjective phrase as *prenominal, postnominal,* or *predicate* (or *other*, if none of these).

(f) Identify any participial adjectives in the excerpt.

(g) Discuss, briefly, any problematic examples that you found, and how you analyzed them. Did they turn out to be adjective phrases or phrases of some other category? What made them difficult to analyze?

I know what it is: Am I Jewish …? Yes, I am. From an observant family. During the Occupation, I had false papers and passed as Aryan. And that was how I was assigned to a forced labor unit. When they deported me to Germany, I eluded being sent to a concentration camp. At the depot, nobody knew that I spoke German; it would have aroused suspicion. It was imprudent of me to say those few words to you, but I knew that you would not betray me … (From *Night*, by Elie Wiesel.)

In the United States, indigenous youth continue to experience the historically oppressive rhetoric of Mexico's ethnic and racial classifications. Anti-indigenous beliefs, sentiments, and old prejudices migrate to the United States along with immigrants. Within the broader Mexican immigrant community, nonindigenous Mexicans hold stereotypes that construct indigenous Mexicans as stubborn, lazy, backward, primitive, and intellectually inferior. Because of the colorism that permeates all sectors of Mexican society, indigenous youth are often marginalized due to their "darker" skin color and "indio" features. (From *Zapotec, Mixtec, and Purepecha Youth,* by William Perez, Rafael Vasquez, and Raymond Buriel.)

Moose was a plain, largish man with a flaring Roman nose that drooped to a bulbous end; his shoulders drooped, too; and yes, there was a kind of homely, even lumbering majesty about him. We, American-born kids of our Pakistani-born parents, also struggled with saying his name, for though of course he was never Moose to us, our parents said his name one way, and he offered it to us – native American speakers with our own varying levels of Punjabi incompetence – in the bizarre, labored accent he'd come upon to make himself sound more American, his diphthongs flattened by ever-widening contortions of his lips, his affricates shoved so far forward he couldn't seem to get through a sentence without baring unnecessary teeth. (From *Homeland Elegies: A novel,* by Ayad Akhtar.)

8

Adverbs

Introduction

We have already discussed adverbs (briefly) in the previous chapters, and here we will take a look at the semantics, morphology, and syntax of this category in more detail. As you already know, verbs can be modified by adverb phrases and we can therefore use modification by an adverb (in particular, by a *manner* adverb) as a "test" for a verb (the *softly* babbling brook, for example). Given what we've talked about so far in this book, you may think that adverbs are always manner adverbs (paraphrased as "in X manner") and that they

Navigating English Grammar: A Guide to Analyzing Real Language, Second Edition.
Anne Lobeck and Kristin Denham.
© 2025 Anne Lobeck and Kristin Denham. Published 2025 by John Wiley & Sons Ltd.

always end in *-ly*. But, as you'll see in this chapter, adverbs actually come in a variety of different shapes and sizes, and they can modify many things besides just verbs. We'll start the discussion of adverbs with a look at their basic meanings, and the kinds of information they contribute to the clause.

Adverb Semantics

As mentioned above, we typically think of adverbs as words that modify the verb ("in X manner"), many of which end in *-ly*.

> *manner* (paraphrased as "in X manner")
> He ran *quickly/slowly/energetically*.
> The dog *happily/ecstatically/slowly* wagged its tail.

It turns out, though, that *-ly* "manner adverbs" are only one semantic class of adverb. Adverbs can also express *time, possibility,* or *speaker attitude*:

> *time* (including aspect, frequency)
> He runs *often/immediately*.
> The dog *never/usually/always* barks.

> *possibility* (conveys information about the truth of an event)
> She will *probably/certainly/possibly* be able to attend the ceremony.
> (Notice that *-ly* doesn't express manner here!)
> The defendant *allegedly* hid the stolen car in the barn.
> *Perhaps/maybe* you could catch the next train.

> *attitude* (of the speaker)
> She will *obviously/fortunately/regrettably* be able to attend the ceremony.

Adverbs can also focus or emphasize different constituents in the clause:

> *focus*
> *Even/only* you know how to get there.
> I *just* don't think you should do that.
> Lonnie wants to see the movie *too*.

And we negate sentences with the negative adverb *never*.

> *negation*
> We *never* talk anymore!

(We leave *not* aside here as there is syntactic evidence that it does not behave like the adverbs under discussion here. See discussion of Negation in Chapter 6.)

As you can see from this list, adverbs have a variety of different meanings, but what they all have in common is that they function as *modifiers*. Though manner adverbs can modify a verb (she talked *quickly*), they can also modify other components in a clause, including the entire clause itself (or more specifically, the event expressed by the clause). Also, adverbs can be used for focus and negation and to express information about time and location. We will see later that the syntactic behavior of adverbs, or more accurately, of adverb phrases, reflects their function as modifiers that express several kinds of "additional information" in the clause.

Adverb Morphology

As we have seen already with the other categories, including nouns, verbs, and adjectives, adverbs too have unique affixes. We examine here both the derivational and inflectional affixes that occur on adverbs.

Derivational affixation and other ways we form adverbs

We form adverbs using a variety of different derivational affixes, though the most familiar one is *-ly*. Other affixes include *-wise, -like, -ward, -ways, -ally, -wide*:

The carpenter set the board *gently* on the workbench.
The carpenter set the board *lengthwise/crosswise* on the workbench.
The baby crawled *crablike* across the floor.
You may flip over *backward* if you aren't careful.
He looked at her *sideways*.
Tragically, someone had eaten all the blueberries.
The internet is used *worldwide*.

A large class of adverbs is derived from adjectives by adding *-ly*:

adjectives: possible, obvious, probable, clear, evident, political, financial
adverbs: possibly, obviously, probably, clearly, evidently, politically, financially

We can also form adverbs from participles by adding *-ly*:

excitedly, interestingly, disgustingly, shockingly

As the above examples illustrate, the category Adverb is an open rather than closed class, and we therefore add new adverbs to the language all the time, often using derivational affixation (*majorly*, *neologistically*, and *globally*).

We also have a number of adverbs, called *conjunctive adverbs*, which were originally compounds: *therefore*, *henceforth*, *heretofore*, etc. (We discuss conjunctive adverbs in Chapter 10 in more detail.) We also form phrases with adverbial meanings through compounding, such as *hand-in-hand* and *back-to-back*.

Toward or towards? Forward or forwards?

Have you ever noticed that people say both *backward* and *backwards*? Or *forward* and *forwards*? *Toward* and *towards*? Each of these has been in common use for hundreds of years, and the -*s* is what remains of a long-lost Old English genitive case ending. Some grammar and style guides say that the -*s* versions are more common in British English, but it's not clear that evidence bears that out. Some suggest that when the words are being used as adjectives, the *s*-less form is preferred: *a backward view*, *a forward thinker*. It's interesting that most people don't have a strong feeling about these varying forms and that the -*s* and -*s*-less forms of these adverbs coexist quite happily.

Flat adverbs

We've seen in previous discussions of nouns, verbs, and adjectives that some words can have the same form across categories; that is, the same word can be a noun in some contexts and a verb in others. This is true for some adverbs as well; the same word can show up as either an adjective or an adverb. Some adverbs have the same morphological form as their related adjectives. These are called *flat adverbs*.

Adverb	Adjective
He ran *fast/hard*	the *fast/hard* run
Drive *safe*!	the *safe* drive
The light shone *bright*	the *bright* light

These adverbs sometimes have corresponding -*ly* forms, but not always:

*He ran *fastly/hardly*.
Drive *safely*!
The light shone *brightly*.

And sometimes, there is a meaning distinction between the adverb with and without an -*ly* form. Note that we can say something like *He hardly ran*, but this doesn't have the same meaning as *he ran hard*. We can also say *Sleep tight* where *tight* doesn't have the same meaning as *tight* or *tightly* in *The child held my hand tight/tightly*.

Inflectional affixation

Like adjectives, adverbs can (sometimes) take comparative and superlative affixes *-er* and *-est* (though not all adverbs that take comparative *-er* can also take superlative *-est*).

> The marathoner ran *harder/faster* during the last mile.
> The marathoner ran *hardest/fastest* during the last mile.
> They ate dinner *earlier/later / ?latest*.
> She arrived *earliest/latest*.
> They stayed *longer/longest*.
> The raft drifted *farther/farthest* out to sea.

Some adverbs show comparative / superlative with *more/most* and *less*.

> The students read articles *more/less often* than books.
> The students *most often* read articles.

And as with adjectives, some adverbs have *suppletive* comparative and superlative forms:

> The team played *bad/badly/worse/worst* last night.
> The team played *good/well/better/best* last night.

Adverb Syntax

We turn now to a brief discussion of the internal structure of the adverb phrase, or AdvP, and to the positions in which we find AdvP in the clause.

Modifiers of adverbs

As you've probably already noticed, adverbs can be modified by the same degree words that modify adjectives, including *very, so, too, rather*, or *quite*. And as we mentioned above, they can sometimes be modified by comparative and superlative *more/less* and *most*.

> *very/more* quickly
> *rather* badly
> *so* fast

We can now write a simple phrase structure rule for AdvP (where we can include *more/less* and *more* in the class DEG):

AdvP → (DEG) Adv

We can draw some simple tree diagrams for adverb phrases, or AdvP, as follows:

As we saw in Chapter 7 on adjectives, certain adverbs express degree or intensity and show up in the same position as other members of the category DEG, like *very*. For example, *amazingly*, *incredibly*, and *fantastically*, which look like manner adverbs, actually express degree in sentences such as the one below.

The child ate *amazingly/incredibly/fantastically* quickly.

When words such as *amazingly* or *fantastically* express degree and modify adverbs or adjectives, we'll assume they are functioning as members of DEG.

The child ate *amazingly* *quickly*.
            DEG   Adv

The *amazingly* *talented* child.
   DEG   A

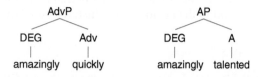

These degree words – *amazingly*, *incredibly*, and so on – can also function as manner adverbs for some speakers; in the following sentence, they modify the verb *plays* and can be paraphrased as in X manner.

Bert plays the piano *extraordinarily/incredibly/amazingly*.
(Bert plays the piano in an extraordinary/incredible/amazing manner.)

When they function in this way, we diagram them as AdvP:

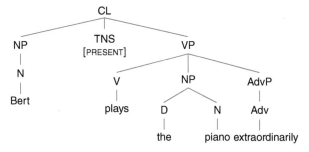

Some speakers find such constructions awkward without an accompanying adverb.

Bert plays the piano *amazingly* well.

In this case, *amazingly* would simply be a degree word modifying the adverb *well*.

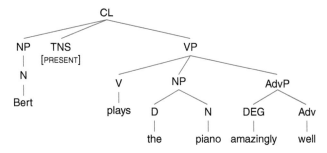

Quickly friendly: Adverbs, adjectives, and -*ly*

The -*ly* suffix that attaches to form adverbs and adjectives appears in a similar form in all of the Germanic languages. Its most common form in Old English was -*lic* or -*lice*, and it attached to nouns to form adjectives, and meant, as it still does, "having the qualities or characteristics of something" – *queenly, knightly, princely, scholarly, friendly, cowardly, beastly*. Another common use of the suffix in English and other Germanic languages is to form adjectives that denote a periodic recurrence: *daily, weekly, monthly, yearly*. It was not until the late Middle English and Early Modern English period that -*ly* could attach to adjectives to form adverbs: *quickly, importantly, unfortunately, merrily*.

Adverb phrase positions

Because they are modifiers of different categories, adverb phrases can occur in a variety of different positions. For this reason, we can say they are *movable*, because they appear to be able to move around. Sometimes moving them to different spots can change the meaning; other times, the varying positions of the adverb phrase do not seem to affect meaning much, if at all.

> She *carefully* rubbed the stone.
> She rubbed the stone *carefully*.
> *Carefully* she rubbed the stone.

> *Evidently*, someone forgot to close the door.
> Someone forgot to close the door, *evidently*.
> Someone *evidently* forgot to close the door.

> He *still* believes the moon is made of green cheese.
> He believes the moon is *still* made of green cheese.
> He believes the moon is made of green cheese *still*.
> *Still*, he believes the moon is made of green cheese.

Though adverb phrases can usually occur in more than one position in the clause, there are some positions in which they sound less natural, if not ungrammatical. For example, adverb phrases cannot occur between the verb and its complement.

> *She rubbed *carefully* the stone.
> *Someone forgot *evidently* to close the door.
> *He believes the moon is made *still* of green cheese.

Adverb phrases can therefore occur in different positions, but not without some restrictions. In this way, adverb phrases differ quite dramatically from phrases of other categories, whose syntactic positions are much more restricted. Why would this be?

One reason that adverb phrases can occur in different positions within the clause is that, unlike phrases of other categories, they are rarely selected as complements by verbs (or any other head, for that matter). Rather, adverb phrases function almost exclusively as modifiers, providing extra or additional information to a clause or other phrase. It follows, then, that adverb phrases, unlike complements of different categories, can occur in clauses with any kind of verb; here, *fortunately* can occur with a linking verb like *seems* or with a transitive verb like *kick*:

> *Fortunately*, Martin seems happy.
>   linking verb

> *Fortunately*, Martin kicked the ball.
>   transitive verb

Analyzing clauses that include adverb phrase modifiers can be a little tricky, because it isn't always clear what the adverb phrase actually modifies. We've given a few examples below to illustrate common positions in which we find adverb phrase modifiers.

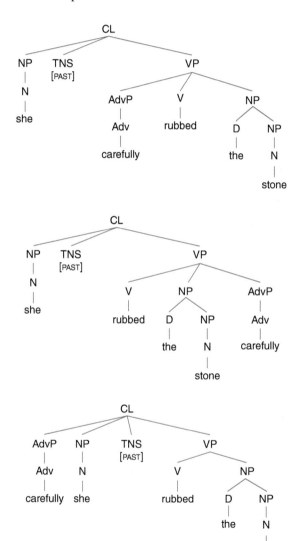

Adverb phrases as modifiers in AP, NP, and PP
We have seen that degree words such as *very, quite,* and *so* can modify adjectives, and that adverbs that express degree can also do so (*extraordinarily*

happy). Adverbs with lexical meanings (and which don't express degree) can also often modify adjectives. Here are some examples of speaker attitude and possibility adverbs that modify adjectives:

possibly happy
evidently superior
obviously surprised
clearly ingenious

Manner adverbs can also modify adjectives:

quietly thoughtful
thoughtfully quiet

As we might expect, such adverb phrases can themselves be modified by degree words:

very *possibly* happy
so quietly thoughtful

We can diagram these AP with AdvP modifiers as follows:

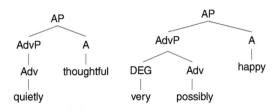

Adverb phrase modifiers also occur in PPs and NPs. Consider the following examples, where the AdvP is in italics.

almost at the top
perfectly in a row
nearly out the door

only camels   (have humps)
even the dog   (went along on the trip)

These phrases can be diagrammed in different ways, depending on whether we analyze the adverb phrase as part of the PP or NP it modifies or not. For simplicity, we will add the AdvP to the NP or PP, illustrated as follows:

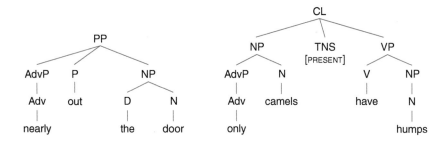

Adverb phrases as complements

You have seen that adverb phrases are nearly always modifiers that provide additional, optional information. However, adverbs can also function very occasionally as complements of verbs. In fact, we can think of only one verb that requires an AdvP complement, the verb *word* (and any of its synonyms – *phrased*, for example).

> She worded/phrased the letter *carefully*.

The AdvP *carefully* seems to be a complement, rather than a modifier, here because it seems required by the verbs *worded/phrased*. The sentence would be ungrammatical (or at least rather strange?) without the AdvP.

> *?She worded/phrased the letter.

More on Modifiers

As we've seen above, adverb phrases express a variety of different kinds of information, such as focus, negation, time, manner, and speaker attitude. Adverb phrase modifiers can, as a result of functioning almost exclusively as modifiers, appear in a variety of different positions in the clause and don't seem to depend on occurring with a particular verb. That is, they are rarely (if ever) complements, required by the verb.

We will find that there are other phrases, including NP and PP (and even verb phrases and clauses) that show up as modifiers, expressing, like adverbs, similar kinds of additional information, about reason, place, cause, condition, etc. Some examples of such modifiers are given as follows:

> *Guiltily*, the dog looked at me. (AdvP)
> The dog looked at me *in a guilty way*. (PP)
> *Guilty*, the dog looked at me. (AP)
> The dog looked at me *yesterday*. (NP)

Barking hysterically, the dog chased the car down the street. (VP)
Its lips curled in a smile, the dog wagged its tail. (CL)

As you may have noticed, the above modifiers occur in both clause-initial and clause-final positions, positions in which we also find AdvP. We return to modifiers such as these in Chapter 11.

Summary

In this chapter, we have discussed a variety of interesting properties that distinguish the category Adverb from other categories. In particular, although adverbs in English bear some similarity to adjectives, they are distinct in terms of semantics, morphology, and syntax. Adverbs express a range of information about time, manner, attitude, negation, focus, and more. Adverbs are often, but not always, affixed with *-ly*; we discussed other **derivational affixes** that derive adverbs (*-wise*, *-like*, and others) and adverbs such as *now* and *still* that have no derivational morphology at all. Still other adverbs, namely, **flat adverbs** (*hard*, *fast*), have the same form as their corresponding adjectives, and **conjunctive adverbs** (*henceforth*, *therefore*, *however*, *nevertheless*) are compounds. Syntactically, adverb phrases typically function as **modifiers** and are rarely complements. For this reason, they occur in a wide range of syntactic positions. We ended the chapter with a brief overview of modifiers of other categories, which, like AdvP, express additional information, and occur in both clause-initial and clause-final positions.

Exercises

1. Add an adverb

Add at least one adverb phrase modifier to each of the following sentences. Try to use adverb phrases (of different types, not just those with *-ly*!) that change the meaning of each clause in a significant way. Try to explain how the meaning changes.

Here's an example:

Maria will write a novel. → *Maybe* Maria will *still* write a novel.

By adding the adverb phrase *maybe*, the meaning of the assertion *Maria will write a novel* becomes quite a bit more interesting and mysterious – *maybe* adds possibility. *Still* suggests that Maria was going to write a novel and may yet do so.

(a) A bat flew under the eaves.
(b) Jan enjoys playing scrabble.

(c) Four ships appeared on the horizon.
(d) The bus driver waved at the children.
(e) Lonnie told me that you should get a haircut.

2. Adjective or adverb?

Identify the category of each italic word as an adjective or adverb. Briefly explain your answers and provide any evidence in support of your analysis. If you analyze the italic word as an adverb, try to come up with a sentence in which it would be an adjective. And if you analyzed the word as an adjective, give an example sentence where it would be an adverb, if you can.

(a) The pitcher held the ball *tight*.
(b) The child held the rope *slack*.
(c) We ate a *late* dinner.
(d) We ate dinner *late*.
(e) Sybil looks *well*.
(f) Lee sings *well*.
(g) Jorge feels *sick*.
(h) They ate the pie *slow*.

3. AdvP modifiers

Each of the following sentences includes an adverb phrase. Try to identify the word or phrase that each AdvP modifies. Diagram the sentences too, for practice!

(a) The crew left early.
(b) The wind filled the sails very gently.
(c) The sailors always loved the ocean.
(d) They sail ships quite expertly.
(e) Only the captain can make that decision.
(f) Apparently, a storm may delay the trip.

4. Degree or adverb?

Determine whether the adverbs in each of the following phrases are modified by a degree word or by a degree adverb, or by an adverb that does not have a degree interpretation. Justify your answer.

(a) I am *impossibly* happy!
(b) That story rings *quite* true.
(c) The car was *significantly* damaged.

(d) I was *unexpectedly* nervous before my presentation.
(e) The toddler was *visibly* frustrated.
(f) The owl is known as *inherently* wise.
(g) The obstacle course was *incredibly* easy.
(h) This *rather* large couch is hard to move.
(i) The textbooks for this course are *outrageously* expensive.

5. Practice

Here are some text excerpts to use for practice in finding adverbs and adverb phrases. We've (as always) provided a few suggestions about what to look for. Remember that there may not be examples in these texts of everything listed here, and we encourage you to explore texts of your own choosing to find additional examples.

(a) Find all the adverb phrases and try to identify their semantic class (time, manner, etc.).
(b) Which adverbs, if any, are derived from adjectives?
(c) Are there any *flat* adverbs?
(d) Analyze the morphology of the adverbs you find. Are any comparative or superlative?
(e) What words or phrases do the adverb phrases that you identified modify?
(f) Find any conjunctive adverbs.
(g) What modifiers of adverbs did you find? Are the modifiers degree words or adverb phrases?
(h) Discuss briefly any problematic examples that you found, and how you analyzed them.

The pony, shaggy as a wintering bear, eased himself into a grudging trot, while the boy, bowed over with his cap pulled down over his ears and eyebrows, held the reins slack and fell into a brown study. I studied the harness, a real mystery. It met and clung in all sorts of unexpected places; it parted company in what appeared to be strategic seats of jointure. It was mended sketchily in risky places with bits of hairy rope. Other seemingly unimportant parts were bound together irrevocably with wire. The bridle was too long for the pony's stocky head, so he had shaken the bit out of his mouth at the start, apparently, and went his own way at his own pace. (From *Holiday*, by Katherine Anne Porter.)

Outside, butterflies and bees were hovering lazily over the grass and hedgerow. Harry was rather uncomfortable. The Muggle boy whose appearance he was affecting was slightly fatter than him, and his dress

Adverbs

robes felt hot and tight in the full glare of a summer's day. (*Harry Potter and the Deathly Hallows*, by J.K. Rowling.)

Harry looked back at Travers, who was still rooted to the spot looking abnormally vacant, and made his decision: With a flick of his wand he made Travers come with them, walking meekly in their wake as they reached the door and passed into the rough stone passageway beyond, which was lit with flaming torches. (*Harry Potter and the Deathly Hallows*, by J.K. Rowling.)

Soon, he was writing about crime and growing acquainted with the more sordid side of city life. Yet, later in his career, when Simenon spoke of his style, he generally avoided creding newspaper work or the shaping practice of motion pictures. Instead, he loftily gave credit to Gogol and Cezanne – Gogol for the surreal edge of dark fable and Cézanne for the weighty individual stroke, the repetitive rhythm. ("The Secret Source," by Ken Okri, *The New Yorker*, September 19, 2022.)

Adverbs

Prepositions and Particles

Introduction

We've already mentioned prepositional phrases (PPs) here and there throughout the book. You know, for example, that PPs show up as subjective complements, as in *My plans are up in the air*. In this chapter, we investigate

Navigating English Grammar: A Guide to Analyzing Real Language, Second Edition.
Anne Lobeck and Kristin Denham.
© 2025 Anne Lobeck and Kristin Denham. Published 2025 by John Wiley & Sons Ltd.

the semantics, morphology, and syntax of prepositions and prepositional phrases in more detail. We will discuss different prepositions and their meanings, and see that unlike the categories Noun, Verb, Adjective, and Adverb, the category Preposition is a closed, rather than open class. Prepositions are similar to other categories, however, in selecting complements of a variety of different categories. We will investigate the grammatical functions of prepositional phrases as complements and modifiers. We will also discuss the differences between *objects of prepositions* and *indirect objects*, adding two more complement types to our list. We close the chapter with a discussion of a special set of prepositions called *particles*, which have the unique property of being able to "shift" around the object of the verb. We will explore *particle shift* and other properties that distinguish particles from prepositions, and what these differences tell us about syntactic structure.

Preposition Semantics

In general, prepositions are words whose meanings are really best described in terms of their relationship to a noun phrase. That is, prepositions typically express some kind of grammatical relationship of their NP object to the rest of the sentence. A traditional trick to help you remember what prepositions are is to think of them as "any way an airplane can fly in relation to a cloud" or "anything a rabbit can do to a hill." For example, the following prepositions express spatial or directional relationships of the noun phrases they combine with:

space, direction:
below, between, under, across, along, beyond, past, by, into, in, behind, down, over, around, up, through, at, to

Prepositions can also express location:

location:
at, in, on

Still other prepositions express neither spatial, directional, nor locative relationships. Some prepositions express temporal relationships:

time:
The party started *at/by/after* 10 p.m.
The party went on *until* 10 p.m.
The party had been going on *since* 10 p.m.

But that's not all; here are some more relationships expressed by prepositions:

reason:
He was fired *because* he took the money.

cause:
He was fired *for* the offense.

means:
We traveled *by* air.

accompaniment:
I would like my sandwich *with* lettuce.

support/opposition:
We're *for/against* the idea.

possession:
It was a glass *with* a gold rim.
They bought a book *of* poems.

exception/addition:
We had a great time *apart from/despite* the snowstorm.

instrument:
We cut the cheesecake *with* a knife.

benefactive:
I baked a cake *for* the party.

Prepositions can have quite complex semantics, as indicated by their many possible meanings. And a single preposition can also have more than one meaning:

a book *by* the famous author
a path *by* the river

Their differences in meaning can be quite subtle:

walk *into* a room
walk *into* a wall

But, although prepositions may seem more like lexical categories with complex meanings, notice that their meanings are also functional, expressing different relationships of their noun phrase complements. The preposition *into*, for example, has a certain meaning that is best described in terms of its relationship to a room or a wall.

Which prepositions are used varies among English speakers. If you live in New York you might wait *on line* for a movie, while you wait *in line* most other places. Many younger speakers do something *on accident* while older ones do it *by accident*. And are you sick *to your stomach* or sick *at your stomach* or sick *on your stomach*?

Prepositions as inflections

We have discussed how Old English was a more synthetic language than Present Day English, conveying grammatical information through inflectional affixation. Prepositions have taken over a lot of this work since English became more analytic. For example, consider the following Old English phrases: *þæs cyninges* meant "of the king," while *þæm cyninge* meant "to the king." In these examples, the forms of the determiner *þæs/þæm*, together with the inflectional ending on the noun *cyning* (-es/-e, respectively), express the relationships we now express with prepositions (*of* and *to*).

Preposition Morphology

Although some prepositions have "contentful" and complex meanings, as do other lexical categories, they are also like functional categories in expressing grammatical relationships. Some prepositions seem purely functional; for example, the preposition *of* in *a cup of coffee* has no lexical meaning but only expresses a relationship between *cup* and *coffee*. Another reason to think of prepositions as a functional category is that they are a closed class; we haven't added new members to the class of English prepositions for hundreds of years.

Yet another reason to analyze the category Preposition as a functional category is that in some other languages, prepositions are inflections, not separate words (see the box "Prepositions as Inflections" on prepositions replacing case endings). Though English prepositions take no inflectional affixes, they do have interesting morphology. Some are formed historically from derivational affixation (prefixation) and compounding, as illustrated in the following examples.

prefixing:
a-: aboard, above, about, across, against, along, amid, amidst, among, around

be-: before, behind, below, beneath, beside, besides, between, betwixt, beyond

compounding:
into, throughout, toward(s), underneath, until, unto, upon, within, without

There are also prepositions that derive from participles, affixed with *-ing*.

No one could visit the prisoner, *barring* her lawyer.
We left *during* halftime.

We don't invent new prepositions, but we do borrow them from other languages from time to time. Both *during* and *barring* derive from Old French words (*dure* "endure" and *barre* "bar") borrowed into Old English (and, interestingly, affixed with an Old English suffix *-ing*). English has also borrowed *vis-à-vis* ("face to face") and *sans* ("without") from French.

The politician's position has changed *vis-à-vis* the energy bill.
An elegant breakfast was served, *sans* eggs.

And the Latin prepositions *super* (above), *sub* (under), and *circum* (around) among others are commonly used to form English words such as *Superwoman*, *subhuman*, and *circumnavigate*. Greek prepositions show up in English words too: *peri* (around, near), *epi* (upon), *hyper* (over), *hypo* (under), as in *perimeter*, *epiphenomenon*, *hyperextend*, or *hypochondriac*.

Preposition Syntax

In this section, we explore the internal syntax of the PP, and the types of complements that prepositions take. We will then turn to the grammatical functions of these PPs in the clause, as modifiers or as complements themselves.

Complements of prepositions

Prepositions typically take complements, and the most common complement of a preposition is a noun phrase. As we'll see, prepositions can also take VP, PP, and even clause complements.

Objects of prepositions
Typically, prepositions express relationships between noun phrases and the rest of the sentence, and so it's not surprising that they form phrases with

NPs. In the following examples of PPs, the head preposition (P) is in italics, and the complement of the preposition (NP) is bracketed.

The goats frolicked *in* [the meadow].
A mouse scampered *up* [the drainpipe].
We got home *before* [midnight].

In these examples, the head P takes an NP complement. This complement is called simply an *object of a preposition*. We can write a basic phrase structure rule for PP as below:

PP → P NP

Other complements of prepositions
Though the most common type of PP has the structure P+NP, prepositions actually select a range of different complements other than NPs, including VP, PP, and CL complements.

without [saying anything to Mary]
P   VP complement

up [on the hill]
P PP complement

after [we ate dinner]
P   CL complement

Here are some tree diagrams of these PPs:

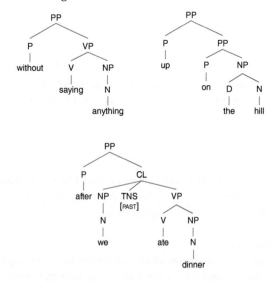

Here is a partial list of prepositions that take VP and CL complements.

after/before/without/while/despite/by [signing the peace treaty]$_{\text{VP}}$

since/because/although/even though/until/when [they signed the peace treaty]$_{\text{CL}}$

As you may have noticed, some of these words are not typically what you might have considered prepositions (*even though*, *because*, *when*, and so on). Prepositions that select clause complements are often called *subordinating prepositions* (or more traditionally, "subordinating conjunctions"), because they take subordinate clause complements. We return to a full discussion of subordinating prepositions in Chapter 11.

In order to accommodate the various kinds of phrases that can show up as complements of prepositions, we'll revise our phrase structure rule using XP, where X can be any category (NP, VP, CL, etc.).

PP → P XP   X = any category

Modifiers of prepositions

Many (but not all) prepositions can be preceded by a certain set of function words that express degree. Though these degree words differ from those that modify adjectives and adverbs, we will assume these words are also members of the category DEG. These degree words may vary from dialect to dialect, so not all of them might be familiar to you.

The squirrel ran *flat/straight/right/plumb/clear* up the tree.

We can now diagram simple PPs with degree modifiers as follows:

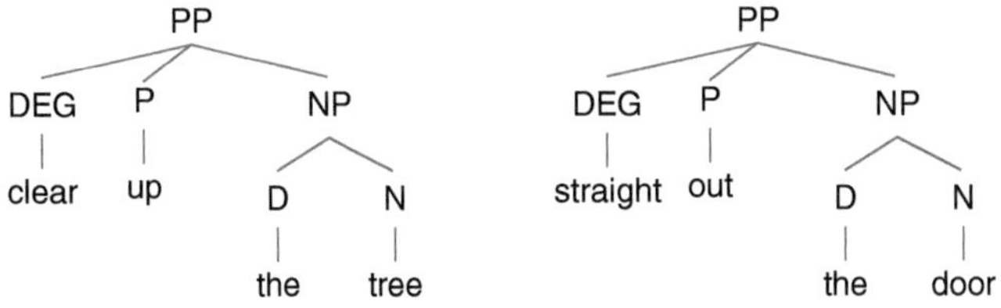

Each of these PPs contains an object of a preposition: *the tree* and *the door*, respectively.

Certain adverbs can also modify prepositions:

just below the surface
almost at the top

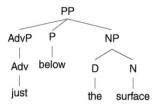

Sometimes, prepositions that select other complements, such as VP or CL complements, can also be modified by degree words or adverbs:

> **Right** *before they signed the treaty*, the news was leaked to the press.
> They won't necessarily get along **just** *because they signed a treaty*.

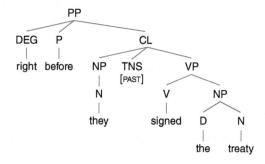

Just as with AdvP and AP, we can include (DEG) in our phrase structure rule for PP.

PP → (DEG) P XP

Prepositional phrases as modifiers and complements

Now that we have a basic understanding of the internal structure of PPs, in the following sections we'll investigate the different grammatical functions of PPs in the clause. We will first look at how PPs modify nouns, and then at how they can modify verb phrases and clauses. We will then explore PP complements of verbs and other categories and we introduce another type of complement, *indirect objects*.

PP modifiers of nouns
Like APs, PPs can modify nouns. PP modifiers usually occur in postnominal position as illustrated in these examples (the modified nouns are in italics here and the PP in brackets).

the *cat* [with a collar]
my *brother* [from North Carolina]
six *books* [about insects]
the little *girl* [down the street]

Like AP modifiers, PP modifiers add more information to the description of the noun and restrict or limit the denotation of the noun. That is, *a book*, without a PP modifier, refers to a member of the set of books. But *a book about insects*, on the other hand, refers to a more limited set, namely, a member of the set of books about insects.

PP modifiers of verbs and clauses
As we mentioned at the end of Chapter 8, PPs can sometimes modify the verb or the clause much in the same way as an adverb phrase.

She smiled at me *happily*. (AdvP)
She smiled at me *in a happy way*. (PP)

She isn't very happy *now*. (AdvP)
She isn't very happy *at this moment*. (PP)

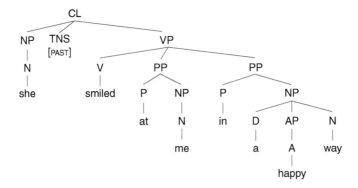

In these examples, the PP, like the AdvP, is not a complement of the verb; each simply adds extra information to the clause or verb phrase, including information about speaker attitude, time, or reason. Below we give some more examples of PP modifiers, which occur in either clause-initial or clause-final position:

At noon we will be on our way.
We left the restaurant *after the party was over*.
Without asking permission, Lulu rode her sister's bicycle.
They went skiing yesterday *because they had the day off*.

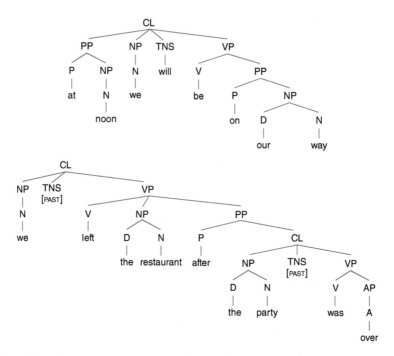

We will return to a more in-depth discussion of these and other modifiers in Chapter 11.

PPs as complements
Recall from the above discussion that a PP can sometimes be the complement of another preposition.

> The water gushed *out* [of the pipe].
> We found the hat *up* [in the attic].
> They looked *in* [on the kids].

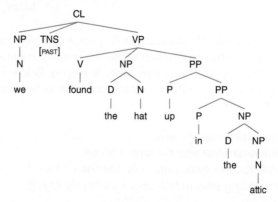

Prepositions and Particles

Certain verbs also take PPs as complements. You are already familiar with *PP subjective complements* of linking verbs. These PP subjective complements have nonliteral interpretations (similar in meaning to AP subjective complements).

Hillary was feeling *under the weather*. (= sick)
I'm feeling *over the hill*. (= old)
The building was *in bad shape*. (= decrepit)

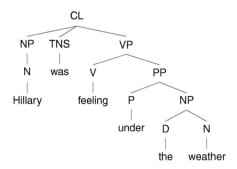

And other verbs can take PP complements that express direction or location.

The kids skipped *down the street*.
They walked *to the station*.
Her friend works *in that office building*.

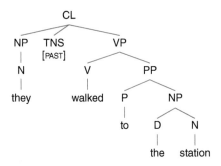

PPs also show up as complements of a variety of other types of verbs. The verbs *blame* and *put* take PP complements and also take direct object NPs, as in the following examples.

177

Rue and Lon always blame [everything] [on each other].
                          NP   PP

They put [their old clothes] [in a box].
          NP   PP

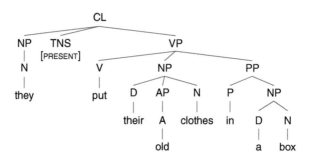

Adjectives can also take PP complements.

fond [*of horses*]
proud [*of her children*]
happy [*about the promotion*]
crazy [*for you*]

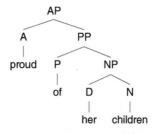

Indirect object complements
In this section, we will discuss a particular subset of PP complements, PPs
that include *indirect object* NPs. As we'll see, these PP complements differ in
important ways from those discussed above, and we will learn about some
of their properties, and about how to distinguish these PPs from others. To
begin, consider the following sentences:

The students gave [their exams] [to the professor].
                   NP   PP

Ursula baked [a cake] [for her brother].
             NP   PP

These sentences look very much like those we just discussed with *blame* and *put*; in each example, the verb is followed by a direct object NP, and then by another complement, a PP (which also contains another NP). So, each verb takes two complements, NP and PP.

Rue and Lon always blame [everything] [on each other].
                               NP   PP

They put [their old clothes] [in a box].
       NP   PP

The objects of the prepositions in these two sets of sentences, however, are syntactically and semantically quite distinct. The prepositions *to* and *for* in the first two sentences select *indirect object NP complements*, but the prepositions *in* and *on* in the second set of sentences select objects of prepositions.

We can distinguish indirect objects from other objects of prepositions quite easily. Just as we saw with Passive as a test for direct objects, there is a syntactic operation that applies only to indirect objects, but not to objects of prepositions. We can use this rule, *Indirect Object Movement*, as a test for indirect objects. We illustrate how this rule works below:

The students gave [their exams] [to the professor].
                     direct object   indirect object

The students gave [the professor] [their exams]
                    indirect object direct object

Ursula baked [a cake]   [for her brother].
             direct object   indirect object

Ursula baked [her brother]   [a cake].
           indirect object direct object

Informally, Indirect Object Movement "moves" the direct object to the right and the indirect object to the left. The preposition, either *to* or *for*, is deleted. Below, we give tree diagrams for a clause before and after Indirect Object Movement applies.

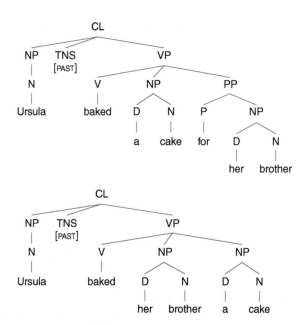

There are a number of verbs in English that take indirect objects, and these verbs have many different labels. They are called "double object" verbs, "ditransitive" verbs, or "dative" verbs. We'll call them *ditransitive* verbs here, a label which means "takes two objects." Here are some more examples of ditransitive verbs: *give, sell, take, bake, send, write, offer, tell, find.*

As you can see from the following examples, *blame* and *put* don't allow Indirect Object Movement, which tells us that the objects of the prepositions *on* and *in* here are not indirect objects, they're just garden-variety objects of prepositions (and *blame* and *put* therefore are not ditransitive verbs).

Rue and Lon always blame [everything] [on each other].
                                    NP   PP

*Rue and Lon always blame [each other] [everything].
                                  object of P   direct object

They put [their old clothes] [in a box].
                 NP   PP

*They put [a box]   [their old clothes].
                object of P   direct object

We know that the complements of *on* and *in* are not possible indirect objects, not only because they don't undergo Indirect Object Movement but also because only the prepositions *to* and *for* take indirect objects complements;

on and *in* do not. We really, then, only need to test whether an NP is an indirect object or not when it is the object of *to* or *for*.

That indirect objects occur with the prepositions *to* or *for* in English is not accidental. An indirect object is typically understood as the beneficiary/recipient (or "goal" in this sense) of the direct object. It makes sense, then, that indirect objects will not occur as objects of other prepositions such as *on, at, with,* and so on, because the objects of these prepositions don't have the appropriate meanings to be indirect objects. This also suggests that objects of the prepositions *to* and *for*, when they are *not* beneficiaries or recipients, are also not indirect objects. To test this hypothesis, see if Indirect Object Movement applies in the following sentences. If not, why not?

We drove [the truck] [to Baltimore].
*We drove [Baltimore] [the truck].

The children played [the game] [for three hours].
*The children played [three hours] [the game].

In these examples, Indirect Object Movement clearly fails, which tells us that neither *Baltimore* nor *three hours* is an indirect object. Rather, these NPs are simply objects of the prepositions (directional) *to* and (durative) *for*.

Below, we summarize the basic properties of indirect objects. You can use these as a way to test whether an NP is an indirect object or not.

Indirect objects:

- occur only with ditransitive verbs
- occur only in PP with *to* and *for*
- are typically goals, beneficiaries, or receivers of the direct object
- undergo Indirect Object Movement

Indirect objects in other languages

Indirect objects don't always show up in other languages as they do in English. In French, for example, indirect object NPs look similar to their English counterparts:

Il achète des livres pour les filles.
he buys some books for the girls
"He buys books for the girls."

Continued on p. 182

Prepositions and Particles

Continued

But when the indirect object is a pronoun, it precedes the verb.

Il leur achète des livres.
He them buys books.
"He buys books for them."

In German and other case-marking languages, indirect objects show up with distinct case markings.

Er kauft die Bücher für das Mädchen.
he buys the books for the girl
"He buys the books for the girl."

Er kauft dem Mädchen die Bücher.
he buys the girl the books
"He buys the girl the books."

In the first example, *das* is in Accusative case as the object of für "for." But in the second sentence (where Indirect Object Movement has applied as in English, and *für* disappears), *dem* has Dative case, the case that marks the indirect object in German.

Particles

In this section, we turn to a subset of prepositions in English, called *particles*. Particles have unique syntax and semantics that distinguish them from prepositions.

Particle semantics

Here are some examples of particles. Consider their meanings and their relationship to the verb.

I looked *up* the number.
We ran *down* the batteries.

What do *up* and *down* mean here? Do they mean the same thing as in the following sentences?

I looked *up* the tree.
We ran *down* the street.

Clearly, the particles *up* and *down* differ in meaning from the prepositions *up* and *down*. Particles form a semantic unit with the verb, with a unique, often idiomatic meaning.

look up = search for
run down = deplete

Neither of these meanings has anything obvious to do with the directional meanings of the prepositions *up* and *down*. This is one reason why verb + particle combinations are often called *phrasal verbs*. (These combinations are also called *multi-word verbs, two-word verbs, separable compounds, poly-word verbs,* and *separable verbs*.) They are generally described as being a verb plus a second element – a particle – which, combining closely with the verb, expresses a verbal concept that the verb alone does not express.

Here are some more examples of verb-particle combinations, with particles *on, out,* and *in*. Consider their meanings and how they differ from the corresponding prepositional meanings in the second set of sentences.

particles:
Please turn *on* the lights.
Rue will pick *out* a present.
Leola should hand *in* the papers.

prepositions:
Please don't step *on* that beetle!
Rue has run *out* the door.
Leola should be *in* that class.

In these examples, the meanings of the particles differ from the corresponding prepositional meanings. As we'll see in the following section, there is quite a bit of evidence that particles and prepositions differ syntactically as well.

Particle syntax

Recall that prepositions can take NP complements, called objects of prepositions. At first glance, particles look like they might take objects as well. But on closer inspection, we see that the object in a verb-particle construction behaves quite differently from the object of a preposition. This evidence suggests that the object in a verb-particle construction is not the object of a preposition at all, but rather a direct object.

One way that particles differ from prepositions is that particles can move to the right, around the object NP. Prepositions can't. We call this rule *Particle Shift*.

particles:
We looked *up* the number. → We looked the number *up*.
We turned *on* the light. → We turned the light *on*.
I handed *in* my paper. → I handed my paper *in*.

prepositions:
We climbed *up* the tree. → *We climbed the tree *up*.
We ran *up* a hill. → *We ran a hill *up*.
I walked *out* the door. → *I walked the door *out*.

How do we explain these differences, and what do they tell us? That a particle, but not a preposition, can move about on its own suggests that the particle does not form a constituent with the NP object. In other words, the particle and NP do not form a phrase, or PP. Rather, the particle is better analyzed as a (separable) part of the verb.

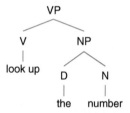

A preposition, on the other hand, forms a constituent with its complement, namely, a PP.

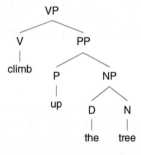

A particle, then, can separate from the verb and move around the NP object, but a preposition can't.

A preposition and its object, which together form a PP, can move as a constituent:

I climbed up the tree.
Up the tree, I climbed.
It was *up the tree* that I climbed.

Because the particle does not form a constituent with the NP object, it can't move with NP:

I looked up the number.
Up the number I looked.
*It was *up the number* I looked.

This different syntactic behavior tells us that while a preposition and its object form a constituent, particles do not form a constituent with the NP object. What does that mean about the NP object in particle constructions? If it's not the object of a preposition, what is it? Notice that the NP object in a particle construction can undergo Passive:

The operator looked up *the number*.
The number was looked up (by the operator).

The child turned on *the light*.
The light was turned on (by the child).

The students handed in *the papers*.
The papers were handed in (by the students).

But objects of prepositions don't passivize as easily.

The child climbed up *the tree*.
The tree was climbed up (by the child).

The man ran up *the hill*.
The hill was run up (by the man).

The dog ran out *the door*.
The door was run out (by the dog).

Only direct objects passivize, so this suggests that the object in a particle construction is a direct object of the [verb + particle] unit. Even though the particle can separate from the verb (and move around the direct object) it is still part of the verb in some sense (hence the term "two-word verbs" for verb + particle constructions). Particles are therefore distinct from prepositions, which form a constituent, namely, a PP, with their NP complement, an object of a preposition.

Given what we now know about particles, how can we analyze constructions such as the following?

Shut *up*!
I never give *up*.
Oh, come *on*.
If you go *out*, don't try to come back *in*.

In these examples, there is no object at all. Are the words *up*, *on*, *out*, and *in*
particles here, or prepositions? We can't test them by moving them around
the object, because there isn't one. We'll leave further analysis of these up
to you!

Summary

Prepositions come in a variety of shapes and sizes, and express a range of
different meanings, though they are morphologically **a closed class**. We
don't add new prepositions to the language in any productive way, but
English has borrowed prepositions from other languages, and some
English prepositions have remnants of inflectional and derivational morphology. Like members of the lexical categories Adverb and Adjective,
prepositions can be modified by (a certain small set of) **degree words**
(*right* or *clear*, for example), and sometimes by adverbs (*just*, *almost*).
Prepositions can also take a range of complements, including **NP objects
of prepositions**, as well as **VP**, **PP**, and even **CL complements**, the complements of **subordinating prepositions**. PPs often function as **modifiers**
(of nouns, verbs, and clauses), and also as complements of linking verbs,
as **PP subjective complements**, and as the complements of other verbs
such as *put*, which we simply refer to as **PP complements**. PPs also show
up as complements of **ditransitive** verbs, verbs that take both direct object
and **indirect object complements**. Indirect objects show up in PPs headed
by *to/for* and differ from other NPs in their semantic role as recipient or
beneficiary of the direct object. Indirect objects are also distinct from other
NP complements in being able to undergo **Indirect Object Movement**.
We concluded the chapter with a short discussion of a subset of prepositions, called **particles**, which form a syntactic and semantic unit with the
verb. Particles are distinct from prepositions in not forming a constituent
with an NP object. Rather, the verb and its particle take a direct object
complement, and the particle can undergo **Particle Shift**, moving around
that direct object.

Exercises

1. Finding prepositional phrases

Here, just practice finding PPs. Some sentences have them and some don't, and some may have more than one!

(a) Columns of smoke rose from the chimney.
(b) She will eat peanut butter sandwiches only with blueberry jelly.
(c) Morgan and Stacy left for Portugal on the same day.
(d) It is clear to the researchers that the gemstones found in the ship-wreck are from Africa.
(e) The subway runs under the city and out to the suburbs.

2. Diagramming practice

Draw tree diagrams for the following PPs. What is the complement of each P? Label the category of each complement (NP, PP, VP, CL). Some PPs here have modifiers – are they degree words or adverbs?

(a) straight out the door
(b) by the house
(c) after the store closed
(d) over under the tree
(e) while eating pizza
(f) just beyond the fence
(g) without having a reason
(h) up in the air
(i) right behind my chair
(j) only at night

3. PP complements of verbs and adjectives

Each of the following sentences contains a PP that is the complement of either a verb or an adjective. Identify each PP and label each as a complement of V or A.

(a) The people were sad about the outcome.
(b) The squirrel scampered up the tree.
(c) She placed the knife on the table.
(d) The child glanced at the teacher.
(e) She was ecstatic about the promotion.

(f) All the students are sick of working so hard.

(g) That haircut of yours seems over the top.

4. PP modifiers of nouns and verbs

Each of the following sentences contains (at least one) PP modifier. Find each PP modifier and try to identify the category of the word that it modifies. Does it modify a noun, or a verb?

(a) The students read a book about climate change.

(b) We found two frogs that were hiding under the leaves.

(c) The hikers brought extra bottles of water just in case.

(d) I checked the dates before texting my friend.

(e) Lois met two sisters from New Jersey on the ferry.

(f) The store will open at 10.

5. Subordinating PPs

We will discuss subordinating PPs much more in Chapter 11, but for now, simply see if you can identify them in the following sentences. Remember that a subordinating PP is a PP modifier that has the syntactic structure of P+CL, so be looking for clauses as complements of P. Not all of the following sentences include a subordinating PP.

(a) After the professor left the room the students cheered.

(b) Reese was annoyed because we forgot the keys.

(c) Although it was late, they decided to finish the movie.

(d) Out behind the barn they discovered a huge pile of old lumber.

(e) Never talk to the chef when they are in the middle of cooking!

(f) We hear owls hooting almost every night of the week.

(g) Across the river the fire continued to burn uncontrollably.

6. Indirect object movement

Remember that we can distinguish indirect objects from objects of prepositions by using Indirect Object Movement as a test.

The doctor gave [a vaccine] to [the patient]. →
The doctor gave [the patient] [a vaccine].

Using Indirect Object Movement, determine whether the italic NPs within PPs are indirect objects or objects of prepositions.

(a)   Bo put the bike in *the shed*.
(b)   We gave a biscuit to *the dog*.
(c)   The child made the card for *her friend*.
(d)   They took the best route to *the beach*.
(e)   Noah sent some flowers to *his mother*.
(f)   Sheila cut the salami with *a knife*.
(g)   They hadn't seen each other for *a long time*.

7.   Preposition or particle?

Determine whether the italic words are prepositions or particles. Use Particle Shift as a test!

(a)   We often refer *to* your paper.
(b)   They climbed *up* the fence.
(c)   We coped *with* the neighbor's visit.
(d)   The teacher took *off* their hat.
(e)   The children ran *down* the stairs.
(f)   The children ran *down* the batteries.
(g)   Rue looked *for* a banana.
(h)   Rue picked *up* a banana.
(i)   The kids rode their bikes *around* the block.

8.   Passive and indirect object movement

Recall that when Indirect Object Movement occurs, the indirect object and direct object "change places."

Lucy sent *a letter* to *Pete*. → Lucy sent *Pete a letter*.

What happens when Passive applies to the first sentence above? What happens when it applies in the second sentence? The result should be two different passive sentences. Why?

9.   Practice

Here are some text excerpts to use for practice in finding prepositional phrases. We provide a few suggestions about what to look for. As always, if you find something difficult to analyze, explain as best as you can why. And as always, remember that there may not be examples in these texts of everything listed here, and we encourage you to explore texts of your own choosing to find additional examples.

(a) Find all the prepositional phrases.
(b) Identify any PP modifiers of nouns or other categories.
(c) Identify some NP objects of prepositions.
(d) Identify any PP complements of verbs or adjectives.
(e) Are any of the PPs you find contained inside larger PPs?
(f) Are any of the PPs you find subjective complements?
(g) Do any of the PPs you find contain indirect objects (and how do you know?)
(h) Are there any particles in the text? How do you know?
(i) Can you identify any subordinating PPs?

On a Wednesday afternoon in the student union café, Corliss looked up from her American history textbook and watched a young man and younger woman walk in together and sit two tables away. The student union wasn't crowded, so Corliss clearly heard the young couple's conversation. He offered her coffee from his thermos, but she declined. Hurt by her rejection, or feigning pain – he always carried two cups because, well, you never know, do you? – he poured himself one, sipped and sighed with theatrical pleasure, and monologued. (From *Ten Little Indians*, by Sherman Alexie.)

About the most cheerful person in Le Roy, New York, the other day was Lynne Belluscio, the curator of the local Jell-O museum, which commemorates the town's history as the "birthplace of Jell-O." "We've had visitors from Canada, from Sri Lanka," she said, reciting highlights from a recent uptick in traffic. … She stood at the entrance to the museum's main gallery and cast a satisfied glance at the guestbook, open to a page filled with ink, which was displayed under a jaunty archway – a structure featuring the word "JELL-O" in red wood suspended between two enormous white spoons. (From "Le Roy Postcard: Hysterical," by Emily Eakin, *The New Yorker*, March 5, 2012.)

Although organisms have evolved to live in diverse conditions, closely related species often inhabit vastly different environments. This is particularly true for aquatic animals such as squid and octopus, which are common in tropical waters but are also found at the poles. These cephalopods have highly developed nervous systems, and one challenging question is how temperature-sensitive neuronal synaptic transmission has adapted to function at a near-freezing temperature. (From "A Cold Editor Makes the Adaptation," by Marie Öhman, *Science* 335, February 17, 2012.)

Coordination and Subordination

Introduction

You are now familiar with basic clause structure, which we can represent with the phrase structure rule below:

CL → NP (TNS) VP

You are also familiar with independent clauses, tensed clauses that are not embedded in or part of another phrase. In this chapter, we'll investigate

Navigating English Grammar: A Guide to Analyzing Real Language, Second Edition.
Anne Lobeck and Kristin Denham.
© 2025 Anne Lobeck and Kristin Denham. Published 2025 by John Wiley & Sons Ltd.

ways that we combine clauses, using *coordination* or *subordination*. Coordination allows us to string clauses together like this:

[The sky is blue] and [the earth is flat]
CL   CL

And subordination allows us to "embed" a clause within a larger one like this:

[Cary thinks [that the earth is flat]].
CL   CL

Coordination and subordination allow us to form sentences of infinite length, but these processes are distinct from each other in important ways, which we discuss in this chapter. In the course of our discussion, we'll find that not all clauses must be tensed; in fact, subordinate clauses are often not tensed (which is why TNS in the above phrase structure rule is optional).

Coordination

Coordination is the process by which we connect phrases and clauses with one or more of the *coordinating conjunctions*. (The acronym FANBOYS can help you remember these conjunctions.)

coordinating conjunctions:
for, and, nor, but, or, yet, so

We can coordinate almost any phrase or word with another one, as long as they are of the same category. This property of coordination is called *parallelism*. To illustrate how parallelism works, consider the following examples:

Juno ate [chocolate chip cookies] and [potato chips].
                NP   NP

*Juno ate [chocolate chip cookies] and [voraciously].
                NP   ADVP

Coordination is grammatical in the first example, where we've coordinated two phrases of the same category (NP) with the coordinating conjunction *and*. Parallelism is violated in the second sentence, where we have conjoined two non-like categories, NP and AdvP.

Here's another example, where parallelism is violated in the second clause, but not the first:

Rue walked [a collie] and [a schnauzer].
        NP   NP

*Rue walked [a collie] and [to the store].
         NP   PP

We can also coordinate single words (numerals and verbs for example), not just phrases:

I can eat [six] or [seven] pancakes for breakfast.
      NUM   NUM

The child [kissed] and [hugged] the doll.
      V   V

Syntactic parallelism doesn't always hold, particularly with complements of linking verbs. This might be because subjective complements, regardless of category, describe the subject NP. They are therefore semantically, if not syntactically, parallel regardless of category.

Mark is a [great person] and [fun to be around].
      NP   AP

My brother was [upset] and [in a total funk].
        AP   PP

As we might expect, we can coordinate independent clauses, just as we coordinate phrases of other categories:

[Mark is a great person] and [he is fun to be around].
CL   CL

[My brother was upset] and [he was in a total funk].
CL   CL

Two independent clauses can be conjoined not just by one of the FANBOYS, but also by *conjunctive adverbs*, which we introduced in Chapter 8.

nevertheless, consequently, furthermore, therefore, hence, moreover, etc.

The party was over; *nevertheless,* the guests refused to leave.
They didn't do the homework; *consequently,* their grade dropped.

As we'll see, coordination is syntactically quite different from subordination. When we coordinate two or more elements, one is not contained within the other. We can represent coordination schematically like this:

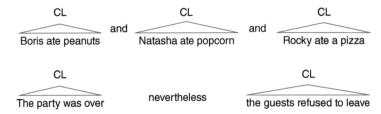

Though coordination might seem pretty straightforward, it's not always clear which constituent is coordinated with which. For example, which constituents are coordinated in the following sentence?

Wiley likes beans and rice.

If you came up with *beans* and *rice*, two NPs, you're right. But, you may have come up with the following analysis, where the NP *rice* is coordinated with the phrase *Wiley likes beans*. This analysis violates parallelism:

[Wiley likes beans] and [rice].

A useful way to determine which constituents are coordinated is to analyze coordination "from right to left." Take the sentence,

Wiley likes beans and rice.

Find the constituent on the right of the coordinating conjunction, and then find a parallel constituent on the left. In the above example, the constituent on the right of *and* is *rice*. *Rice* is in this case an NP, so it must be coordinated with another NP, namely, *beans*, but not the phrase *Wiley likes beans*. This distinction becomes more clear when we take a look at the tree diagram for this sentence:

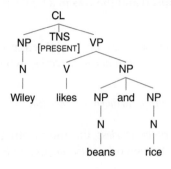

194

As you can see here, *beans and rice* form the object of the verb *likes*. We can replace this larger NP with a pronoun, providing further evidence that *beans and rice* form a constituent:

Wiley likes *them*.   (*them* = *beans and rice*)

Subordination

Subordination differs in important ways from coordination, though both allow us to combine phrases into larger units. Subordination involves only clauses, where one clause is contained within another, like this:

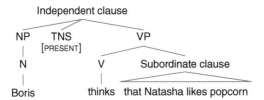

A *subordinate clause* (also called an *embedded* or *dependent* clause) is a clause that is dominated by another constituent. This can occur in a variety of ways. In this example, the clause *that Natasha likes popcorn* is the complement of the verb *think* and occurs in the same position as other complements of verbs we have discussed in previous chapters. The clause *that Natasha likes popcorn* is therefore contained in another phrase, here, the VP, and so it is by definition a subordinate clause.

Subordination provides us with a good example of *recursion*, the means by which we can form phrases of unlimited length by embedding one within another. (We discuss the word *that*, which introduces each subordinate clause in this example, later in the chapter.)

[Olive said [that Wyatt passed the exam]].
CL   CL

We can embed the above clause within yet another clause:

[Peter thinks [that Olive said [that Wyatt passed the exam]]].
CL   CL   CL

195

And we can make this independent clause ever longer, by using more subordination:

[Peter thinks [that Olive said [that Wyatt hopes [that his teacher believes [that he passed the exam]]]]]
CL   CL   CL   CL   CL

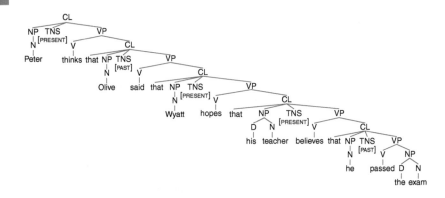

The above examples and diagrams illustrate how subordination differs from coordination. Recall that with coordination, phrases are linked to each other (on the same level) by coordinating conjunctions. With subordination, a clause is contained inside another phrase.

Clauses and sentences

We can now make a clear distinction between clauses and sentences. The following is both an independent clause *and* a sentence.

The child thinks that Wyatt likes beans.

And so is this:

The child believes that Bo said that Juno hoped that Rue had decided that Wyatt likes beans.

In this example, the sentence is made up of one (rather long) independent clause, one that contains several subordinate clauses, each bracketed below:

[The child believes [that Bo said [that Juno hoped [that Rue had decided [that Wyatt likes beans]]]]].
CL   CL   CL   CL   CL

196

Are independent clauses and sentences the same thing? In the examples we've looked at so far, we can say that independent clauses are sentences. But are *clauses* the same as sentences? No, because a sentence can contain more than one clause, for example, when an independent clause contains a subordinate one.

We can also create long sentences with coordination rather than subordination:

[Wyatt likes beans] *and* [Juno likes ice cream], *but* [Rue really loves potato chips].
CL   CL   CL

This sentence is made up of three independent clauses, coordinated with the conjunctions *and* and *but*. And here is a sentence in which two subordinate clauses are coordinated. This sentence therefore involves both coordination and subordination:

The child believes [that Wyatt likes beans] *and* [that Juno likes rice].

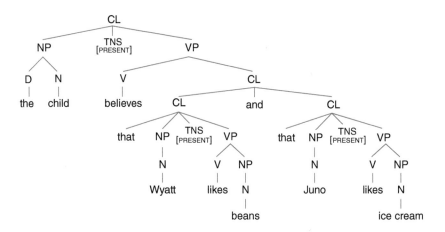

Using coordination and subordination, we can combine clauses to make longer sentences. A *sentence*, then, can be made up of numerous independent and/or subordinate clauses, so it can't really be defined in terms of the syntactic concept of *clause*. We can, however, define *sentence* in terms of written language and define *clause* in terms of syntactic structure:

sentence:
everything from the capital to the period

clause:
CL → NP (TNS) VP

independent clause:
a clause that is not dominated by another phrase

subordinate clause:
a clause that is dominated by another phrase

In the following section, we discuss different types of subordinate clauses. Recall from earlier chapters that independent clauses are by definition tensed clauses. As we will see, this is not the case for all subordinate clauses, for reasons we discuss below.

Subordinate Clause Types

A clause, as we've defined it, is a syntactic unit, which we expressed using the phrase structure rule:

CL → NP (TNS) VP

According to this definition, the following would all be clauses:

She *writes* biographies of famous people
The rain *pounding* on the roof
The students *to solve* the problem

In the first example, the main verb *writes* is in present tense (we use morphological inflections for illustration, but the points made here hold whether tense is expressed morphologically or not). In the second, the main verb *pounding* is a present participle, and in the third, *to solve* is an infinitive. Only the first example has a tensed verb. For this reason, only the first sentence above can be defined as an independent clause. Nevertheless, the other two are also clauses; each is made up of an NP subject and a VP predicate. The difference between the second and third clauses and the first one is simply that they lack tense, or, to put it another way, they lack a TNS position. This is allowed by our phrase structure rule, where TNS is optional.

We can easily "fix" the untensed clauses above by changing the verb from a participle and an infinitive, respectively, to a tensed verb.

The students *to solve* the problem → The students *solved* the problem.
The rain *pounding* on the roof → The rain *pounds* on the roof.

Each of these tensed clauses is also (now) an independent clause; neither clause is dominated by another phrase. Subordinate clauses, on the other hand, are by definition embedded in tensed independent clauses. It might come as no surprise, then, that clauses with tensed *or* untensed verbs work just fine as subordinate clauses:

I believe [she *writes* biographies of famous people].
CL

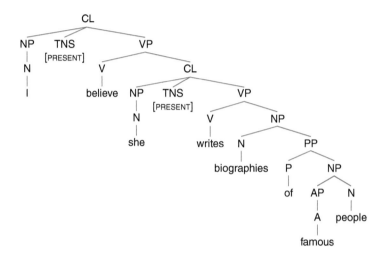

We heard [the rain *pounding* on the roof].
CL

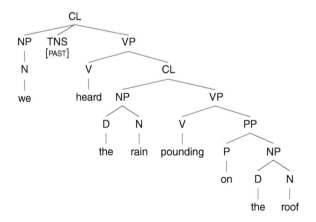

199

The teacher expects [the students *to solve* the problem].
CL

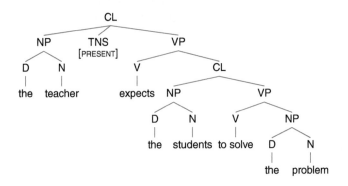

In the following sections, we'll go into a bit more detail to discuss different types of subordinate clauses and provide you with some tools to identify them.

Tensed clause complements

Tensed clause complements of verbs (here, *think, believe,* and *hope*) are fairly easy to identify because they include tensed verbs/verb strings.

The kids think [that the beans *grew* quickly].
CL

Susie believes [that the rain *will make* her depressed].
CL

The teacher hopes [that the students *understood* the theorem].
CL

And what about *that*? This little word is called a "complementizer" because it introduces a (tensed) clause complement. The complementizer *that* can't introduce an independent clause (we don't interpret the clauses below as independent clauses):

That the beans grew quickly.
That the rain will make her depressed.
That the students understood the theorem.

The complementizer *that* is also optional in tensed subordinate clause complements:

The kids think [the beans grew quickly].
           CL

Susie believes [the rain will make her depressed].
           CL

The teacher hoped [the students understood the theorem].
           CL

We can diagram tensed subordinate clause complements (with *that*) as follows:

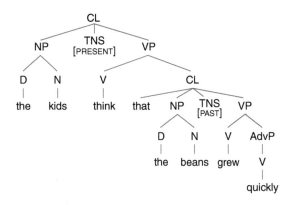

Complementizers in other languages

Other languages also have complementizers. Here's an example from Spanish where *que* is the complementizer (here, similar to English *that*); the subordinate clause, introduced by *que* is in brackets. Spanish, like English, has SVO word order.

Creo   [que Juan compro un perro].
believe.1sg that Juan bought a dog
"I believe that Juan bought a dog."

Japanese, a language with SOV word order, has a complementizer *to*:

Taroo-wa [Hanako-ga Ziroo-ni atta. to]   omotteiru
Taroo   Hanako   Ziroo   met that thinks
"Taroo thinks that Hanako met Ziroo."

Continued on p. 202

Continued

And here is an example from Irish, a VSO language, with the subordinate clause introduced by the complementizer *go*:

Ceapaim [go mbuaileann sé le   Séan inniu]
think.1sg that meets   he with John today.
"I think that he meets with John today."

(from Carnie, 2013, p. 282)

Adjectives can also take tensed clause complements.

Millicent seems [annoyed [that Bert won the award]].
             AP   CL

The players were [sad [that the game was postponed]].
             AP CL

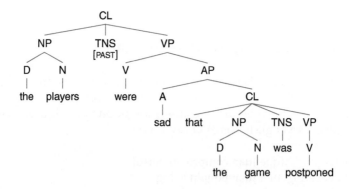

Certain prepositions can also take tensed clause complements (but note that *that* is not possible here, for reasons we leave aside):

Millicent brushed her teeth [after [she ate the cupcake]].
                       PP   CL

Lionel read the paper [before [he got on the bus]].
               PP   CL

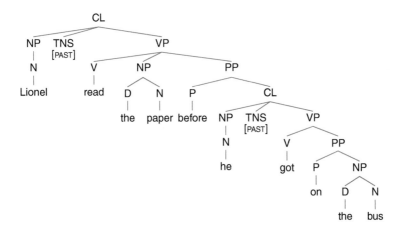

And finally, tensed clauses can also be complements of some nouns:

His [belief/guess [that the earth is round]] turned out to be right.
    NP   CL

Her [admission [that she had seen the incident]] influenced the verdict.
    NP   CL

Bare infinitival clause complements

As we mentioned above, subordinate clause complements are not always tensed; here's another type:

The crowd watched [the girl juggle some very sharp knives].
              CL

This subordinate clause differs from those discussed above in terms of the form of the verb. The verb *juggle* here is a *bare infinitive*. If it were tensed (using tense morphology for illustration), it would show up as *juggles/juggled* (but both forms are ungrammatical here).

Bare infinitival complements typically occur with perception verbs such as *watch, observe, hear, see,* and *feel,* among some others.

The kids saw [the cat catch the bird].
        CL

The climber felt [her strength give out].
         CL

We heard [the dog bark angrily].
    CL

Bare infinitival clause complements are one example of a type of subordinate clause that lacks tense, providing us with evidence for our definition of clause as:

$$CL \rightarrow NP \text{ (TNS) } VP$$

As we can see from the above, we can diagram bare infinitival clause complements simply as clauses without a TNS position:

Bare infinitives and subjunctive mood

Another place that bare infinitives show up in English verbal constructions is where there are remnants of the subjunctive mood. If you have studied a Romance or Germanic language, you may be familiar with the subjunctive. Certain verbs, such as the *esperar*, "to hope," require the subjunctive form of the verb to follow in their complements. Here's an example from Spanish. Compare the verb forms for *estar* (to be) first in the indicative and then in the subjunctive:

Veo que <u>estás</u> bien   (indicative)
"I see that you're well."

Espero que <u>estés</u> bien   (subjunctive)
"I hope you're well."

There are only a few places where it remains in English, however.

We insisted that she *be* in charge.
It is important that they *sign* the petition.

The use of the subjunctive has never been robust in English and is still on the decline. Thus, you are just as likely to hear

It is crucial that she *locks* the door.

as you are to hear the subjunctive form *lock* (a bare infinitive, indicating subjunctive):

It is crucial that she *lock* the door. (subjunctive)

And you might hear *was* rather than subjunctive *were* in sentences like this:

If I *was* you, I wouldn't do that.
If I *were* you, I wouldn't do that. (subjunctive)

However, there are some formulaic sayings where the subjunctive remains: *So be it! Be that as it may. Far be it from me. Truth be told. God forbid!*

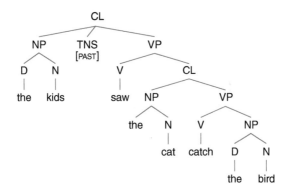

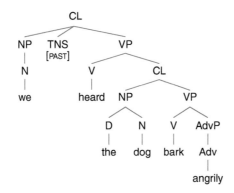

To-infinitive clause complements

Another type of infinitival clause complement, which is much easier to spot than a bare infinitival clause complement, is a to-*infinitival clause complement*. Like bare infinitival clause complements, *to*-infinitival complements lack tense but differ in some interesting ways from other types of clause complements.

Verbs that take *to*-infinitival clauses as complements include *want, expect, prefer,* and *like,* as in the following examples:

My brother wants [my nephew to buy a new car].
                CL

Juno expects/prefers [the exam to be on Tuesday].
                CL

The neighbors like [the newspaper to be delivered].
                CL

In some varieties of English, these *to*-infinitival complements can be introduced by the complementizer *for*. Some or all may sound ok to you? We provide a tree diagram below, where *for* occurs in the same position as the complementizer *that* in tensed subordinate clauses. We'll assume that in *to*-infinitives there is no TNS position.

My brother wants [for my nephew to buy a new car].
                CL

Juno expects/prefers [for the exam to be on Tuesday].
                CL

The neighbors like [for the newspaper to be delivered].
                CL

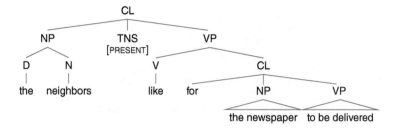

Adjectives can also take *to*-infinitival clause complements:

She seems eager [for Juno to leave].
                CL

We can diagram infinitival clause complements of adjectives as below:

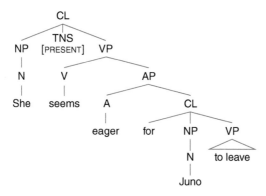

Infinitival clause complements can also have unexpressed or unpronounced subjects as in the following examples:

My brother wants [Ø to buy a new car].
                  CL

Juno expected/prefers [Ø to take the exam on Tuesday].
                  CL

The neighbors like [Ø to get a newspaper].
                  CL

She is happy [Ø to leave].
           CL

There is quite a bit of evidence that these *to*-infinitival complements actually have NP subjects, but that these subjects are unpronounced. Notice that in each example, we interpret the subject of the infinitival clause as identical to the subject of the independent clause:

My brother wants [Ø to buy a new car].   Ø = my brother
                  CL

There is additional evidence (see the exercises if you want to learn more!) that these *to*-infinitival subjects are a type of null pronoun. The convention linguists use to represent this null pronoun is PRO:

My brother wants [PRO to buy a new car].
                  CL

Juno expected/prefers [PRO to take the exam on Tuesday].
                  CL

The neighbors like [PRO to get a newspaper].
                  CL

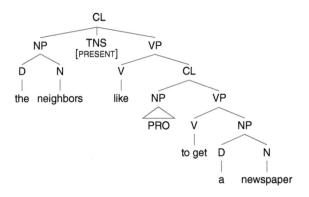

Participial clause complements

Perception verbs such as *watch*, *observe*, or *hear*, which take bare infinitival complements as we saw above, can take *participial clause complements* as well.

> We watched [the dog running after the goose].
>   CL
>
> The protestors heard [the senator jeered by the mob].
>   CL

Participial clause complements are by definition untensed; the verb is in participial form, and there is no auxiliary or modal to express tense. Participial clause complements therefore lack a TNS position. We can diagram participial clause complements like this:

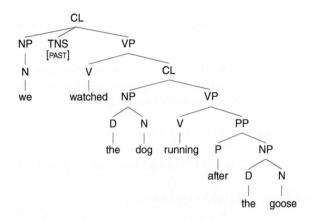

Participial clause complements also occur with other verbs such as *find* and *discover* and more:

The police found/discovered [the suspect hiding in the garage].
  CL

Wh-clause complements

So far, we've seen that some clause complements can be introduced by complementizers, namely, *that* and *for*. Two other complementizers, *whether* and *if*, introduce another type of subordinate clause complement.

I wonder [*whether* Ama will get a raise].
  CL

We can't decide [*if* the story is true or not].
  CL

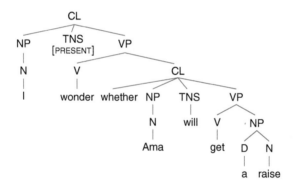

Whether and *if* are interrogative or "question" words, and in this way, they are different from both *that* and *for*. Also, *whether* is distinct from *if* in that only *whether* can introduce either a tensed clause complement or a *to*-infinitival complement. The complementizer *if*, on the other hand, occurs only with tensed clause complements.

I wonder [*whether/if* the storm will be over by morning].
  CL

We wondered [*whether/*if* to leave].
  CL

What you may already have realized is that it isn't just *whether* and *if* that can introduce interrogative clause complements; other interrogative words (and phrases too, as we show below) can as well. Interrogative words and phrases in English begin with *wh*: *who, which, whose, what, when, where* (and the apparent exception *how* derives from the same root). We call these complements *wh-clause complements*.

I wonder [*who* the hosts will invite to the party].
CL

We figured out [*what* to do].
CL

The hikers didn't know [*where* the camp was].
CL

The girls decided [*when* to leave].
CL

They understand [*how* this works].
CL

Shay wondered [*which person* can answer that question].
CL

He remembered [*whose book* was on sale].
CL

We can diagram *wh*-clause complements the same way we have diagrammed other clause complements. Here is an example:

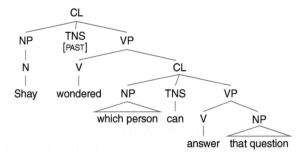

There is much more to say about *wh*-clause complements, in particular in how they are structurally similar to *wh*-questions such as *Who did you talk to?* We explore *wh*-questions in the exercises and return to *wh*-clauses in Chapter 11.

Summary

In this chapter, we have discussed two syntactic operations, **coordination** and **subordination,** and how they differ from each other. Coordination allows us to string heads and phrases (of parallel categories) together, using **coordinating conjunctions** or **conjunctive adverbs**. Subordination also allows us to create longer phrases by embedding one clause within another using **recursion**. Both coordination and subordination allow us to create long and often complex strings of clauses, or **sentences**. We devoted much of the chapter to a discussion of different types of **subordinate clause complements**, including **tensed, bare infinitival, *to*-infinitival, participial**, and ***wh*-clause complements**. Each type of clause complement occurs with certain verbs and can sometimes be introduced by a **complementizer** (*that* for tensed clause complements, *for* for *to*-infinitival complements, and *whether/if* for *wh*-clause complements).

Exercises

1.   Coordination

Recall that a general requirement of coordination is that the coordinated elements are syntactically (or in some cases semantically) parallel. We also saw that an easy way to determine which constituents are coordinated is to analyze coordination "from right to left" – find the constituent on the right of the coordinating conjunction,

Wiley likes beans and [rice]
                     NP

and then find a parallel constituent on the left.

Wiley likes [beans] and [rice].
           NP   NP

For practice, figure out which constituents are coordinated in the following sentences.

(a)   The children ran out the door and down the street.
(b)   Marnie is still playing basketball and also running cross country.
(c)   Eloise started singing and dancing.
(d)   No one wants to go nor expects to stay.
(e)   These four bagels and those three oranges are for you.
(f)   Peter thinks that pigs can fly and that the moon is made of green cheese.
(g)   She laughed politely and looked away.

2. Coordination and ambiguity

Coordination can sometimes lead to ambiguity. Are any of the following sentences ambiguous? If so, why? Be as specific as you can.

(a) She drew big squares and circles.
(b) We like to eat eggs and potatoes with ketchup.
(c) Black cats and spiders are terrifying.
(d) Mel loves wine and chocolates from France.

3. Coordination challenge

For more of a challenge, identify the coordinated constituents in the following excerpt. Does using coordination here have any stylistic effect?

> The old man dropped the line and put his foot on it and lifted the harpoon as high as he could and drove it down with all his strength, and more strength he had just summoned, into the fish's side just behind the great chest fin that rose high in the air to the altitude of a man's chest. He felt the iron go in and he leaned on it and drove it further and then pushed all his weight after it.
>
> (From *The Old Man and the Sea*, by Ernest Hemingway)

4. Independent clauses and sentences

Find the independent clauses in the following sentences. Some independent clauses will also include subordinate clauses, so try to find them too! Which clauses are coordinated, and are they independent or subordinate?

(a) The climbers decided that the route up the cliff was too dangerous and they chose another way to the summit.
(b) Martha said that she had left her jacket on the subway; nevertheless, she made it to the party on time.
(c) They wondered what her truest feelings were, exactly, and what she meant by the contents of the letter.
(d) Juno wanted to go out to dinner but Rue believed it was a bad idea.

5. Identifying clause types

Find the subordinate clause complements (of both verbs and adjectives) in the following sentences. Label each clause as *tensed*, *to-infinitival*, *bare infinitival*, or *participial*. Also identify any *wh*-clause complements. There

212

may be more than one subordinate clause in each sentence, and some may have none at all!

(a) I already answered that question.
(b) Chicken Little squawked that the sky was falling.
(c) I never really understood why we had to move or how we sold our house so fast.
(d) They found the kitten hiding behind the tree.
(e) She was very happy that papers came in the mail today.
(f) Only the chef knows what to buy at the market.
(g) Oona persuaded Lee to leave.
(h) Louis wished the boring show would end.
(i) They heard the tree fall in the woods.
(j) The team hopes the game will get rained out.
(k) The students were anxious for class to end.
(l) No one thought that the senator really believed that he'd get away with the crime.
(m) My sister wants to fly to Vegas.

6. Diagramming practice

Diagram five of the sentences in (5) above. Remember that not all subordinate clauses will have a TNS node, and some may have PRO subjects!

7. Create your own sentences

Create sentences that include the following types of clauses. Use your own examples, rather than those from the chapter.

(a) an independent clause containing a tensed subordinate clause
(b) an independent clause containing a *to*-infinitival subordinate clause
(c) two coordinated independent clauses (without conjunctive adverb)
(d) an independent clause containing a participial subordinate clause
(e) an independent clause containing two subordinate coordinated clauses
(f) two coordinated independent clauses (with a conjunctive adverb)
(g) an independent clause with a *wh*-clause complement

8. Sentence fragments

You may have learned to avoid sentence "fragments" in your writing. Sentence fragments can be defined as "anything that isn't an independent clause." Though sentence fragments might be considered writing "errors," many writers use them very effectively.

213

Find all the fragments in the following excerpt. What makes the fragments? How would you "fix" them, and would fixing them have an effect on the meaning of the excerpt?

Haymitch doesn't protest when I walk out. Down the hall. Through the bee-hive of compartments. Find a warm pipe to hide behind in a laundry room. It takes a long time before I get to the bottom of why I'm so upset. When I do, it's almost too mortifying to admit. All those months of taking it for granted that Peeta thought I was wonderful are over. Finally, he can see me for who I really am. Violent. Distrustful. Manipulative. Deadly. (From *Mockingjay*, by Suzanne Collins.)

9. PRO puzzles

As we mentioned in this chapter, there is quite a bit of evidence for null subjects in *to*-infinitival complements. (PRO subjects are different from null subjects of tensed clauses found in languages like Spanish and Italian, but we leave those differences aside here.)

We hope [PRO to be on time].
CL

Here's another piece of evidence for not only a null subject but also a null object in *to*-infinitival complements, in this case, complements of the adjectives *easy* and *eager*.

The teacher is easy to please.
The teacher is eager to please.

These sentences look identical, except for the difference in adjective *easy/eager*. Yet, the subject and object of the infinitive *to please* is interpreted completely differently in each sentence. How do we explain the two different interpretations of each sentence? (Hint – how can proposing that there are null subjects and objects in each subordinate clause help?)

Here's another example just for fun! Why is this sentence ambiguous? Can a null subject/object of a *to*-infinitival clause help us explain the ambiguity?

The crab is too hot to eat.

10. *Wh*-movement

You may have noticed that *wh*-clause complements (bracketed below) look a lot like *wh*-questions:

(a) I wonder [which radio station you listen to].
(b) Which radio station do you listen to?

(c) Noah decided [when we should meet].
(d) When should we meet?

(e) They don't know [who to invite to the party].
(f) Who can we invite to the party?

In English, *wh*-questions are formed by moving the questioned word or phrase to sentence-initial position, a process called *wh*-movement. This movement leaves a "gap," indicated here by the underscore, indicating the original position of the moved *wh*-phrase. We also provide possible answers to the question, where the "gap" is filled.

(g) [Which radio] station do you listen to ___?
(h) I listen to *the campus radio station*.

(i) When should we meet ___?
(j) We should meet *at 6 pm*.

(k) Who will the hosts invite ____ to the party?
(l) The hosts will invite *two friends* to the party.

The same process of *wh*-movement applies in subordinate clause complements, again leaving a "gap":

(m) I wonder [which radio station you listen to ___].
(n) Noah decided [when we should meet ___].
(o) They don't know [who the hosts will invite ____ to the party].

Apply *wh*-movement in the following sentences. We have indicated which phrase to "question" by bolding it. Indicate the gap created by *wh*-movement with an underscore.

(p) You talked to **Norma** yesterday.
(q) You talked to Norma **yesterday.**
(r) **You** talked to Norma yesterday.

Now, do the same in the subordinate clauses below. Is anything different? Does *wh*-movement apply in the same way? Briefly explain.

I wonder [you talked to **Norma** yesterday].
[you talked to Norma **yesterday**].
[**you** talked to Norma yesterday].

11. Practice

Here are some sentences from texts to use for practice. You may also want to find other text passages to practice what you learned in this chapter. Try to do the following:

(a) Identify all the independent clauses.
(b) Identify any subordinate clause complements.
(c) Label each subordinate clause complement as tensed, infinitival, or participial. Label any *wh*-clause complements.
(d) Identify any examples of coordination. What is the conjunction and which constituents are coordinated?
(e) Find all the complementizers.
(f) You may find subordinate clauses that are not complements. Can you determine their function?

Dwight drove in a sullen reverie. When I spoke he answered curtly or not at all. Now and then his expression changed, and he grunted as if to claim some point of argument. He kept a Camel burning on his lower lip. Just the other side of Concrete he pulled the car hard to the left and hit a beaver that was crossing the road. Dwight said he had swerved to miss the beaver, but that wasn't true. He had gone out of his way to run over it. He stopped the car on the shoulder of the road and backed up to where the beaver lay. (From *This Boy's Life*, by Tobias Wolff.)

In the old country in South America, Carlotta's grandmother, Zedé, had been a seamstress, but really more of a sewing magician. These capes were worn by dancers and musicians and priests at traditional village festivals and had been worn for countless generations. It had puzzled her at first why a creature so beautiful (though admittedly with hideous feet) emitted a sound so like a soul in torment. This old woman thought each feather she found was a gift from the Gods ... (From *The Temple of My Familiar*, by Alice Walker.)

Gabriella nodded, then signed Austin's name, eyebrows raised in request. Charlie waved across the table to get his attention – asking someone to tap or flag down a friend was common practice in a world where calling one by name was pretty much useless – but regretted it as soon as he looked up. The fact that her body had chosen this particular moment to fully integrate this cultural norm into her muscle memory was annoying; she certainly did not want to help Gabriella. Plus, now everyone was staring at her. (From *True Biz*, by Sara Nović.)

More on Modification

Introduction

In this chapter, we'll turn once again to *modification,* ways in which we add additional information to phrases and clauses. We have discussed modifiers in previous chapters, but here we'll introduce some that are more syntactically complex. First, we explore ways in which we use subordinate clauses to modify nouns; these are called *relative clauses.* Then we discuss a

Navigating English Grammar: A Guide to Analyzing Real Language, Second Edition.
Anne Lobeck and Kristin Denham.
© 2025 Anne Lobeck and Kristin Denham. Published 2025 by John Wiley & Sons Ltd.

large class of *moveable modifiers,* phrases that can occur in clause-initial and clause-final positions. We provide you with some tools to recognize these different kinds of modifiers, tools that will help you analyze ever larger and more complex clauses and sentences.

Clauses that Modify Nouns: Relative Clauses

We have already discussed a number of ways to modify nouns within NP: by adding prenominal modifiers that can be verbs, adjectives, or nouns, for example.

the *galloping* horse   the *pretty* horse   the *iron* horse

We can also modify nouns by adding postnominal modifiers, APs and PPs:

something *wild*   the horse *with a long tail*

Here we'll see that we can also modify nouns with clauses, or *relative clauses.* Relative clauses can modify nouns in different ways. We turn first to *restrictive* relative clauses.

Restrictive relative clauses

Restrictive relative clauses are, like the clause complements we discussed in Chapter 10, subordinate clauses, but they are different from the other ones we've seen so far because they modify nouns, and are constituents of NP. Relative clause modifiers can express the same kinds of information as the other modifiers of nouns we're familiar with, but as clauses, they can include even more information. Here are some examples of relative clauses that modify the noun *horse.*

the horse   [that was galloping across the pasture]
         [that was really pretty]
         [that was made of iron]
         [that has a long tail]
         [that they bought from a ranch in Montana]

Like other modifiers of nouns, relative clauses provide more information about the noun: they limit, or "restrict" the denotation of the noun. For example, by itself, the NP *the horse* refers to a particular horse that is a member of a larger set of horses. But when we add a relative clause modifier to this NP, the relative clause in the NP *the horse* [*that has a long tail*] limits the description of the horse being referred to as the one with the long tail.

Relative clauses, like other modifiers we'll discuss in this chapter, are one more tool we have in our syntactic toolbox to express additional information, in this case, through subordination: a clause modifier that is dominated by NP.

Relative clauses provide us with a way to combine separate independent clauses:

> The horse was out in the pasture. The horse has a long tail.
>
> [The horse [that was out in the pasture]] has a long tail.
> NP   CL
>
> We bought a horse *and* we bought it from a ranch *and* the ranch was in Montana.
>
> [The horse [that we bought from a ranch [that was in Montana]]]
> NP   CL   CL

Relative clauses can be introduced by *relative pronouns, that, who, which, when, where,* etc. (You may prefer some over others, depending on your variety of English.) And sometimes, relative pronouns can be omitted. Can you omit any of the relative pronouns in the examples below?

> [The movie [*that* we saw last night]] was scary.
> NP   CL
>
> [Someone [*who* plays the piano]] will be at the party tonight.
> NP   CL
>
> [The place [*where* we meet on Tuesdays]] is closed today.
> NP   CL
>
> [The things [*which* bother Rue]] seem weird.
> NP   CL

We know that relative clauses are part of NP because they must be included when we replace the NP with a pronoun:

> *The movie that we saw last night* was scary.
> *It* was scary.
>
> *The things which bother Rue* seem weird.
> *They* seem weird.

The relative clauses we are discussing here are called *restrictive relative clauses,* because they "restrict" the meaning of the noun they modify, and are constituents of NP. Restrictive relative clauses, like other modifiers, modify only common nouns, because only common nouns can take modifiers! Recall from Chapter 2 that proper nouns can't be modified, because they already "pick out" a unique referent. Restrictive relative clauses therefore sound odd, if not ungrammatical, when they modify proper nouns.

[The movie [that we saw last night]]
NP   CL

*[*The Empire Strikes Back* [that we saw last night]]
NP   CL

The second example here sounds funny if not completely ungrammatical, because it leads us to understand *The Empire Strikes Back* as a common noun, which conflicts with what we know about movie titles (namely, that they are, at least in this case, proper nouns/names). The same situation arises when we modify proper nouns with other restrictive modifiers, such as adjective phrases (*exciting*) or prepositional phrases (*in theaters today*):

*[The exciting *The Empire Strikes Back*] is fun to watch.
NP

*[*The Empire Strikes Back* in theaters today] is fun to watch.
NP

Just like other modifiers of nouns, we diagram restrictive relative clauses as modifiers of N in NP. For simplicity, we use a triangle for the relative clause:

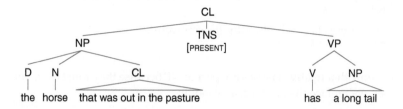

In the next section, we take a closer look at the internal structure of relative clauses. As we might expect given what we know about subordinate clauses, relative clauses can be tensed or infinitival. Relative clauses can also be participial, or "reduced," in ways we discuss below.

Tensed, reduced, and infinitival relative clauses
So far, we've looked only at *tensed relative clauses*, or relative clauses with tensed verbs.

[someone [who *plays* the piano]]
NP   CL

Tensed relative clauses, as we might expect, can include longer tensed verb strings:

[someone [who *has been playing the piano*]]
NP   CL

[someone [who *will play the piano*]]
NP   CL

[someone [who *was playing the piano*]]
NP   CL

Tensed relative clauses can also sometimes be *reduced,* by omitting the relative pronoun and the form of auxiliary verb *be:*

[someone [who *was playing the piano*]]
NP   CL

[someone [___ *playing the piano*]] (*who was* is omitted)
NP   CL

In this last example with *who was* omitted, we still understand the reduced relative clause as modifying the noun *someone*. As we saw above, we can replace the entire NP, including the reduced modifier, with a pronoun.

I could hear *someone playing the piano.*
I could hear *them.*

But, you might also have noticed that the following sentence is also possible:

I could hear *them playing the piano.*

What's going on here? Reduced relative clauses can sometimes create ambiguity because they look identical to participial clauses. Recall from Chapter 10 that participial subordinate clauses can be complements of verbs.

We found [*the kitten hiding under the porch*].

This sentence is syntactically ambiguous because it has two different structures. *The kitten hiding under the porch* can be a participial subordinate clause:

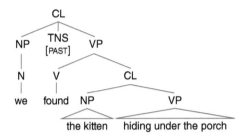

We can replace the subject of this participial clause with a pronoun. When we do this, the sentence is no longer ambiguous because its syntax is clear:

We found [*it* *hiding under the porch*]. *it* = the kitten
       CL

But we can also understand *We found the kitten hiding under the porch* as including a direct object NP of *found,* an NP that includes a relative clause modifier.

We found [*the kitten* [who was *hiding under the porch*]]
          NP   CL

This relative clause modifier can in turn be reduced, leaving us with an ambiguous sentence:

We found [*the kitten* [___ *hiding under the porch*]]
          NP   CL

But note that we can replace the NP object of *found* with a proform, and any ambiguity disappears:

We found [*it*].   *it* = the kitten (who was) hiding under the porch
          NP

A tree diagram of this clause, with *the kitten hiding under the porch* as the direct object NP containing a reduced relative clause modifier, is given below:

224

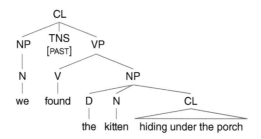

It may not always be clear on the surface whether a phrase such as *the kitten hiding under the porch* or *someone playing the piano* is a participial clause or an NP that includes a participial or reduced relative clause, but pronoun substitution (and context) provides us with tools to distinguish one from the other.

Like other subordinate clauses, relative clauses can also be infinitival (and more specifically, *to*-infinitival):

the person *who we met*	(tensed relative clause)
the person *to meet*	(infinitival relative clause)
four emus *that Juno saw in the zoo*	(tensed relative clause)
four emus *for Juno to see in the zoo*	(infinitival relative clause)

Infinitival relative clauses differ from tensed ones not only in the form of the verb. As you can see in the above examples, unlike tensed relative clauses, infinitival relative clauses typically do not occur with relative pronouns.

the person (**who*) *to meet*
four emus (**that/which*) *to see in the zoo*

the place (**where*) *to go*
the time (**when*) *to meet*

And as with other *to-infinitival* subordinate clauses, infinitival relative clauses may or may not have expressed subjects, introduced by the complementizer *for*:

the person (*for you*) *to meet*

As we saw in Chapter 6, *to*-infinitival clauses that do not have lexical subjects can be analyzed as having PRO subjects. We can assume the same structure here, though for simplicity, we'll diagram infinitival relative clauses with a triangle, as part of NP (whether they have PRO subjects or not).

the person [PRO *to meet*]
the person [*for you to meet*]

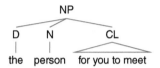

Nonrestrictive relative clauses

Relative clauses fall into two classes, *restrictive* and *nonrestrictive*. Those we've looked at so far are all restrictive, because they limit, or "restrict" what the noun refers to.

The woman *who I met* was very tall.
Hawaii is the place *where we go on vacation*
We met the man *who was singing* after the show.
The person *to ask* can be found behind the counter.
The champagne *for you to try* is on sale.

Nonrestrictive relative clauses, on the other hand – though they might provide similar information – do not restrict the reference of the noun. They are also usually set off by commas in writing, and you can also usually detect "comma intonation" in a speaker's voice, distinguishing the two types.

restrictive:
The woman *who I met* was very tall.

nonrestrictive:
The woman, *who I met*, was very tall.

The restrictive relative clause limits which woman we're referring to, namely, to *the woman who I met*. It picks out a particular woman from the set of women. The nonrestrictive relative clause, on the other hand, does not restrict the reference of the noun *woman*; it is simply incidental information. This distinction may be difficult to see at first, but evidence comes from modification of proper nouns. We know that restrictive relative clauses can't modify proper nouns:

*Cary *who I met* was very tall.

But nonrestrictive relative clauses can:

Cary, *who I met,* was very tall.

This evidence, together with the difference in intonation, suggests that nonrestrictive relative clauses don't form a constituent with the noun they modify in the same way that restrictive relative clauses do, and thus don't modify them in the same way.

Another difference between restrictive and nonrestrictive relative clauses is that unlike restrictive relative clauses, nonrestrictive relative clauses appear to require a relative pronoun:

The woman *(who) I met* is very tall. (restrictive)
*The woman, *I met,* is very tall. (nonrestrictive)
The woman, *who I met,* is very tall.

Like restrictive relative clauses, nonrestrictive relative clauses can appear to be reduced, or participial:

The kitten, *who was hiding under the porch,* finally decided to come out.
The kitten, *hiding under the porch,* finally decided to come out.

These reduced participial relative clauses seem indistinguishable from VP (participial) movable modifiers that we discuss later in this chapter. We won't delve into the details here, other than to note that in a position following an NP, the two types of modifiers are, for our purposes here, indistinguishable.

A final, more clear distinction between restrictive relative clauses and nonrestrictive ones is that nonrestrictive relative clauses don't seem to be infinitival, but this may depend on your variety of English:

The woman *(for you) to meet at the station* will be wearing a red hat.
*?The woman, *(for you) to meet at the station,* will be wearing a red hat.

What do you think?

Headless relative clauses

A final type of relative clause we discuss here is called a *headless relative clause.* These relative clauses are "headless" because the noun they modify is absent, though it may be implied or understood. These relative clauses typically occur with compound relative pronouns, such as *whatever, who(m)ever, whenever, however,* and so on.

I will do *what(ever) you want.*
Whenever you want to leave is fine with me.
The committee will invite *who(ever) we put on the list.*

Note that the headless relative clauses in the above examples are functioning as either subjects or complements of the verb, rather than as modifiers in NP.

A similar kind of *wh*-phrase can also show up as a nonrestrictive modifier (of NP or another constituent). In the following example, *which is where the hummus should go too* appears to be a nonrestrictive relative clause modifying the NP *the fridge*.

I put the pudding in the fridge, *which is where the hummus should go too*.

But what about these phrases? They seem to modify the entire clause and therefore aren't clearly examples of nonrestrictive relative clauses modifying a particular NP.

The penguin distracted the emu, *which astonished everyone*.
We left the gate open, *which Hank had asked us not to do*.

We will simply call these nonrestrictive modifiers, distinct from nonrestrictive relative clauses and headless relative clauses.

Appositive NPs

Another way to add additional information to an NP is by adding an *appositive NP*. Appositive NPs are nonrestrictive and are set off by commas in writing and by comma intonation in speech. Like nonrestrictive relative clauses, they don't restrict the denotation of the noun (or NP) they follow; they rename and add more information about that NP.

The bird, *a seagull*, hopped along the beach.
The President, *Commander in Chief*, must make difficult decisions.

Appositive NPs, like the modifiers we've discussed in this section, allow us to pack more information into a single clause, rather than stating this information in two separate clauses.

The bird hopped along the beach. It was a seagull.
The bird hopped along the beach *and* it was a seagull.
The bird, [a seagull], hopped along the beach.
    (appositive NP)

Appositive NPs are just that, NPs rather than clauses, so be sure not to mix them up with nonrestrictive relative clauses.

The bird, *which was a seagull,* hopped along the beach. (nonrestrictive relative clause)
The bird, *a seagull,* hopped along the beach. (appositive NP)

There is much more to say about relative clauses and their complex syntax and semantics. The central point we hope to make is that relative clauses and the modifiers and appositive NPs discussed in this section illustrate how we use subordinate clauses and other phrases to combine information that could be expressed in separate clauses into a single, more complex one.

Movable Modifiers

In this final section, we discuss a set of modifiers that expresses "adverbial" information about time, manner, reason, cause, and so on. These modifiers can be of any category: NP, PP, VP, AP, AdvP, and even CL, and like other nonrestrictive modifiers they add "extra" information to the clause. We call them "movable" because they can occur in either clause-initial or clause-final position.

Movable AdvP modifiers

You are already quite familiar with AdvP modifiers, which, as you recall, can occur in a variety of different positions in the clause. In the example below, the AdvP *quickly* appears clause-finally and clause-initially.

Cary kissed Lee *quickly.*
Quickly, Cary kissed Lee.

AdvP modifiers are by definition "movable" and express information about time, manner, reason, place, cause, etc. We start off with them, because they are familiar examples of movable modifiers. But as we'll see in this section, adverb phrases are not the only kinds of modifiers that express this kind of information, nor are they the only modifiers that are "movable."

Movable PP modifiers

Here are some examples of typical PP movable modifiers. As you can see, they occur in either clause-final or clause-initial position (you can move each around yourself to see why we call them "movable"). These also express "adverbial" information, of time in this case.

Cary kissed Lee *on Sunday*.
At 7:00, she boarded the plane.
Jack went home *after his soccer game*.

In Chapters 9 and 10, we spent some time discussing *subordinating PP modifiers*. Recall that these PPs include a subordinate clause. Subordinating PPs are good examples of movable modifiers:

Mae is happy about the promotion, *though they are worried about job security*.
After the party was over, we left the restaurant.
Lil will apply for a job, *because she needs the income*.
If she gets a chance, Lil will apply for a job.
When she finishes the program, Lil will try to find a job.

Movable NP modifiers

We know that NPs often function as subjects and complements. NPs can also be movable modifiers, expressing time, place, etc.

We weren't late to class *this time*.
Today the jury should give their verdict.
The judge will be on vacation *tomorrow*.
Downtown, you can find everything you need.

Movable AP modifiers

You are quite familiar with AP modifiers of nouns in NP (*the green chair*). APs can also be movable modifiers; they modify NPs and occur in clause-initial or clause-final position (rather than *within* NP).

The children clapped their hands, *ecstatic*.
Totally disgusted, my friends walked out of the theater.
Lil ended the call, *aghast*.

Because these modifiers modify nouns or NPs, they may not "move" as freely as other movable modifiers. For example, in the first sentence below, the clause-initial (coordinated) AP modifier *tired and hungry* clearly modifies the subject NP, *the hikers*. The second sentence seems less clear; the modifier in clause-final position may modify the object NP, *the park ranger*, causing some ambiguity.

Tired and hungry, the hikers talked to the park ranger.
The hikers talked to the park ranger, *tired and hungry.*

So, although we assume here that movable modifiers can occur in different positions, there are some semantic restrictions that may restrict the position in which they are most likely to occur.

Movable VP modifiers

VP movable modifiers are *participial;* the verb in these VP modifiers is either a present or past participle.

> *Splashing water all over the floor,* the child played in the tub.
> *Driven by thirst,* the wildebeests searched for water.
> The kids ran away from the wasp nest, *screaming.*

Although these modifiers can typically occur in either clause-initial or clause-final position, sometimes they are more clear in one position than in the other for semantic reasons – you can probably tell why, based on the following example!

> She put the dog in the house, *barking furiously.*
> *Barking furiously,* she put the dog in the house.

Movable CL modifiers

Movable modifiers can also be clauses, and more specifically, *participial* clauses. (Participial clause modifiers are sometimes called *absolute phrases* in traditional grammar.) Notice that these clause modifiers are composed of a subject and a participial VP.

> *Their eyes squinting in the sun,* the spectators watched the tennis match.
> Ike read the morning paper, *his dog curled up at his feet.*

It's easy to mix these participial clause modifiers up with participial VP modifiers discussed above, but remember that clause modifiers have subjects, and VP modifiers don't.

> VP modifiers – no subject expressed:
> *Squinting in the sun,* the spectators watched the tennis match.
> Ike read the morning paper, *curled up on the couch.*

Infinitival clauses can also be movable modifiers, and when they are, they usually have an "in order" interpretation, such as in the examples below.

Bo wore a fluorescent vest *in order to be seen*.
In order to be on time, Zoe must get up at 6 am.

Sometimes, the *in order* can be omitted:

Bo wore a fluorescent vest *to be seen*.
To be on time, Zoe must get up at 6 am.

To summarize this section, movable modifiers, like relative clauses, allow us to add additional information to the clause. Moveable modifiers sometimes involve subordination (as do relative clauses), and allow us to "combine" separate clauses into larger ones. Here are just a few examples, based on the movable modifiers we've used above:

My friends walked out of the theater. They were totally disgusted.
Totally disgusted, my friends walked out of the theater.

The child played in the tub. She was splashing water all over the floor.
Splashing water all over the floor, the child played in the tub.

Ike read the morning paper *and* his dog was curled up at his feet.
Ike read the morning paper, *his dog curled up at his feet*.

Summary

In this chapter, we have investigated different kinds of modifiers that allow us to combine clauses into larger, more complex units, often using subordination. One way is by using **relative clause modifiers** to modify nouns. **Restrictive relative clauses** can be **tensed, participial/reduced**, or **infinitival**, limiting the denotation of the noun they modify. **Nonrestrictive relative clauses,** which are typically tensed, do not limit the denotation of a noun but provide another way to add additional information to an NP. We briefly discussed **headless relative clauses**, relative clauses that do not appear to modify an overt noun. We briefly introduced **appositive NPs** here as well, which allow us to rename an NP, and in this way express some additional information about that NP. We concluded the chapter with an overview of **movable modifiers** of different categories. These modifiers provide us with yet another way to combine clauses into larger, more complex units.

Exercises

1. Restrictive relative clauses

Identify any restrictive relative clauses in the following sentences. Try using pronoun substitution as a test for an NP with a relative clause modifier. Remember that not all relative clauses require a relative pronoun, and that they may be tensed, infinitival, or reduced/participial.

(a) Have you seen those delicious red berries I like to eat?
(b) The students wanted to vote for the person who was concerned about student loan debt.
(c) The bands to see at the festival are the ones with the funky names.
(d) I ate the cod that was caught by that man over there.
(e) The best person to do that job is out today.
(f) A book that I read for another class is also required for this class.
(g) The doctor sent the information about the physical therapist for you to see next week.

2. Relative clauses and *wh*-movement

Recall from Chapter 10 that *wh*-clauses are derived by *wh*-movement of a phrase to clause-initial position. This movement leaves a "gap," the position from which the moved phrase originated. Here are some examples from Chapter 10 (exercise 10 if you want to review!).

(a) [Which radio] station do you listen to ___?
(b) I listen to *the campus radio station*.

(a) When should we meet ___?
(b) We should meet *at 6 pm*.

(a) Who will the hosts invite ____ to the party?
(b) The hosts will invite *two friends* to the party.

Relative clauses also involve *wh*-movement. Can you find the gap in the following relative clauses?

(a) the person [who Rue met at the party]
(b) the restaurant [where we met]
(c) the teacher [who you talked to]

And what about when the relative pronoun in the relative clause is the subject? How might you analyze the gap there?

the person [who teaches grammar]

3. Nonrestrictive relative clauses and appositive NPs

Find any restrictive or nonrestrictive relative clauses in the following sentences. Identify any appositive NPs. Also identify any nonrestrictive modifiers that may not modify an NP, but rather some other constituent.

(a) The long, slender snake, which lived in a hole under the barn, shed its skin.
(b) Most people like to exercise, which is very good for your health.
(c) We hope to vote for that candidate, who seems to have some great ideas about the new health care plan, which includes additional prescription drug coverage.
(d) The decision on the bill, which was long overdue, came as something of a shock to the committee, a group that has worked very hard on it.
(e) Cameron, who used to be a member of the committee, showed up for the meeting yesterday.
(f) Lil gave the book, which she's had in the attic for years, to her daughter.
(g) Cooking for a large group, which can be really stressful, can also be fun if you have had some experience.
(h) Sally Ride, the first American woman to fly in space, earned many awards, including a top honor, the Presidential Medal of Freedom.

Now, divide a few of these sentences into as many separate clauses as you can. Do you all get the same answers? Compare your work and discuss!

4. Moveable modifiers

Identify any movable modifiers in the following sentences. Label the category of each. Not every sentence includes a movable modifier, and some may include more than one. Not all the modifiers are set off by commas.

(a) In order to reach the summit, they hiked all night.
(b) Angry, Vern scowled at the crowd.
(c) Next week, they plan to have dinner together on Wednesday.
(d) It was sunny yesterday.
(e) Velma sent him a letter about the lease.
(f) Shaking her fist, Alma demanded fresh milk.
(g) They both stood on the steps, smiling happily.
(h) Though no one was around, we tiptoed through the house.
(i) We found a box, its lid rusted shut.

(j) My sister seems on top of the world.
(k) My sister puts her legal papers in a locked box after she signs them.
(l) The elephants stampeded noisily.
(m) Alex hoped to sell the car.
(n) The dog greeted me, his tail wagging.

5. Find the modifier

The following sentences include examples of all of the kinds of modifiers discussed in this chapter. See if you can find them, and then label them!

(a) The couscous, which was cooked for way too long, was soggy.
(b) We wanted to talk to the professor, a leading expert on DNA, about the upcoming project.
(c) Because she wanted to better understand the concepts, Suki asked if she could come to the office early.
(d) Apparently unfazed, Juno walked out of the meeting, smiling.
(e) After the tournament, the players hoped to go to the restaurant to have a snack.
(f) We watched the ship sail away, its flag snapping in the wind.
(g) We go to the courthouse tomorrow, the last day to turn in the documents.
(h) Until we can buy our own, we will use the computer in the library.
(i) Jake, the owner of the restaurant, is standing in the alley.
(j) She washed the car, which was a birthday present from her uncle.
(k) We won't set off fireworks in our backyard this year, to appease our worried neighbors.

6. Modifiers and sentence combining

Choose two or three of the sentences above and "unpack" them into separate sentences. Compare your answers and discuss what you did differently/ the same. Combine the following sets of short sentences into a single clause, using the tools of modification we've discussed in this chapter. Try to avoid using any coordination! Discuss your answers (because they will be different!).

(a) George bought sushi. The sushi was on sale. He bought it on Saturday.
(b) Alice ate the tripe. Alice doesn't really like it. Alice did not want to offend her friends.

(c) My mother traveled to Budapest. She went for free. She stayed with friends. She didn't stay in a hotel.

(d) The students were nervous about the exam. They arrived early and they were hoping to have some time to ask questions. The professor told the students that the exam would be easy.

7. Practice

Here are some sentences from texts to use for practice. You may also want to find other text passages to practice what you learned in this chapter. Try to do the following:

(a) find any restrictive relative clauses
(b) find any nonrestrictive relative clauses
(c) find any appositive NPs
(d) find any movable modifiers
(e) identify any other nonrestrictive modifiers you find

The horse bolted over the pool of ice toward Peter Lake, and lowered his wide white neck. Peter Lake took possession of himself and throwing his arms around what seemed like a swan, sprang up on the horse's back. He was up again, exulting even as the pistol shots rang out in the cold air. Having become his accomplice in one graceful motion, the horse turned and skittered, leaning back slightly on his haunches to get breath and power for an explosive start. In that moment, Peter Lake faced his stunned pursuers, and laughed at them. His entire being was one light perfect laugh. (From *Winter's Tale*, by Mark Helprin.)

The lifeguard enters the pool through a separate entrance marked STAFF ONLY and sits atop a high metal stool in front of the wooden bleachers, gazing out across the water for hours. The lifeguard wears white shorts and a light blue shirt and reports directly to the Aquatics Director, a small, bespectacled man in a battered windbreaker whose windowless office sits opposite the vending machines on the lower-mezzanine landing. The lifeguard is sometimes a skinny teenage boy and sometimes a grown man. Occasionally, the lifeguard is a young woman. Often, the lifeguard is late. Timely or tardy, young or old, male or female, the lifeguard never lasts for long. (From *The Swimmers: A Novel*, by Julie Otsuka.)

The talk didn't bother me much. Folks know'd the Blues were unchurched and didn't associate with the preacher. But I couldn't help fearing he'd be discovered, worry on what Devil John might've seen, worrying more that Doc would let something slip, or someone's hunting dog would come along and dig him up. Lately, I'd been peeking behind Junia's stall, scattering leaves atop the preacher's grave, piling on more sticks, rock, then dragging logs from the woodpile onto it. Made sure he stayed good "n" put, couldn't push his devil-rotted, fire-wagging fingers up from the black earth and grab himself another sinner. (From *The Book Woman of Troublesome Creek: A Novel*, by Kim Michele Richardson.)

Monday, Peña telephoned. The audience with El Jefe was set in the National Palace for the next day. We were to bring a sponsor. Someone willing to give the young offender work and be responsible for him. Someone who had not been in trouble with the government. (From *In the Time of Butterflies*, by Julia Alvarez.)

Navigating and Analyzing: Review

Navigating English Grammar: A Guide to Analyzing Real Language, Second Edition.
Anne Lobeck and Kristin Denham.
© 2025 Anne Lobeck and Kristin Denham. Published 2025 by John Wiley & Sons Ltd.

Introduction

In this final chapter, we'll revisit the central grammatical concepts we've introduced in this book to help you "navigate" English and other languages if you wish to study them. We begin with a brief overview of syntactic categories and phrases and then turn to the functions of those phrases (NP, VP, AP, AdvP, PP, and clauses) as complements and modifiers. We conclude by revisiting subordination and coordination, two syntactic operations that apply to phrases. This chapter is not meant to be a comprehensive review of all the grammatical concepts we have discussed. Rather, our focus here is to provide you with a "capstone" opportunity to practice applying the tools of analysis that we have introduced in the preceding chapters. We encourage you to refer back to relevant chapters should you wish to re-explore some of the concepts we touch on here, or others that you may wish to review.

We conclude this chapter with exercises based on some of the text excerpts you may have already analyzed in earlier chapters. Here, however, we revise and expand on things to look for in those excerpts based on your deeper understanding of and familiarity with the terminology and concepts introduced in this book. The goal of these exercises is to encourage you to apply the tools of grammatical analysis we've discussed and to challenge you to use those tools to practice "analyzing real language." Enjoy!

Navigating and
Analyzing: Review

Syntactic Categories

We assume you are now familiar with the basic syntactic categories of English. Recall that each lexical category is head of a phrase, and that each lexical category can occur with a functional category; for example, a lexical category N can be preceded by a determiner D, a functional category, resulting in a noun phrase: NP → D N, *the gnome*. Table 12.1 provides examples of lexical categories and Table 12.2 of functional categories.

Recall that clauses are also a type of phrase, a unit made up of a **subject** NP and a **predicate** VP. As we've discussed throughout the book, clauses

Table 12.1 Lexical categories with examples.

Noun	Verb	Adjective	Adverb
ocean, intelligence, earth, scissors, furniture, email, vlog	discuss, remember, annoy, feel, run, seem, email	unhappy, fortuitous, beautiful, global, tiny, smart, delicious	hopefully, maddeningly, fast, still, now, often

Table 12.2 Functional categories with examples.

Determiner	the, a, this, that, these, those, his, my	**Preposition**	without, in, on, over, behind, above, around
Numeral	one, five, ten, second, eighth	**Conjunction**	and, or, yet, for, but, so, nor
Quantifier	all, each, every, both, some	**Degree word**	very, so, quite, rather, too
Pronoun	they, he, she, her, theirs, mine, yours	**Auxiliary verb**	have, be, do
		Modal	may, might, can, could, will, would, shall, should, must

are sometimes, but not always, tensed. The phrase structure rule for CL therefore includes an optional Tense (TNS) position.

CL → NP (TNS) VP

In the following sections, we will review the basic functions of phrases that we have discussed in this book. We'll start with **complementation,** how phrases function as complements of different heads (N, V, A, P, and Adv).

Complementation

As you've seen in this book, phrases have a number of different grammatical functions. An NP, for example, can function as a *subject* and a VP as a *predicate*. Together, these two phrases form a larger unit, a clause.

[[The emu] [raced along the fence]].
CL NP   VP

In this section, we'll review yet another function of phrases that you are now familiar with, phrases that function as *complements*. As we have assumed throughout this book, complements "complete" a phrase; put another way, a head "selects" or "takes" a complement, and together the head and its complement form a phrase. For example, a head such as the transitive verb *kiss* selects an NP direct object as a complement, and together V + NP form a unit, VP. A verb such as *think* selects a different phrase as a complement, namely, a clause or PP, to form a larger VP.

I kissed *a frog*. (NP complement)
I think *that I like frogs*. (clause complement)
I think *about frogs*. (PP complement)

Recall as well that some complements have specific labels (direct object, subjective complement, etc.) but not all do, as we'll see below. What complements all have in common, however, is that they are selected by a head (N, V, A, P, or Adv) and together with that head form a larger phrase (NP, VP, AP, PP, or AdvP).

Complements of verbs

Verbs are heads that commonly take complements, and as we've seen throughout the book, verbs can be divided into different classes, based on the type of complement they take. These classes of verbs (transitive verbs, for example) are defined by their syntactic and semantic properties. Below we provide a brief overview of the types of complements of verbs we've discussed, including some we haven't! This overview isn't meant to be exhaustive, but should help you recognize the complement of a verb when you see one!

NP complements of verbs

As you've learned so far, *transitive* verbs ("action" verbs such as *meet, kiss, pat*, etc.) take *direct object* NP complements. *Linking* verbs (*become, remain, be, seem, appear*, etc.) take NP complements, *subjective complement* NPs. Recall that subjective complement NPs and direct object NPs are quite distinct semantically; the following examples illustrate this distinction.

> met *the leader*   (direct object)
> became *the leader*   (subjective complement)

These examples clearly show that although both transitive verb *meet* and linking verb *become* select NP complements (*the leader*) the meanings of those complements are quite different. The direct object NP is the object of an action, while the NP subjective complement *the leader* is a description.

Another NP complement you are familiar with is an *indirect object* NP. Indirect objects are selected by *ditransitive* or "double object" verbs, verbs that take two objects: direct objects and indirect objects.

> gave *Bert* a present   (*Bert* – indirect object; *a present* – direct object)

You may remember that indirect object NPs also occur as complements of prepositions *to/for*. We can rearrange the order of the verb direct and indirect object as follows, where *Bert* is the object of (and thus the complement of) the preposition *to*.

> gave a present to *Bert*   (indirect object)

Verbs can also take other types of NP complements such as those below (these NPs express location, direction, weight, and cost):

ran *downtown*
walked *home*
weighed *ten pounds*
costs *a great deal of money*

AP complements of verbs
APs are often modifiers, but they can also be complements of verbs, in particular complements of *linking verbs,* as shown below. Complements of linking verbs are called *subjective complements* (because they describe the subject of the clause).

remained *very happy*   (subjective complement)
seemed *totally relaxed*   (subjective complement)

AdvP complements of verbs
Adverb phrases are not typically complements, but there are a few instances in which a verb requires an adverb phrase complement:

worded the document *carefully*

PP complements of verbs
Like APs, PPs are often modifiers (as we'll discuss below), but some verbs take PP complements, as illustrated in the following examples:

think *about Mary*
put the dog *in the kennel*

PP complements of linking verbs are *subjective complements,* as we discussed above.

remains *in a funk*   (subjective complement)

VP complements of verbs
Participial VPs can also be complements of verbs, as illustrated by the following examples.

began *speaking quickly*
finished *writing his term paper*

Clause complements of verbs

And finally, certain verbs take clause complements. Clause complements are of different types, depending on the form of the verb in the clause. Recall that we identified five forms of the verb in Chapters 4 and 5: infinitival, present tense, past tense, present participle, past participle. Clause complements can be identified by the form of the verb: as infinitival, tensed, or participial.

> believe *that Cleo likes horses*   (tensed clause complement)
> saw *Fern running a race*   (participial clause complement)
> watched *Fern run a race*   (bare infinitival clause complement)
> want *their daughter to study linguistics*   (*to*-infinitival clause complement)

Clause complements can also be *interrogative* or what we call *wh*-clause complements:

> wonder *whether Cleo likes horses*   (*wh*-clause complement)
> decided *what to wear*

As all these examples illustrate, verbs select a wide range of complements of different categories and meanings. Other heads also select complements, though they don't exhibit quite the same range of complement types as verbs. (This isn't really surprising, given that verbs are an essential part of any clause, while other categories are not.) We turn now to complements of adjectives, prepositions, and adverbs.

Complements of adjectives

Adjectives take different kinds of complements, most commonly PPs, but also clauses:

PP complements of adjectives
> proud *of her son*
> sick *of your complaints*

Clause complements of adjectives
> happy *that he got the promotion*
> certain *we will be there in time*

Complements of prepositions

Prepositions nearly always require complements, most commonly NPs, which we call *objects of prepositions*. Prepositions can also take VPs, PPs, or clauses as complements.

NP complements of prepositions (object of preposition)
in *the woods*
over *that fence*

VP complements of prepositions
before *washing the car*
without *telling her mother*

PP complements of prepositions
in *for a surprise*
up *over the mountain*

Clause complements of prepositions (remember these PPs are called "subordinating" PPs because they include a subordinate clause)
because *Frida wants to play tennis*
after *Bel wrote a check*

Complements of nouns

Though nouns (in contrast to verbs and prepositions) rarely take complements, some do:

PP complements of nouns
the destruction *of the cake by the squirrels*
a book *of poems*

Clause complements of nouns
the belief *that the earth is flat*
her guess *that the answer was no*

This completes our brief overview of how phrases of different categories can function as complements, phrases selected by a head N, V, A, Adv, or P.

Modification

We review here the various types of modifiers you've seen throughout the book. Recall that modification crucially differs from complementation: modifiers add additional information and are therefore not selected by a head. Modifiers, unlike complements, are therefore optional.

Modifiers of nouns

You'll recall that various lexical categories and clauses can function as modifiers of nouns within NP. (As you may also recall, some of these modifiers occur in prenominal position before the noun, and some follow the noun, in postnominal position.)

Adjective modifiers of nouns
   the *fuzzy* cat
   a *strong* wind

Noun modifiers of nouns
   a *rail* fence
   the *rubber* hose

Verb modifiers of nouns
   the *babbling* brook
   a *chirping* sparrow

PP modifiers of nouns
   the cat *in the photo*
   the man *from Vancouver*

Restrictive relative clause modifiers of nouns
   the hat *that was covered with cat fur*
   the person *who Lee met at Starbucks*

Nonrestrictive relative clause modifiers of nouns
   the hat, *that I bought from my friend,* is on the chair
   that person, *who Lee met at Starbucks,* is a linguist

Modifiers of adjectives

Modifiers of adjectives include degree words DEG (we include here adverbs that express degree) and AdvPs.

DEG modifiers of adjectives
   very quick
   rather sharp
   amazingly happy

AdvP modifiers of adjectives
   financially troubled
   uncharacteristically silent

Navigating and
Analyzing: Review

Modifiers of adverbs

Degree words also modify adverbs.

DEG modifiers of adverbs
  very/so/too quickly
  amazingly happily

Modifiers of prepositions

Degree words can also modify prepositions.

DEG modifiers of prepositions
  right up the tree
  straight/clear out the door

Modifiers of verbs

Verbs are typically modified by AdvPs.

AdvP modifiers of verbs
  Fern talked to the horses *quietly*.
  Juno *usually* runs after work.

Modifiers of clauses: Movable modifiers

In Chapter 11, we discussed what we referred to as "movable modifiers," phrases that modify clauses, occurring either clause-initially or clause-finally. As we saw in that chapter, movable modifiers can be of any category and typically convey additional or extra information of time, manner, reason, place, or cause.

NP movable modifiers
  We weren't late to class *this time*.
  Today the jury should give their verdict.
  The judge will be on vacation *tomorrow*.
  Downtown, you can find everything you need.

AP movable modifiers
  The virtuoso plays the violin *naked*.
  Totally disgusted, Beulah left the room.
  Ella hung up the phone, *aghast*.

VP (participial) movable modifiers
> *Splashing water all over the floor*, the child played in the tub.
> *Driven by thirst*, the wildebeests searched for water.
> Ivy ran away from the wasp nest, *screaming*.

PP movable modifiers
> Cary kissed Lee *on Sunday*.
> *At 7:00*, she boarded the plane.
> Jack went home *after his soccer game*.

Subordinating PP movable modifiers:
> Mary is happy about the raise, *though she is worried about job security*.
> *After the party was over*, we left the restaurant.
> *If she gets a chance*, Lil will apply for a job.
> *When she graduates from college*, Lil will try to find a job.

Participial clause movable modifiers
> *Her eyes squinting in the sun*, Beulah watched the tennis match.
> Ike read the morning paper, *his dog curled up at his feet*.

Infinitival clause movable modifiers
> Hugh wore a fluorescent vest *in order to be seen*.
> *To catch the #7 bus* you have to be at the stop at exactly 6:00.

This concludes our brief review of the grammatical function of modification. In the final section, we turn to a review of two important aspects of syntactic structure that overlap with complementation and modification, namely, subordination and coordination.

Subordination

You are aware by now that syntactic structure is *hierarchical*; phrases occur within other phrases, and clauses and sentences are not simply linear strings of words. Hierarchical structure is formed in various ways, but one particular way is through *subordination* of one clause within another clause.

Clause complements, of verbs and other categories, provide good examples of subordination, and we repeat the relevant examples we've discussed above here:

Clause complements of verbs
    believe *that Cleo likes horses*   (each clause complement is a subordinate clause)
    see *Fern running a race*
    watch *Fern run a race*
    wants *his kid to study linguistics*
    wonder *whether Cleo likes horses*
    decide *what to wear*

Clause complements of nouns
    the belief *that the earth is flat*
    her guess *that the answer was no*

Clause complements of adjectives
    happy *that he got the promotion*
    certain *we'll be there in time*

Clause complements of prepositions
    because *Frida wants to play tennis*
    after *Bel wrote a check*

Subordination can also overlap with modification; subordinate clauses can occur as modifiers, for example, as relative clause modifiers of nouns.

Relative clause modifiers of nouns
    the hat *that was covered with cat fur*
    the man *who Lee met in Seattle*

Several kinds of clauses show up as movable modifiers. These clauses are also subordinate clauses, because they are contained inside a larger phrase (namely, a larger independent clause).

Subordinating PP movable modifier:
    Mary is happy about the raise, *though she is worried about job security.*
    After the party was over, we left the restaurant.
    If she gets a chance, Lil will apply for a job.
    When she graduates from college, Lil will try to find a job.

Participial clause movable modifiers
    Her eyes squinting in the sun, Beulah watched the tennis match.
    Ike read the morning paper, *his dog curled up at his feet.*

Infinitival clause movable modifiers
Hugh wore a fluorescent vest *in order to be seen.*
To catch that bus you have to be at the stop at exactly 6:00.

These are just some examples of how subordination gives rise to hierarchical syntactic structure (and also to examples of *recursion* of a clause within a clause, which we have also discussed in this book).

Coordination

Recall that coordination is quite different from subordination. Although both allow us to create longer and more complex clauses and sentences, coordination does so by connecting words and phrases using coordinating conjunctions: *for, and, nor, but, or, yet* and *so* (FANBOYS).

My friends brought [two pizzas] *and* [a lasagne] to the party. (coordinated NPs)

We love these chocolate [cakes] *and* [cookies]. (coordinated Ns)

Jojo [loves pizza] *but* [detests lasagne]. (coordinated VPs)

[My mom loves pizza] *but* [she refuses to make it from scratch]. (coordinated clauses)

These examples illustrate that coordination involves *parallelism;* we typically coordinate heads or phrases of the same category.
We can also coordinate clauses using *conjunctive adverbs* such as *therefore, consequently,* and *however.*

[The student missed the exam]; however, [they can still get some credit for taking it late].
CL   CL

Summary

This concludes our brief review of some of the more central grammatical concepts that you can use to navigate and analyze language in any of its modalities, oral, written, and signed. We also hope that what you have learned here helps you form your own answers to questions and issues about language and grammar that arise at home, in the classroom, in the workplace, and elsewhere.

Navigating and Analyzing: Review

Practice and Review

We return here to some of the text passages that were in the exercises in previous chapters. Revisiting these now will – we're pretty sure! – reveal how much you have learned about grammatical analysis.

Practice 1

Around the beginning of this century, the Queen of Thailand was aboard a boat, floating along with her many courtiers, manservants, maids, feet-bathers, and food-tasters, when suddenly the stern hit a wave and the queen was thrown overboard into the turquoise waters of the Nippon-Kai, where, despite her pleas for help, she drowned, for not one person on that boat went to her aid. (From *White Teeth*, by Zadie Smith.)

    (a) What's the subject of the independent clause?
    (b) Find some NP complements of prepositions.
    (c) How would you label the first phrase (*around the beginning of this century*)?
    (d) Identify at least one movable modifier. What category is it?

Practice 2

Lydia packed her belongings from her dorm room, placed them in her car, and hugged Niecy. She drove to her granny's house, unloaded the boxes onto the back porch, and gave her the story she'd worked out with Niecy, that Lydia was staying with her roommate in Atlanta. Niecy's parents had a big house and didn't mind company, but she didn't want to bring all her junk to Niecy's house. Here was the number, in case of emergency. Lydia would see her granny in June. (From *The Love Songs of W.E.B. DuBois*, by Honorée Fanonne Jeffers.)

    (a) Identify the complements of 2–3 verbs.
    (b) Identify the complements of 2–3 prepositions.
    (c) Label each of these complements by category (AP, PP, NP, etc.)
    (d) Label each of these complements by any other function labels they may have (direct object, subjective complement, etc.).

Practice 3

The affluent, educated, liberated women of the First World, who can enjoy freedoms unavailable to any women ever before, do not feel as free as they want to. And they can no longer restrict to the subconscious their sense that this lack of freedom has something to do with apparently frivolous issues, things that really should not matter. Many are ashamed to admit that such trivial concerns – to do with physical appearance, bodies, faces, hair, clothes – matter so much. But in spite of shame, guilt, and denial, more and more women are wondering if it isn't that they are entirely neurotic and alone but rather that something important is indeed at stake that has to do with the relationship between female liberation and female beauty. (From *The Beauty Myth*, by Naomi Wolf.)

    (a) What is the subject NP of the first sentence?
    (b) Identify some modifiers that are included in that subject NP.
    (c) What is the subject NP of the second sentence?
    (d) What phrases are coordinated in this excerpt? Find at least two examples.

Practice 4

No wonder we are stretched top to bottom from both ends of our being. No wonder the soul can't decide where to wedge itself. Of course, there are those who aren't troubled by these things, for instance my mother. As I said, she has decided to get her law degree. She moved down here to live with Grandma Zosie and Grandma Mary and go to night school. During the day, she works as a checker in a big discount food warehouse. For this, I guess she has learned to question nothing. She knows that prices change constantly and yet are precisely fixed. Every evening, I run the city lake while she walks the curved shore in startling peace. We meet at the bridge. There, her profile held simple against the sky, it seems to me that my mother is held equally by sky and earth, home and city. Some days with her I feel the perfect suspension, the balance. Other days I know how small a thing it takes to throw us off. (From *The Antelope Wife*, by Louise Erdrich.)

    (a) Find some clause complements of verbs.
    (b) Find some movable modifiers in this passage. Label the syntactic category of each.
    (c) What are some examples of coordination in this passage? What categories/phrases are coordinated?
    (d) Find 2–3 examples of modifiers of nouns. Label the syntactic category of each.

Practice 5

This water is cool and clean as anything I have ever tasted: it tastes of my father leaving, of him never having been there, of having nothing after he was gone. I dip it again and lift it level with the sunlight. I drink six measures of water and wish, for now, that this place without shame or secrets could be my home. Then the woman pulls me back to where I am safe on the grass and goes down alone. The bucket floats on its side for a moment before it sinks and swallows, making a grateful sound, a glug, before it's torn away and lifted. (From *Foster*, by Claire Keegan.)

Find examples of any of the following (you choose!):

    (a)   Complements of verbs (and of other heads, if you wish)
    (b)   Modifiers (of nouns, verbs, adjectives, and adverbs)
    (c)   Modifiers of clauses (movable modifiers)
    (d)   Relative clauses (restrictive and nonrestrictive)
    (e)   Examples of subordinate clauses
    (f)   Examples of coordination

Practice 6

Moose was a plain, largish man with a flaring Roman nose that drooped to a bulbous end; his shoulders drooped, too; and yes, there was a kind of homely, even lumbering majesty about him. We, American-born kids of our Pakistani-born parents, also struggled with saying his name, for though of course he was never Moose to us, our parents said his name one way, and he offered it to us – native American speakers with our own varying levels of Punjabi incompetence – in the bizarre, labored accent he'd come upon to make himself sound more American, his diphthongs flattened by ever-widening contortions of his lips, his affricates shoved so far forward he couldn't seem to get through a sentence without baring unnecessary teeth. (From *Homeland Elegies: A Novel*, by Ayad Akhtar.)

Again, find examples of any of the following (you choose!):

    (a)   Complements of verbs (and of other heads, if you wish)
    (b)   Modifiers (of nouns, verbs, adjectives, and adverbs)
    (c)   Modifiers of clauses (movable modifiers)
    (d)   Relative clauses (restrictive and nonrestrictive)
    (e)   Examples of subordinate clauses
    (f)   Examples of coordination

References

Cameron, Deborah. 1995. *Verbal Hygiene*. London, New York: Routledge.

Carnie, Andrew. 2013. *Syntax: A Generative Introduction*, 3rd edition. Malden, MA: Wiley Blackwell.

Curzan, Anne. 2014. *Fixing English: Prescriptivism and Language History*. Cambridge: Cambridge University Press.

DeBose, Charles E. 2015. "The Systematic Marking of Tense, Modality, and Aspect in African American Language." In: *The Oxford Handbook of African American Language* (eds. Jennifer Bloomquist, Lisa J. Green, and Sonja L. Lanehart), 371–386. Oxford Academic.

Green, Lisa. 2002. *African American English: A Linguistic Introduction*. New York: Cambridge University Press.

Greenfield, Laura and Karen Rowan. 2011. *Writing Centers and the New Racism*. Logan, UT: Utah State Press.

Labov, William. 1972. *Language in the Inner City: Studies in the Black English Vernacular*. Philadelphia: University of Pennsylvania Press.

Labov, William et al. 1968. *A Study of Non-Standard English of Negro and Puerto Rican Speakers in New York City*. Philadelphia: US Regional Survey.

Lippi-Green, Rosina. 2012. *English with an Accent: Language Ideology and Discrimination in the United States*, 2nd edition. London, New York: Routledge.

Milroy, James and Lesley Milroy. 2012. *Authority in Language: Investigating Standard English*, 1st edition. London: Routledge.

Mithun, Marianne. 1999. *The Languages of Native North America: Cambridge Language Surveys*, 1st edition. New York: Cambridge University Press.

Navigating English Grammar: A Guide to Analyzing Real Language, Second Edition.
Anne Lobeck and Kristin Denham.
© 2025 Anne Lobeck and Kristin Denham. Published 2025 by John Wiley & Sons Ltd.

Montgomery, Michael B. and Joseph S. Hall. 2004. *Dictionary of Smoky Mountain English*, 1st edition. Knoxville: University of Tennessee Press.

Pullum, Geoffrey. 2011. "Root Haughtiness." *LanguageLog*, August 20. https://languagelog.ldc.upenn.edu/nll/?p=3377.

Rickford, John R. 1999. "Phonological and Grammatical Features of African American Vernacular English (AAVE)." In: *African American Vernacular English* (ed. John R. Rickford), 3–14. Malden, MA and Oxford, UK: Blackwell.

Siddiqi, Daniel. 2011. "The English Intensifier *Ass.*" *Snippets*. May 23.

Index

Page numbers for tables are in **boldface**. Words or word fragments discussed as topics are in *italic*.

Navigating English Grammar: A Guide to Analyzing Real Language, Second Edition.
Anne Lobeck and Kristin Denham.
© 2025 Anne Lobeck and Kristin Denham. Published 2025 by John Wiley & Sons Ltd.

Index